THE WISDOM OF THE TORAH

THE WISDOM OF THE TORAH

Edited by Dagobert D. Runes

PHILOSOPHICAL LIBRARY
New York

15 East 40th Street, New York 16, N. Y.

Manufactured in the United States of America

Contents

THE WISDOM OF THE TORAH

A Note to the Reader

Torah means, in the literal Hebrew, *instruction,* or *guidance,* and is used in this sense by the ancient prophets and sages.

Prior to the first destruction of the great Temple in Jerusalem, by "Torah" the Hebrews meant the Books attributed to Moses. Shortly after the time of the second Temple, the final settlement of the Canon was made at Jamnia about 100 C.E. leading to the Bible's present form as codified by the seventh century rabbis known as Masoretes. Therefore, the Hebrew Bible *in toto,* as well as all Talmudic and later literature was often referred to as Torah.

The Hebrew Bible as it appears in our texts today is an anthology of thirty-nine books, reckoned as twenty-two, written for the most part in Hebrew, a little of it in Aramaic. (The uncanonized apocryphal sections are in Greek as well as Hebrew.) There is hardly any doubt that these books were written over a time stretching more than a thousand years. A much larger segment than commonly supposed is written in poetic and aphoristic form. In this sense the Torah is to be considered one of the world's greatest collections of pure literature.

Basically it contains five types of material:

(1) the legendary tales, frequently influencing faraway Asian story writers, as in India and Persia;

(2) the historical books (of remarkable accuracy, as shown by recent archaeological findings);

(3) the ritualistic codes with their 613 commandments and prohibitions as to diet, habitat, marriage, prayer service, sacrifices, and legal procedure;

(4) the prophetic sermons on current political and social issues;

(5) the philosophical and poetical works.

In this present selection, based, with only a few changes, on the still and forever majestic King James translation, we have concentrated on the Hebrew Bible as a book of philosophy and literature, with no disrespect to the historic, prophetic, legendary, or ritualistic attributes which have served and continue to serve many millions of believers as a guide in life and faith.

The present selection is to be taken as a treasury of divinely inspired poets and philosophers of perhaps the most heroic era in human history. It has been truly said that the Bible is an *inspired* as well as an *inspiring* book.

Pray tell me if there is anywhere, or was at any time, another volume of writings such as this, whose impact set aflame the lands between the Nile and the Euphrates more than three thousand years ago—a flame that has never ceased to burn all these millennia and has leapt from continent to continent, from tongue to tongue, from heart to heart.

Show me a village of people and I will find somewhere among them a trace of the Mosaic flame, be it in a book, a house of worship, a painting, a sculptured figurine, a phrase of music, or the memory of a sage proverb from Solomon, the king of kings. And even in places where the Torah has been defiled and its people erased, you will find the ashes of Israel still glimmering to remind the forgetful.

The Torah cannot be forgotten nor can it be thrown aside. If one had such intent, he would have to rip out a thousand books from a thousand shelves, a thousand statues and portraits from a thousand walls, and a thousand temples and churches from land to land. For millennia the people of the East and the West have grown and flourished in the breath of the Torah. The songs of its inspired sages reverberated in the poets, the dramatists, the painters, the sculptors, the fabulists, the preachers, the statesmen, the legislators, the philosophers, and the people at large, forever seeking justice.

If there ever was a book that has moved the world, this is it. It was of this Torah that Jesus said, "I come to fulfill it, not to destroy it." And it was because of the Torah that Mohammed called the Hebrews the People of the Book.

The Hebrew Bible as assembled here in excerpts is for the most part a wreath of poetry and aphoristic rhythm. Except for the historic-prophetic and ritualistic citations, this book consists, most significantly, of poems and aphorisms of the two kings, David and his son Solomon.

So much has been written on the subject of the authorship of the various Biblical books that I certainly do not wish to add to the already existing commentaries. There is no doubt that the majesty of Moses appears in many a page attributed to him, as does the wisdom of King Solomon in the writings named after him, and the incomparable poetry of his father in the Psalms.

Little difference would it make today if these three greatest of the children of Jacob were princes in the palace, as in truth they were, or shepherds on a hill.

The Lord showed His face to none of them, but if ever man's soul spoke His word, they did. Jew, gentile, even pagan, can listen to His word without professing religion or ritual and traditional ties.

The Torah shuns neither the believing nor the faithless, be it written in the Hebrew or the vernacular. While the traditional revelations of God in the books known as Holy Writ have been transmitted to us in Hebrew, His word can be heard in any language. And if this present offering of poetry and philosophy reaches someone who could not hurdle the obstacles of a foreign tongue or foreign-seeming rituals, the purpose of this volume will have been fulfilled.

As our sages have said, the ways to our Lord are wondersome, and who knows which is the better one?

D. D. R.

The Men Behind the Book

MOSES:

Of the teachings of this greatest of the Hebrew sages, far too little has come down to us. Through the theological and legendary setting of the five-chaptered book attributed to him shines the indomitable light of a great Teacher, imbued with the spirit and vision of a God-devoted life for his people under a social order founded on justice, neighbor-love, and self-discipline.

All available historical writings serve to emphasize the unique and precious personality of the profound lawmaker who carved in imperishable stone the very breath and beauty of the Lord's commandments. We do not know which of the legendary, historical, or ritualistic segments of the Mosaic books were written by this strange and princely shepherd, but dull must be the reader of the Bible who fails to detect the thunderous step of this benign and melancholy giant, wandering through the scrolls of the desert.

This is the immortal tribute the Torah pays to its relentless leader: "So Moses, the servant of the Lord, died there in the land of Moab . . . and he was buried in the valley of Moab . . . and no man knoweth of his grave unto this day . . . And there hath not arisen a prophet since in Israel like unto Moses whom the Lord knew soul to soul."

DAVID:

Like Moses, he was a shepherd before he became a leader of his people. This second of the Hebrew kings, conqueror of Jerusalem and unifier of the Hebrew nation, was by far the most colorful of Biblical authors.

Called to the court of King Saul as a young man because of his musical talents, he was a bear and lion killer as a boy, a mercenary soldier, a captain of outlaws, a shining hero who bested Goliath, a magnanimous adversary who more than once spared the life of his enemy king while the monarch was at his mercy, a saintly servant of the Lord, and a very great sinner indeed.

David was the most human among kings and, with all his blunders and failings, a kingly human.

SOLOMON:

By far the most eminent personality of the era of the tenth century B.C.E., Solomon put his stamp on the world of his time as well as all times to follow. He developed Israel into a highly organized empire, reformed its government, sponsored voyages of discovery to West Africa and probably India, and encouraged an architecture the traces of which even a cruel three millennia did not eradicate. He was, as his name bespeaks, a lover of peace, and while wealth was his share, he was unfailingly true to his prayerful wish to become endowed with the blessings of true judgment first and last.

This gifted king of kings gave himself to the study of living nature, and so widely known was his scholarship that for a hundred generations people of all three continents thought him a ruler not only of men, but also of the spirits of the air and the waters. They even attributed magical powers to the plant that bears his name, and many a mystic order claims him as its founder.

Solomon made Jerusalem, the city of his birth, a religious and literary center, the fame of which spread to the East and West. This first of the great polyhistors, who was as much at home in the warrior's chariot as at the writing table, became the symbol of story and thought from Iceland to India. Wherever and whenever people spoke or wrote of a wise monarch it was he they envisioned.

The Biblical books are a great (but not the only) document to this astounding man; no wonder that even a thousand years after his death scholars and poets named their writings after this king. Be it so that not every chapter and verse of Solomonic literature is of his pen, they all are of his devoted heart and soul.

JOB:

One of the most profound of all dramatic poems, this centers around an ancient chieftain endeavoring to interpret the purposefulness of divine providence. The present version may be dated to the fifth century B.C. It is traditionally attributed to Moses.

JESHU BEN SIRAH:

An erudite philosopher of Palestine in the second century B.C.E. whose writings, while kept outside the Canon, rank with its finest.

ISAIAH:

First of the major prophets. His pathos stemmed from a deep righteousness; his words resound with almost lyrical rhythm and refrains. According to legend, he perished, like Jeremiah, at the hands of assassins.

JEREMIAH:

This undaunted messenger of doom became witness to his gloomy forebodings when the first Temple was destroyed. His utterances are marked by rare poetic beauty. He died at the hands of assassins.

From the Books of Moses

IN THE THIRD MONTH, when the children of Israel were gone forth out of the land of Egypt, the same day came they into the wilderness of Sinai.

For they were departed from Rephidim, and were come to the desert of Sinai, and had pitched in the wilderness; and there Israel encamped before the mount.

And Moses went up unto God, and the Lord called unto him out of the mountain, saying, Thus shalt thou say to the house of Jacob, and tell the children of Israel;

Ye have seen what I did unto the Egyptians, and how I bare you on eagles' wings, and brought you unto myself.

Now therefore, if ye will obey my voice indeed, and keep my covenant, then ye shall be a peculiar treasure unto me above all people: for all the earth is mine.

And ye shall be unto me a kingdom of priests, and a holy nation. These are the words which thou shalt speak unto the children of Israel.

Exodus, xix

And God spake all these words, saying,

I am the Lord thy God, which have brought thee out of the house of bondage.

Thou shalt have no other gods before me.

Thou shalt not make unto thee any graven image, or any likeness of any thing that is in heaven above, or that is in the earth beneath, or that is in the water under the earth:

Thou shalt not take the name of the Lord thy God in vain: for the Lord will not hold him guiltless that taketh his name in vain.

Remember the sabbath-day to keep it holy.

Six days shalt thou labour, and do all thy work:

But the seventh day is the sabbath of the Lord thy God: in it thou shalt not do any work, thou, nor thy son, nor thy daughter, thy man-servant, nor thy maid-servant, nor thy cattle, nor thy stranger that is within thy gates.

Honour thy father and thy mother; that thy days may be long upon the land which the Lord thy God giveth thee.

Thou shalt not kill.

Thou shalt not commit adultery.

Thou shalt not steal.

Thou shalt not bear false witness against thy neighbour.

Thou shalt not covet thy neighbour's house, thou shalt not covet thy neighbour's wife, nor his man-servant, nor his maid-servant, nor his ox, nor his ass, nor any thing that is thy neighbour's.

Exodus, xx

Now these are the judgments which thou shalt set before them.

If thou buy a Hebrew servant, six years he shall serve: and in the seventh he shall go out free for nothing.

If he came in by himself, he shall go out by himself: if he were married, then his wife shall go out with him.

He that smiteth a man, so that he die, shall be surely put to death.

And he that stealeth a man, and selleth him, or if he be found in his hand, he shall surely be put to death.

Eye for eye, tooth for tooth, hand for hand, foot for foot.

Burning for burning, wound for wound, stripe for stripe.

Exodus, xxi

Thou shalt not raise a false report: put not thy hand with the wicked to be an unrighteous witness.

Thou shalt not follow a multitude to do evil; neither shalt thou speak in a cause to decline after many to wrest judgment:

Neither shalt thou countenance a poor man in his cause.

If thou meet thine enemy's ox or his ass going astray, thou shalt surely bring it back to him again.

If thou see the ass of him that hateth thee lying under his burden, and wouldest forbear to help him, thou shalt surely help with him.

Thou shalt not wrest the judgment of thy poor in his cause.

Keep thee far from a false matter; and the innocent and righteous slay thou not: for I will not justify the wicked.

And thou shalt take no gift; for the gift blindeth the wise, and perverteth the words of the righteous.

Also thou shalt not oppress a stranger: for ye know the heart of a stranger, seeing ye were strangers in the land of Egypt.

And six years thou shalt sow thy land, and shall gather in the fruits thereof:

But the seventh year thou shalt let it rest and lie still; that the poor of thy people may eat: and what they leave the beasts of the field shall eat. In like manner thou shalt deal with thy vineyard, and with thy oliveyard.

Six days thou shalt do thy work, and on the seventh day thou shalt rest: that thine ox and thine ass may rest, and the son of thy handmaid, and the stranger, may be refreshed.

***Exodus,* xxiii**

And when ye reap the harvest of your land, thou shalt not wholly reap the corners of thy field, neither shalt thou gather the gleanings of thy harvest.

And thou shalt not glean thy vineyard, neither shalt thou gather every grape of thy vineyard; thou shalt leave them for the poor and stranger: I am the Lord your God.

Ye shall not steal, neither deal falsely, neither lie one to another.

And ye shall not swear by my name falsely, neither shalt thou profane the name of thy God: I am the Lord.

Thou shalt not defraud thy neighbour, neither rob him: the wages of him that is hired shall not abide with thee all night until the morning.

Thou shalt not curse the deaf, nor put a stumbling-block before the blind, but shalt fear thy God: I am the Lord.

Ye shall do no unrighteousness in judgment; thou shalt not respect the person of the poor, nor honour the person of the mighty: but in righteousness shalt thou judge thy neighbour.

Thou shalt not go up and down as a tale-bearer among thy people; neither shalt thou stand against the blood of thy neighbour; I am the Lord.

Thou shalt not hate thy brother in thy heart: thou shalt in any wise rebuke thy neighbour, and not suffer sin upon him.

Thou shalt not avenge, nor bear any grudge against the children of thy people, but thou shalt love thy neighbour as thyself: I am the Lord.

Ye shall not eat any thing with the blood: neither shall ye use enchantment, nor observe times.

Regard not them that have familiar spirits, neither seek after wizards, to be defiled by them: I am the Lord your God.

Thou shalt rise up before the hoary head, and honour the face of the old man, and fear thy God: I am the Lord.

And if a stranger sojourn with thee in your land, ye shall not vex him.

But the stranger that dwelleth with you shall be unto you as one born among you, and thou shalt love him as thyself; for ye were strangers in the land of Egypt: I am the Lord your God.

Ye shall do no unrighteousness in judgment, in mete-yard, in weight, or in measure.

Just balances, just weights, a just ephah, and a just hin shall ye have: I am the Lord your God, which brought you out of the land of Egypt.

Therefore shall ye observe all my statutes, and all my judgments, and do them: I am the Lord.

Leviticus, xix

And the Lord spake unto Moses in mount Sinai, saying, Speak unto the children of Israel, and say unto them, When ye come into the land which I give you then shall the land keep a sabbath unto the Lord.

Six years thou shalt sow thy field, and six years thou shalt prune thy vineyard, and gather in the fruit thereof;

But in the seventh year shall be a sabbath of rest unto the land, a sabbath for the Lord: thou shalt neither sow thy field, nor prune thy vineyard.

That which groweth of its own accord of thy harvest, thou shalt not reap, neither gather the grapes of thy vine undressed: for it is a year of rest unto the land.

And the sabbath of the land shall be meat for you; for thee, and for thy servant, and for thy maid, and for thy hired servant, and for thy stranger that sojourneth with thee,

And for thy cattle, and for the beasts that are in thy land, shall all the increase thereof be meat.

And thou shalt number seven sabbaths of years unto thee, seven times seven years; and the space of the seven sabbaths of years shall be unto thee forty and nine years.

Then shalt thou cause the trumpet of the jubilee to sound, on the tenth day of the seventh month, in the day of atonement shall ye make the trumpet sound throughout all your land.

And ye shall hallow the fiftieth year, and proclaim liberty throughout all the land unto all the inhabitants thereof: it shall be a jubilee unto you; and ye shall return every man unto his possession, and ye shall return every man unto his family.

A jubilee shall that fiftieth year be unto you: ye shall not sow, neither reap that which groweth of itself in it, nor gather the grapes in it of thy vine undressed.

For it is the jubilee; it shall be holy unto you: ye shall eat the increase thereof out of the field.

In the year of this jubilee ye shall return every man unto his possession.

And if thou sell aught unto thy neighbour, or buyest aught

of thy neighbor's hand, ye shall not oppress one another:

According the number of years after the jubilee, thou shalt buy of thy neighbour, and according unto the number of years of the fruits he shall sell unto thee:

According to the multitude of years thou shalt increase the price thereof, and according to the fewness of years thou shalt diminish the price of it: for according to the number of the years of the fruits doth he sell unto thee.

Ye shall not therefore oppress one another; but thou shalt fear thy God: for I am the Lord your God.

Wherefore ye shall do my statutes, and keep my judgments, and do them; and ye shall dwell in the land in safety.

And the land shall yield her fruit, and ye shall eat your fill, and dwell therein in safety.

And if ye shall say, What shall we eat the seventh year? behold, we shall not sow nor gather in our increase:

Then I will command my blessing upon you in the sixth year, and it shall bring forth fruit for three years.

And ye shall sow the eighth year, and eat yet of old fruit until the ninth year; until her fruits come in ye shall eat of the old store.

The land shall not be sold for ever; for the land is mine, for ye are strangers and sojourners with me.

And in all the land of your possession ye shall grant a redemption for the land.

If thy brother be waxen poor, and hath sold away some of his possession, and if any of his kin come to redeem it, then shall he redeem that which his brother sold.

And if the man have none to redeem it, and himself be able to redeem it;

Then let him count the years of the sale thereof, and restore the overplus unto the man to whom he sold it; that he may return unto his possession.

But if he be not able to restore it to him, then that which is sold shall remain in the hand of him that hath bought it until the year of jubilee: and in the jubilee it shall go out, and he shall return unto his possession.

And if a man sell a dwelling-house in a walled city, then he may redeem it within a whole year after it is sold: within a full year may he redeem it.

And if it be not redeemed within the space of a full year, then the house that is in the walled city shall be established for ever to him that bought it, throughout his generations: it shall not go out in the jubilee.

But the houses of the villages which have no walls round about them, shall be counted as the fields of the country: they may be redeemed, and they shall go out in the jubilee.

Notwithstanding the cities of the Levites, and the houses of the cities of their possession, may the Levites redeem at any time.

And if a man purchase of the Levites, then the house that was sold, and the city of his possession shall go out in the year of jubilee; for the houses of the cities of the Levites are their possession among the children of Israel.

But the field of the suburbs of their cities may not be sold, for it is their perpetual possession.

And if thy brother be waxen poor, and fallen in decay with thee; then thou shalt relieve him: yea, though he be a stranger, or a sojourner; that he may live with thee.

Take thou no usury of him, or increase; but fear thy God; that thy brother may live with thee.

Thou shalt not give him thy money upon usury, nor lend him thy victuals for increase.

I am the Lord your God, which brought you forth out of the land of Egypt, to give you the land of Canaan, and to be your God.

And if thy brother that dwelleth by thee be waxen poor, and be sold unto thee; thou shalt not compel him to serve as a bond-servant:

But as a hired servant, and as a sojourner he shall be with

thee, and shall serve thee unto the year of jubilee:

And then shall he depart from thee, both he and his children with him, and shall return unto his own family, and unto the possession of his fathers shall he return.

For they are my servants which I brought forth out of the land of Egypt; they shall not be sold as bond-men.

Thou shalt not rule over him with rigour, but shalt fear thy God.

Leviticus, xxv

❧

At the end of every seven years thou shalt make a release.

And this is the manner of the release: Every creditor that lendeth aught unto his neighbour, shall release it; he shall not exact it of his neighbour, or of his brother; because it is called the Lord's release.

Save when there shall be no poor among you; for the Lord shall greatly bless thee in the land which the Lord thy God giveth thee for an inheritance to possess it:

If there be among you a poor man of one of thy brethren within any of thy gates in thy land which the Lord thy God giveth thee, thou shalt not harden thy heart, nor shut thy hand from thy poor brother:

But thou shalt open thy hand wide unto him, and shalt surely lend him sufficient for his need, in that which he wanteth.

Beware that there be not a thought in thy wicked heart saying, The seventh year, the year of release, is at hand; and thine eye be evil against thy poor brother, and thou givest him nought; and he cry unto the Lord against thee, and it be sin unto thee.

Thou shalt surely give him, and thy heart shall not be grieved when thou givest unto him: because that for this thing the Lord thy God shall bless thee in all thy works, and in all that thou puttest thy hand unto.

For the poor shall never cease out of the land: therefore I command thee, saying, Thou shalt open thy hand wide unto thy brother, to thy poor, and to thy needy, in thy land.

And if thy brother, a Hebrew man, or a Hebrew woman, be sold unto thee, and serve thee six years; then in the seventh year thou shalt let him go free from thee.

And when thou sendest him out free from thee, thou shalt not let him go away empty:

Thou shalt furnish him liberally out of thy flock, and out of thy floor, and out of thy wine-press: of that wherewith the Lord thy God hath blessed thee thou shalt give unto him.

And thou shalt remember that thou wast a bond-man in the land of Egypt, and the Lord thy God redeemed thee: therefore I command thee this thing to-day.

Deuteronomy, xv

Judges and officers shalt thou make thee in all thy gates, which the Lord thy God giveth thee, throughout thy tribes: and they shall judge the people with just judgment.

Thou shalt not wrest judgment; thou shalt not respect persons, neither take a gift: for a gift doth blind the eyes of the wise, and pervert the words of the righteous.

That which is altogether just shalt thou follow, that thou mayest live, and inherit the land which the Lord thy God giveth thee.

Thou shalt not plant thee a grove of any trees near unto the altar of the Lord thy God, which thou shalt make thee.

Neither shalt thou set up any image; which the Lord thy God hateth.

Deuteronomy, xvi

Thou shalt separate three cities for thee in the midst of thy land which the Lord thy God giveth thee to possess it.

Thou shalt prepare thee a way, and divide the coasts of thy land which the Lord thy God giveth thee to inherit, into three parts, that every slayer may flee thither.

And this is the case of the slayer, which shall flee thither, that he may live: Whoso killeth his neighbour ignorantly, whom he hated not in time past;

As when a man goeth into the wood with his neighbour to hew wood, and his hand fetcheth a stroke with the axe to cut down the tree, and the head slippeth from the helve, and lighteth upon his neighbour, that he die; he shall flee unto one of these cities, and live:

Lest the avenger of the blood pursue the slayer, while his heart is hot, and overtake him, because the way is long, and slay him; whereas he was not worthy of death, inasmuch as he hated him not in time past.

Wherefore I command thee, saying, Thou shalt separate three cities for thee.

Thou shalt not remove thy neighbour's land-mark, which they of old time have set in thine inheritance, which thou shalt inherit in the land that the Lord thy God giveth thee to possess it.

One witness shall not rise up against a man for any iniquity, or for any sin, in any sin that he sinneth; at the mouth of two witnesses, or at the mouth of three witnesses, shall the matter be established.

If a false witness rise up against any man to testify against him that which is wrong;

Then both the men between whom the controversy is shall stand before the Lord, before the priests and the judges, which shall be in those days; and the judges shall make diligent inquisition: and behold, if the witness be a false witness, and hath testified falsely against his brother;

Then shall ye do unto him, as he had thought to have done unto his brother: so shalt thou put the evil away from among you.

And those which remain shall hear, and fear, and shall henceforth commit no more any such evil among you.

And thine eye shall not pity; but life shall go for life, eye for eye, tooth for tooth, hand for hand, foot for foot.

***Deuteronomy*, xix**

When thou goest out to battle against thine enemies, and seest horses, and chariots, and a people more than thou, be not afraid of them: for the Lord thy God is with thee, which brought thee up out of the land of Egypt.

Deuteronomy, xx

⁂

Thou shalt not see thy brother's ox or his sheep go astray, and hide thyself from them: thou shalt in any case bring them again unto thy brother.

And if thy brother be not nigh unto thee, or if thou know him not, then thou shalt bring it unto thine own house, and it shall be with thee until thy brother seek after it, and thou shalt restore it to him again.

In like manner shalt thou do with his ass; and so shalt thou do with his raiment; and with all lost things of thy brother's, which he hath lost, and thou hast found, shalt thou do likewise: thou mayest not hide thyself.

Thou shalt not see thy brother's ass or his ox fall down by the way, and hide thyself from them: thou shalt surely help him to lift them up again.

The woman shall not wear that which pertaineth unto a man, neither shall a man put on a woman's garment; for all that do so are abomination unto the Lord thy God.

If a bird's nest chance to be before thee in the way in any tree, or on the ground, whether they be young ones, or eggs, and the dam sitting upon the young, or upon the eggs, thou shalt not take the dam with the young:

But thou shalt in any wise let the dam go, and take the young to thee; that it may be well with thee, and that thou mayest prolong thy days.

Deuteronomy, xxii

⁂

Thou shalt not deliver unto his master the servant which is escaped from his master unto thee:

He shall dwell with thee, even among you in that place which he shall choose in one of thy gates where it liketh him best: thou shalt not oppress him.

That which is gone out of thy lips thou shalt keep and perform; even a free-will-offering, according as thou hast vowed unto the Lord thy God, which thou hast promised with thy mouth.

When thou comest into thy neighbour's vineyard, then thou mayest eat grapes thy fill, at thine own pleasure; but thou shalt not put any in thy vessel.

When thou comest into the standing corn of thy neighbour, then thou mayest pluck the ears with thy hand: but thou shalt not move a sickle unto thy neighbour's standing corn.

Deuteronomy, xxiii

When thou dost lend thy brother any thing, thou shalt not go into his house to fetch his pledge:

Thou shalt stand abroad, and the man to whom thou dost lend shall bring out the pledge abroad unto thee:

And if the man be poor, thou shalt not sleep with his pledge:

In any case thou shalt deliver him the pledge again when the sun goeth down, that he may sleep in his own raiment, and bless thee; and it shall be righteousness unto thee before the Lord thy God.

Thou shalt not oppress a hired servant that is poor and needy, whether he be of thy brethren, or of thy strangers that are in thy land within thy gates:

At his day thou shalt give him his hire, neither shall the sun go down upon it, for he is poor, and setteth his heart upon it: lest he cry against thee unto the Lord, and it be sin unto thee.

The fathers shall not be put to death for the children, neither shall the children be put to death for the fathers: every man shall be put to death for his own sin.

Thou shalt not pervert the judgment of the stranger, nor of

the fatherless, nor take the widow's raiment to pledge:

But thou shalt remember that thou wast a bond-man in Egypt and the Lord thy God redeemed thee thence: therefore I command thee to do this thing.

When thou cuttest down thy harvest in thy field, and hast forgot a sheaf in the field, thou shalt not go again to fetch it: it shall be for the stranger, for the fatherless, and for the widow: that the Lord thy God may bless thee in all the work of thy hands.

When thou beatest thine olive-tree, thou shalt not go over the boughs again: it shall be for the stranger, for the fatherless, and for the widow.

When thou gatherest the grapes of thy vineyard, thou shalt not glean it afterward: it shall be for the stranger, for the fatherless, and for the widow.

And thou shalt remember that thou wast a bond-man in the land of Egypt: therefore I command thee to do this thing.

***Deuteronomy*, xxiv**

Give ear, O ye heavens, and I will speak; and hear, O earth, the words of my mouth.

My doctrine shall drop as the rain, my speech shall distil as the dew, as the small rain upon the tender herb, and as the showers upon the grass:

Because I will publish the name of the Lord: ascribe ye greatness unto our God.

He is the rock, his work is perfect: for all his ways are judgment: a God of truth and without iniquity, just and right is he.

They have corrupted themselves, their spot is not the spot of his children: they are a perverse and crooked generation.

Do ye thus requite the Lord, O foolish people and unwise? Is not he thy father that hath bought thee? Hath he not made thee, and established thee?

Remember the days of old, consider the years of many generations: ask thy father, and he will shew thee; thy elders, and they will tell thee.

When the most High divided to the nations their inheritance, when he separated the sons of Adam, he set the bounds of the people according to the number of the children of Israel.

For the Lord's portion is his people; Jacob is the lot of his inheritance.

He found him in a desert land, and in the waste howling wilderness; he led him about, he instructed him, he kept him as the apple of his eye.

As an eagle stirreth up her nest, fluttereth over her young, spreadeth abroad her wings, taketh them, beareth them on her wings:

So the Lord alone did lead him, and there was no strange god with him.

He made him ride on the high places of the earth, that he might eat the increase of the fields; and he made him to suck honey out of the rock, and oil out of the flinty rock;

Butter of kine, and milk of sheep, with fat of lambs, and rams of the breed of Bashan, and goats, with the fat of kidneys of wheat; and thou didst drink the pure blood of the grape.

But Jeshurun waxed fat, and kicked: thou art waxen fat, thou art grown thick, thou art covered with fatness; then he forsook God which made him, and lightly esteemed the rock of his salvation.

They provoked him to jealousy with strange gods, with abominations provoked they him to anger.

They sacrificed unto devils, not to God; to gods whom they knew not, to new gods that came newly up, whom your fathers feared not.

Of the Rock that begat thee thou art unmindful, and hast forgotten God that formed thee.

And when the Lord saw it, he abhorred them, because of

the provoking of his sons, and of his daughters.

And he said, I will hide my face from them, I will see what their end shall be: for they are a very froward generation, children in whom is no faith.

They have moved me to jealousy with that which is not God; they have provoked me to anger with their vanities: and I will move them to jealousy with those which are not a people; I will provoke them to anger with a foolish nation.

For a fire is kindled in mine anger and shall burn unto the lowest hell, and shall consume the earth with her increase, and set on fire the foundations of the mountains.

I will heap mischiefs upon them; I will spend mine arrows upon them.

They shall be burnt with hunger, and devoured with burning heat, and with bitter destruction: I will also send the teeth of beasts upon them, with the poison of serpents of the dust.

The sword without, and terror within, shall destroy both the young man and the virgin, the suckling also with the man of gray hairs.

I said, I would scatter them into corners, I would make the remembrance of them to cease from among men:

Were it not that I feared the wrath of the enemy, lest their adversaries should behave themselves strangely, and lest they should say, our hand is high and the Lord hath not done all this.

For they are a nation void of counsel, neither is there any understanding in them.

O that they were wise, that they understood this, that they would consider their latter end!

How should one chase a thousand, and two put ten thousand to flight, except their rock had sold them, and the Lord had shut them up?

For their rock is not as our rock, even our enemies themselves being judges.

For their vine is of the vine of Sodom, and of the fields of

Gomorrah: their grapes are grapes of gall, their clusters are bitter;

Their wine is the poison of dragons, and the cruel venom of asps.

Is not this laid up in store with me, and sealed up among my treasures?

To me belongeth vengeance, and recompence; their foot shall slide in due time: for the day of their calamity is at hand, and the things that shall come upon them make haste.

For the Lord shall judge his people, and repent himself for his servants, when he seeth that their power is gone, and there is none shut up, or left.

And he shall say, where are their gods, their rock in whom they trusted;

Which did eat the fat of their sacrifices, and drank the wine of their drink offerings? Let them rise up and help you, and be your protection.

See now that I, even I, am he, and there is no god with me: I kill, and I make alive; I wound, and I heal: neither is there any that can deliver out of my hand.

For I lift up my hand to heaven, and say, I live for ever.

If I whet my glittering sword, and mine hand take hold on judgment; I will render vengeance to mine enemies, and will reward them that hate me.

I will make mine arrows drunk with blood, and my sword shall devour flesh; and that with the blood of the slain and of the captives, from the beginning of revenges upon the enemy.

Rejoice, O ye nations, with his people: for he will avenge the blood of his servants, and will render vengeance to his adversaries, and will be merciful unto his land, and to his people.

And Moses came and spake all the words of this song in the ears of the people, he, and Hoshea the son of Nun.

And Moses made an end of speaking all these words to all Israel:

And he said unto them, set your hearts unto all the words which I testify among you this day, which ye shall command your children to observe to do, all the words of this law.

For it is not a vain thing for you; because it is your life: and through this thing ye shall prolong your days in the land, whither ye go over Jordan to possess it.

***Deuteronomy*, xxxii**

The Ballad of Job

There was a man in the land of Uz, whose name was Job; and that man was perfect and upright, and one that feared God, and eschewed evil.

And there were born unto him seven sons and three daughters.

His substance also was seven thousand sheep, and three thousand camels, and five hundred yoke of oxen, and five hundred she-asses, and a very great household; so that this man was the greatest of all the men of the east.

And his sons went and feasted in their houses, every one his day; and sent and called for their three sisters to eat and to drink with them.

And it was so, when the days of their feasting were gone about, that Job sent and sanctified them, and rose up early in the morning, and offered burnt-offerings according to the number of them all: for Job said, It may be that my sons have sinned, and cursed God in their hearts. Thus did Job continually.

Now there was a day when the sons of God came to present themselves before the Lord, and Satan came also among them.

And the Lord said unto Satan, Whence comest thou? Then Satan answered the Lord, and said, From going to and fro in the earth, and from walking up and down in it.

And the Lord said unto Satan, Hast thou considered my servant Job, that there is none like him in the earth, a perfect and an upright man, one that feareth God, and escheweth evil?

Then Satan answered the Lord and said, Doth Job fear God for nought?

Hast not thou made a hedge about him, and about his house, and about all that he hath on every side? thou hast blessed the work of his hands, and his substance is increased in the land.

But put forth thy hand now, and touch all that he hath, and he will curse thee to thy face.

And the Lord said unto Satan, Behold, all that he hath is in thy power; only upon himself put not forth thy hand. So Satan went forth from the presence of the Lord.

And there was a day when his sons and his daughters were eating and drinking wine in their eldest brother's house:

And there came a messenger unto Job, and said, The oxen were ploughing, and the asses feeding beside them:

And the Sabeans fell upon them, and took them away; yea, they have slain the servants with the edge of the sword; and I only am escaped alone to tell thee.

While he was yet speaking, there came also another, and said, The fire of God is fallen from heaven, and hath burned up the sheep and the servants, and consumed them; and I only am escaped alone to tell thee.

While he was yet speaking, there came also another, and said, The Chaldeans made out three bands, and fell upon the camels, and have carried them away, yea, and slain the servants with the edge of the sword: and I only am escaped alone to tell thee.

While he was yet speaking, there came also another, and said, Thy sons and thy daughters were eating and drinking wine in their eldest brother's house:

And behold, there came a great wind from the wilderness, and smote the four corners of the house, and it fell upon the young men, and they are dead; and I only am escaped alone to tell thee.

Then Job arose, and rent his mantle, and shaved his head, and fell down upon the ground, and worshipped,

And said, Naked came I out of my mother's womb, and naked shall I return thither: The Lord gave, and the Lord hath taken away; blessed be the name of the Lord.

In all this Job sinned not, nor charged God foolishly.

❧

Again there was a day when the sons of God came to present themselves before the Lord, and Satan came also among them to present himself before the Lord.

And the Lord said unto Satan, From whence comest thou? And Satan answered the Lord, and said, From going to and fro in the earth, and from walking up and down in it.

And the Lord said unto Satan, Hast thou considered my servant Job, that there is none like him in the earth, a perfect and an upright man, one that feareth God, and escheweth evil? and still he holdeth fast his integrity, although thou movedst me against him, to destroy him without cause.

And Satan answered the Lord, and said, Skin for skin, yea, all that a man hath will he give for his life.

But put forth thy hand now, and touch his bone and his flesh, and he will curse thee to thy face.

And the Lord said unto Satan, Behold, he is in thy hand; but save his life.

So went Satan forth from the presence of the Lord, and smote Job with sore boils from the sole of his foot unto his crown.

And he took him a potsherd to scrape himself withal; and he sat down among the ashes.

Then said his wife unto him, Dost thou still retain thine integrity? curse God, and die.

But he said unto her, Thou speakest as one of the foolish women speaketh. What! shall we receive good at the hand of God, and shall we not receive evil? In all this did not Job sin with his lips.

Now when Job's three friends heard of all this evil that was come upon him, they came every one from his own place; Eliphaz the Temanite, and Bildad the Shuhite, and Zophar the Naamathite: for they had made an appointment together to come to mourn with him, and to comfort him.

And when they lifted up their eyes afar off, and knew him not, they lifted up their voice, and wept; and they rent every one his mantle, and sprinkled dust upon their heads toward heaven.

So they sat down with him upon the ground seven days and seven nights, and none spake a word unto him for they saw that his grief was very great.

❧

After this opened Job his mouth, and cursed his day.

And Job spake, and said,

Let the day perish wherein I was born, and the night in which it was said, There is a man child conceived.

Let that day be darkness; let not God regard it from above, neither let the light shine upon it.

Let darkness and the shadow of death stain it; let a cloud dwell upon it; let the blackness of the day terrify it.

As for that night, let darkness seize upon it; let it not be joined unto the days of the year; let it not come into the number of the months.

Lo, let that night be solitary; let no joyful voice come therein.

Let them curse it that curse the day, who are ready to raise up their mourning.

Let the stars of the twilight thereof be dark; let it look for light, but have none; neither let it see the dawning of the day.

Because it shut not up the doors of my mother's womb, nor hid sorrow from mine eyes.

Why died I not from the womb? why did I not give up the ghost when I came out of the belly?

Why did the knees prevent me? or why the breasts that I should suck?

For now should I have lain still and been quiet, I should have slept: then had I been at rest

With kings and counsellors of the earth, which built desolate places for themselves;

Or with princes that had gold, who filled their houses with silver:

Or as a hidden untimely birth I had not been; as infants which never saw light.

There the wicked cease from troubling; and there the weary be at rest.

There the prisoners rest together; they hear not the voice of the oppressor.

The small and great are there; and the servant is free from his master.

Wherefore is light given to him that is in misery, and life unto the bitter in soul;

Which long for death, but cometh not; and dig for it more than for hid treasures;

Which rejoice exceedingly, and are glad, when they can find the grave?

Why is light given to a man whose way is hid, and whom God hath hedged in?

For my sighing cometh before I eat, and my roarings are poured out like the waters.

For the thing which I greatly feared is come upon me, and that which I was afraid of is come unto me.

I was not in safety, neither had I rest, neither was I quiet; yet trouble came.

Then Eliphaz the Temanite answered and said, If we assay to commune with thee, wilt thou be grieved? but who can withhold himself from speaking?

Behold, thou hast instructed many, and thou hast strengthened the weak hands.

Thy words have upholden him that was falling, and thou hast strengthened the feeble knees.

But now it is come upon thee, and thou faintest; it toucheth thee, and thou art troubled.

Is not this thy fear, thy confidence, thy hope, and the uprightness of thy ways?

Remember, I pray thee, who ever perished, being innocent? or where were the righteous cut off?

Even as I have seen, they that plough iniquity, and sow wickedness, reap the same.

By the blast of God they perish, and by the breath of his nostrils are they consumed.

The roaring of the lion, and the voice of the fierce lion, and the teeth of the young lions are broken.

The old lion perisheth for lack of prey, and the stout lion's whelps are scattered abroad.

Now a thing was secretly brought to me, and mine ear received a little thereof.

In thoughts from the visions of the night, when deep sleep falleth on men,

Fear came upon me, and trembling, which made all my bones to shake.

Then a spirit passed before my face; the hair of my flesh stood up:

It stood still, but I could not discern the form thereof: an image was before mine eyes, there was silence, and I heard a voice, saying,

Shall mortal man be more just than God? shall a man be more pure than his Maker?

Behold, he put no trust in his servants; and his angels he charged with folly:

How much less in them that dwell in houses of clay, whose foundation is in the dust, which are crushed before the moth?

They are destroyed from morning to evening; they perish for ever without any regarding it.

Doth not their excellency which is in them go away? they die, even without wisdom.

❧

Call now, if there be any that will answer thee; and to which of the saints wilt thou turn?

For wrath killeth the foolish man, and envy slayeth the silly one.

I have seen the foolish taking root: but suddenly I cursed his habitation.

His children are far from safety, and they are crushed in the gate, neither is there any to deliver them.

Whose harvest the hungry eateth up, and taketh it even out of the thorns, and the robber swalloweth up their substance.

Although affliction cometh not forth of the dust, neither doth trouble spring out of the ground;

Yet man is born unto trouble, as the sparks fly upward.

I would seek unto God, and unto God would I commit my cause:

Which doeth great things and unsearchable; marvellous things without number.

Who giveth rain upon the earth, and sendeth waters upon the fields:

To set up on high those that be low; that those which mourn may be exalted to safety.

He disappointeth the devices of the crafty, so that their hands cannot perform their enterprise.

He taketh the wise in their own craftiness: and the counsel of the froward is carried headlong.

They meet with darkness in the day-time, and grope in the noon-day as in the night.

But he saveth the poor from the sword, from their mouth, and from the hand of the mighty.

So the poor hath hope, and iniquity stoppeth her mouth.

Behold, happy is the man whom God correcteth: therefore despise not thou the chastening of the Almighty:

For he maketh sore, and bindeth up: he woundeth, and his hands make whole.

He shall deliver thee in six troubles: yea, in seven there shall no evil touch thee.

In famine he shall redeem thee from death: and in war from the power of the sword.

Thou shalt be hid from the scourge of the tongue: neither shalt thou be afraid of destruction when it cometh.

At destruction and famine thou shalt laugh: neither shalt thou be afraid of the beasts of the earth.

For thou shalt be in league with the stones of the field: and the beasts of the fields shall be at peace with thee.

And thou shalt know that thy tabernacle shall be in peace; and thou shalt visit thy habitation, and shalt not sin.

Thou shalt know also that thy seed shall be great, and thine offspring as the grass of the earth.

Thou shalt come to thy grave in a full age, like as a shock of corn cometh in his season.

Lo this, we have searched it, so it is; hear it, and know thou it for thy good.

❧

But Job answered and said,

O that my grief were thoroughly weighed, and my calamity laid in the balances together!

For now it would be heavier than the sand of the sea: therefore my words are swallowed up.

For the arrows of the Almighty are within me, the poison whereof drinketh up my spirit: the terrors of God do set themselves in array against me.

Doth the wild ass bray when he hath grass? or loweth the ox over his fodder?

Can that which is unsavoury be eaten without salt? or is there any taste in the white of an egg?

The things that my soul refused to touch are as my sorrowful meat.

O that I might have my request; and that God would grant me the thing that I long for!

Even that it would please God to destroy me; that he would let loose his hand, and cut me off!

Then should I yet have comfort; yea, I would harden myself in sorrow: let him not spare; for I have not concealed the words of the Holy One.

What is my strength, that I should hope? And what is mine end, that I should prolong my life?

Is my strength the strength of stones? or is my flesh of brass?

Is not my help in me? and is wisdom driven quite from me?

To him that is afflicted pity should be shewed from his friend; but he forsaketh the fear of the Almighty.

My brethren have dealt deceitfully as a brook, and as the stream of brooks they pass away;

Which are blackish by reason of the ice, and wherein the snow is hid:

What time they wax warm, they vanish: when it is hot, they are consumed out of their place.

The paths of their way are turned aside; they go to nothing, and perish.

The troops of Tema looked, the companies of Sheba waited for them.

They were confounded because they had hoped; they came thither, and were ashamed.

For now ye are nothing; ye see my casting down, and are afraid.

Did I say, Bring unto me? or, Give a reward for me of your substance?

Or, Deliver me from the enemy's hand? or, Redeem me from the hand of the mighty?

Teach me, and I will hold my tongue: and cause me to understand wherein I have erred.

How forcible are right words! but what doth your arguing reprove?

Do ye imagine to reprove words, and the speeches of one that is desperate, which are as wind?

Yea, ye overwhelm the fatherless, and ye dig a pit for your friend.

Now therefore be content, look upon me; for it is evident unto you if I lie.

Return, I pray you, let it not be iniquity; yea, return again, my righteousness is in it.

Is there iniquity in my tongue? cannot my taste discern perverse things?

❧

Is there not an appointed time to man upon earth? are not his days also like the days of a hireling?

As a servant earnestly desireth the shadow, and as a hireling looketh for the reward of his work:

So am I made to possess months of vanity, and wearisome nights are appointed to me.

When I lie down, I say, When shall I arise, and the night be gone? and I am full of tossings to and fro unto the dawning of the day.

My flesh is clothed with worms and clods of dust; my skin is broken, and become loathsome.

My days are swifter than a weaver's shuttle, and are spent without hope.

O remember that my life is wind: mine eye shall no more see good.

The eye of him that hath seen me shall see me no more: thine eyes are upon me, and I am not.

As the cloud is consumed and vanisheth away: so he that goeth down to the grave shall come up no more.

He shall return no more to his house, neither shall his place know him any more.

Therefore I will not refrain my mouth; I will speak in the

anguish of my spirit; I will complain in the bitterness of my soul.

Am I a sea, or a whale, that thou settest a watch over me?

When I say, My bed shall comfort me, my couch shall ease my complaint;

Then thou scarest me with dreams, and terrifiest me through visions:

So that my soul chooseth strangling, and death rather than my life.

I loathe it; I would not live always: let me alone: for my days are vanity.

What is man, that thou shouldest magnify him, and that thou shouldest set thy heart upon him?

And that thou shouldest visit him every morning and try him every moment?

How long wilt thou not depart from me, nor let me alone till I swallow down my spittle?

I have sinned; what shall I do unto thee, O thou Preserver of men? why hast thou set me as a mark against thee, so that I am a burden to myself?

And why dost thou not pardon my transgression, and take away mine iniquity? for now shall I sleep in the dust; and thou shalt seek me in the morning, but I shall not be.

❧

Then answered Bildad the Shuhite, and said,

How long wilt thou speak these things? and how long shall the words of thy mouth be like a strong wind?

Doth God pervert judgment; or doth the Almighty pervert justice?

If thy children have sinned against him, and he have cast them away for their transgression;

If thou wouldest seek unto God betimes, and make thy supplication to the Almighty;

If thou wert pure and upright, surely now he would awake

for thee, and make the habitation of thy righteousness prosperous.

Though thy beginning was small, yet thy latter end should greatly increase.

For inquire, I pray thee, of the former age, and prepare thyself to the search of their fathers:

(For we are but of yesterday, and know nothing, because our days upon earth are a shadow:)

Shall not they teach thee, and tell thee, and utter words out of their heart?

Can the rush grow up without mire? can the flag grow without water?

Whilst it is yet in his greenness, and not cut down, it withereth before any other herb.

So are the paths of all that forget God; and the hypocrite's hope shall perish.

Whose hope shall be cut off, and whose trust shall be a spider's web.

He shall lean upon his house, but it shall not stand: he shall hold it fast, but it shall not endure.

He is green before the sun, and his branch shooteth forth in his garden.

His roots are wrapped about the heap, and seeth the place of stones.

If he destroy him from his place, then it shall deny him, saying, I have not seen thee.

Behold, this is the joy of his way, and out of the earth shall others grow.

Behold, God will not cast away a perfect man, neither will he help the evil doers:

Till he fill thy mouth with laughing, and thy lips with rejoicing.

They that hate thee shall be clothed with shame; and the dwelling-place of the wicked shall come to nought.

Then Job answered and said,

I know it is so of a truth: but how should man be just with God?

If he will contend with him, he cannot answer him one of a thousand.

He is wise in heart, and mighty in strength: who hath hardened himself against him, and hath prospered?

Which removeth the mountains, and they know not: which overturneth them in his anger;

Which shaketh the earth out of her place, and the pillars thereof tremble;

Which commandeth the sun, and it riseth not; and sealeth up the stars;

Which alone spreadeth out the heavens, and treadeth upon the waves of the sea;

Which maketh Arcturus, Orion, and Pleiades, and the chambers of the south;

Which doeth great things past finding out; yea, and wonders without number.

Lo, he goeth by me, and I see him not: he passeth on also, but I perceive him not.

Behold, he taketh away, who can hinder him? who will say unto him, What doest thou?

If God will not withdraw his anger, the proud helpers do stoop under him.

How much less shall I answer him, and choose out my words to reason with him?

Whom, though I were righteous, yet would I not answer, but I would make supplication to my judge.

If I had called, and he had answered me; yet would I not believe that he had hearkened unto my voice.

For he breaketh me with a tempest, and multiplieth my wounds without cause.

He will not suffer me to take my breath, but filleth me with bitterness.

If I speak of strength, lo, he is strong: and if of judgment, who shall set me a time to plead?

If I justify myself, mine own mouth shall condemn me: if I say, I am perfect, it shall also prove me perverse.

Though I were perfect, yet would I not know my soul: I would despise my life.

This is one thing, therefore I said it, He destroyeth the perfect and the wicked.

If the scourge slay suddenly, he will laugh at the trial of the innocent.

The earth is given into the hand of the wicked: he covereth the faces of the judges thereof; if not, where, and who is he?

Now my days are swifter than a post; they flee away, they see no good.

They are passed away as the swift ships: as the eagle that hasteth to the prey.

If I say, I will forget my complaint, I will leave off my heaviness, and comfort myself.

I am afraid of all my sorrows, I know that thou wilt not hold me innocent.

If I be wicked, why then labour I in vain?

If I wash myself with snow-water, and make my hands never so clean;

Yet shalt thou plunge me in the ditch, and mine own clothes shall abhor me.

For he is not a man, as I am, that I should answer him, and we should come together in judgment.

Neither is there any daysman betwixt us, that might lay his hand upon us both.

Let him take his rod away from me, and let not his fear terrify me:

Then would I speak, and not fear him; but it is not so with me.

My soul is weary of my life; I will leave my complaint upon myself; I will speak in the bitterness of my soul.

I will say unto God, Do not condemn me; shew me wherefore thou contendest with me.

Is it good unto thee that thou shouldest oppress, that thou shouldest despise the work of thy hands, and shine upon the counsel of the wicked?

Hast thou eyes of flesh? or seest thou as man seeth?

Are thy days as the days of man? are thy years as man's days,

That thou inquirest after mine iniquity, and searchest after my sin?

Thou knowest that I am not wicked; and there is none that can deliver out of thy hand.

Thy hands have made me and fashioned me together round about; yet thou dost destroy me.

Remember, I beseech thee, that thou hast made me as the clay; and wilt thou bring me into dust again?

Hast thou not poured me out as milk, and curdled me like cheese?

Thou hast clothed me with skin and flesh, and hast fenced me with bones and sinews.

Thou hast granted me life and favour, and thy visitation hath preserved my spirit.

And these things hast thou hid in thine heart: I know that this is with thee.

If I sin, then thou markest me, and thou wilt not acquit me from mine iniquity.

If I be wicked, wo unto me; and if I be righteous, yet will I not lift up my head. I am full of confusion; therefore see thou mine affliction;

For it increaseth. Thou huntest me as a fierce lion: and again thou shewest thyself marvellous upon me.

Thou renewest thy witnesses against me, and increasest thine indignation upon me; changes and war are against me.

Wherefore then hast thou brought me forth out of the womb? Oh that I had given up the ghost, and no eye had seen me!

I should have been as though I had not been; I should have been carried from the womb to the grave.

Are not my days few? cease then, and let me alone, that I may take comfort a little,

Before I go whence I shall not return, even to the land of darkness, and the shadow of death,

A land of darkness, as darkness itself; and of the shadow of death, without any order, and where the light is as darkness.

❧

Then answered Zophar the Naamathite, and said,

Should not the multitude of words be answered? and should a man full of talk be justified?

Should thy lies make men hold their peace? and when thou mockest, shall no man make thee ashamed?

For thou hast said, My doctrine is pure, and I am clean in thine eyes.

But Oh that God would speak, and open his lips against thee;

And that he would shew thee the secrets of wisdom, that they are double to that which is! Know therefore that God exacteth of thee less than thine iniquity deserveth.

Canst thou by searching find out God? canst thou find out the Almighty unto perfection?

It is as high as heaven; what canst thou do? deeper than hell; what canst thou know?

The measure thereof is longer than the earth, and broader than the sea.

If he cut off, and shut up, or gather together, then who can hinder him?

For he knoweth vain men: he seeth wickedness also; will he not then consider it?

For vain man would be wise, though man be born like a wild ass's colt.

If thou prepare thy heart, and stretch out thy hands toward him;

If iniquity be in thy hand, put it far away, and let not wickedness dwell in thy tabernacles.

For then shalt thou lift up thy face without spot; yea thou shalt be steadfast, and shalt not fear:

Because thou shalt forget thy misery, and remember it as waters that pass away;

And thine age shall be clearer than the noon-day: thou shalt shine forth, thou shalt be as the morning.

And thou shalt be secure, because there is hope; yea, thou shalt dig about thee, and thou shalt take thy rest in safety.

Also thou shalt lie down, and none shall make thee afraid; yea, many shall make suit unto thee.

But the eyes of the wicked shall fail, and they shall not escape, and their hope shall be as the giving up of the ghost.

And Job answered and said,

No doubt but ye are the people, and wisdom shall die with you.

But I have understanding as well as you; I am not inferior to you: yea, who knoweth not such things as these?

I am as one mocked of his neighbour, who calleth upon God, and he answereth him: the just upright man is laughed to scorn.

He that is ready to slip with his feet is as a lamp despised in the thought of him that is at ease.

The tabernacles of robbers prosper, and they that provoke God are secure; into whose hand God bringeth abundantly.

But ask now the beasts, and they shall teach thee; and the fowls of the air, and they shall tell thee:

Or speak to the earth, and it shall teach thee; and the fishes of the sea shall declare unto thee.

Who knoweth not in all these that the hand of the Lord hath wrought this?

In whose hand is the soul of every living thing, and the breath of all mankind.

Doth not the ear try words? and the mouth taste his meat?

With the ancient is wisdom; and in length of days understanding.

With him is wisdom and strength, he hath counsel and understanding.

Behold, he breaketh down, and it cannot be built again: he shutteth up a man, and there can be no opening.

Behold, he withholdeth the waters, and they dry up: also he sendeth them out, and they overturn the earth.

With him is strength and wisdom: the deceived and the deceiver are his.

He leadeth counsellors away spoiled, and maketh the judges fools.

He looseth the bond of kings, and girdeth their loins with a girdle.

He leadeth princes away spoiled, and overthroweth the mighty.

He removeth away the speech of the trusty, and taketh away the understanding of the aged.

He poureth contempt upon princes, and weakeneth the strength of the mighty.

He discovereth deep things out of darkness, and bringeth out to light the shadow of death.

He increaseth the nations, and destroyeth them: he enlargeth the nations, and straiteneth them again.

He taketh away the heart of the chief of the people of the earth, and causeth them to wander in a wilderness where there is no way.

They grope in the dark without light, and he maketh them to stagger like a drunken man.

Lo, mine eye hath seen all this, mine ear hath heard and understood it.

What ye know, the same do I know also: I am not inferior unto you.

Surely I would speak to the Almighty, and I desire to reason with God.

But ye are forgers of lies, ye are all physicians of no value.

O that ye would altogether hold your peace; and it should be your wisdom.

Hear now my reasoning, and hearken to the pleadings of my lips.

Will ye speak wickedly for God? and talk deceitfully for him?

Will ye accept his person? will ye contend for God?

Is it good that he should search you out? or as one man mocketh another, do ye so mock him?

He will surely reprove you, if ye do secretly accept persons.

Shall not his excellency make you afraid? and his dread fall upon you?

Your remembrances are like unto ashes, your bodies to bodies of clay.

Hold your peace, let me alone, that I may speak, and let come on me what will.

Wherefore do I take my flesh in my teeth, and put my life in my hand?

Though he slay me, yet will I trust in him: but I will maintain mine own ways before him.

He also shall be my salvation: for a hypocrite shall not come before him.

Hear diligently my speech, and my declaration with your ears.

Behold, now, I have ordered my cause I know that I shall be justified.

Who is he that will plead with me? for now, if I hold my tongue, I shall give up the ghost.

Only do not two things unto me: then will I not hide myself from thee.

Withdraw thy hand far from me: and let not thy dread make me afraid.

Then call thou, and I will answer: or let me speak, and answer thou me.

How many are mine iniquities and sins? make me to know my trangression and my sin.

Wherefore hidest thou thy face, and holdest me for thine enemy?

Wilt thou break a leaf driven to and fro? and wilt thou pursue the dry stubble?

For thou writest bitter things against me, and makest me to possess the iniquities of my youth.

Thou puttest my feet also in the stocks, and lookest narrowly unto all my paths; thou settest a print upon the heels of my feet.

And he, as a rotten thing, consumeth, as a garment that is moth-eaten.

❧

Man that is born of a woman is of few days, and full of trouble.

He cometh forth like a flower, and is cut down: he fleeth also as a shadow, and continueth not.

And dost thou open thine eyes upon such a one, and bringest me into judgment with thee?

Who can bring a clean thing out of an unclean? not one.

Seeing his days are determined, the number of his months are with thee, thou hast appointed his bounds that he cannot pass;

Turn from him, that he may rest, till he shall accomplish, as a hireling, his day.

For there is hope of a tree, if it be cut down, that it will sprout again, and that the tender branch thereof will not cease.

Though the root thereof wax old in the earth, and the stock thereof die in the ground;

Yet through the scent of water it will bud, and bring forth boughs like a plant.

But man dieth, and wasteth away: yea, man giveth up the ghost, and where is he?

As the waters fail from the sea, and the flood decayeth and dryeth up:

So man lieth down, and riseth not: till the heavens be no more, they shall not awake, nor be raised out of their sleep.

O that thou wouldest hide me in the grave, that thou wouldest keep me secret, until thy wrath be past, that thou wouldest appoint me a set time, and remember me!

If a man die, shall he live again? all the days of my appointed time will I wait, till my change come.

Thou shalt call, and I will answer thee: thou wilt have a desire to the work of thy hands.

For now thou numberest my steps: dost thou not watch over my sin?

My transgression is sealed up in a bag, and thou sewest up mine iniquity.

And surely the mountain falling cometh to nought, and the rock is removed out of his place.

The waters wear the stones: thou washest away the things which grow out of the dust of the earth; and thou destroyest the hope of man.

Thou prevailest for ever against him and he passeth: thou changest his countenance, and sendest him away.

His sons come to honour, and he knoweth it not; and they are brought low, but he perceiveth it not of them.

But his flesh upon him shall have pain, and his soul within him shall mourn.

Then answered Eliphaz the Temanite, and said,

Should a wise man utter vain knowledge, and fill his belly with the east wind?

Should he reason with unprofitable talk? or with speeches wherewith he can do no good?

Yea, thou casteth off fear, and restrainest prayer before God.

For thy mouth uttereth thine iniquity, and thou choosest the tongue of the crafty.

Thine own mouth condemneth thee, and not I: yea, thine own lips testify against thee.

Art thou the first man that was born? or wast thou made before the hills?

Hast thou heard the secret of God? and dost thou restrain wisdom to thyself?

What knowest thou that we know not? what understandest thou, which is not in us?

With us are both the gray-headed and very aged men, much elder than thy father.

Are the consolations of God small with thee? is there any secret thing with thee?

Why doth thy heart carry thee away? and what do thine eyes wink at,

That thou turnest thy spirit against God, and lettest such words go out of thy mouth?

What is man, that he should be clean? and he which is born of a woman, that he should be righteous?

Behold, he putteth no trust in his saints; yea, the heavens are not clean in his sight.

How much more abominable and filthy is man, which drinketh iniquity like water?

I will shew thee, hear me; and that which I have seen, I will declare;

Which wise men have told from their fathers, and have not hid it:

Unto whom alone the earth was given, and no stranger passed among them.

The wicked man travaileth with pain all his days, and the number of years is hidden to the oppressor.

A dreadful sound is in his ears: in prosperity the destroyer shall come upon him.

He believeth not that he shall return out of darkness, and he is waited for of the sword.

He wandereth abroad for bread, saying, Where is it? he knoweth that the day of darkness is ready at his hand.

Trouble and anguish shall make him afraid; they shall prevail against him, as a king ready to the battle.

For he stretcheth out his hand against God, and strengtheneth himself against the Almighty.

He runneth upon him, even on his neck, upon the thick bosses of his bucklers:

Because he covereth his face with his fatness, and maketh collops of fat on his flanks.

And he dwelleth in desolate cities, and in houses which no man inhabiteth, which are ready to become heaps.

He shall not be rich, neither shall his substance continue, neither shall he prolong the perfection thereof upon the earth.

He shall not depart out of darkness; the flame shall dry up his branches, and by the breath of his mouth shall he go away.

Let not him that is deceived trust in vanity: for vanity shall be his recompense.

It shall be accomplished before his time, and his branch shall not be green.

He shall shake off his unripe grape as the vine, and shall cast off his flower as the olive.

For the congregation of hypocrites shall be desolate, and fire shall consume the tabernacles of bribery.

They conceive mischief, and bring forth vanity, and their belly prepareth deceit.

Then Job answered and said,

I have heard many such things: miserable comforters are ye all.

Shall vain words have an end? or what emboldeneth thee that thou answerest?

I also could speak as ye do: if your soul were in my soul's stead, I could heap up words against you, and shake my head at you.

But I would strengthen you with my mouth, and the moving of my lips should assuage your grief.

Though I speak, my grief is not assuaged: and though I forbear, what am I eased?

But now he hath made me weary: thou hast made desolate all my company.

And thou hast filled me with wrinkles, which is a witness against me: and my leanness rising up in me beareth witness to my face.

He teareth me in his wrath, who hateth me: he gnasheth upon me with his teeth; mine enemy sharpeneth his eyes upon me.

They have gaped upon me with their mouth; they have smitten me upon the cheek reproachfully; they have gathered themselves together against me.

God hath delivered me to the ungodly, and turned me over into the hands of the wicked.

I was at ease, but he hath broken me asunder: he hath also taken me by my neck, and shaken me to pieces, and set me up for his mark.

His archers compass me round about; he cleaveth my reins asunder, and doth not spare; he poureth out my gall upon the ground.

He breaketh me with breach upon breach; he runneth upon me like a giant.

I have sewed sackcloth upon my skin, and defiled my horn in the dust.

My face is foul with weeping, and on my eyelids is the shadow of death;

Not for any injustice in my hands: also my prayer is pure.

O earth, cover not thou my blood, and let my cry have no place.

Also now, behold, my witness is in heaven, and my record is on high.

My friends scorn me: but mine eye poureth out tears unto God.

O that one might plead for a man with God, as a man pleadeth for his neighbour!

When a few years are come, then I shall go the way whence I shall not return.

❧

My breath is corrupt, my days are extinct, the graves are ready for me.

Are there not mockers with me? and doth not mine eye continue in their provocation?

Lay down now, put me in a surety with thee: who is he that will strike hands with me?

For thou hast hid their heart from understanding; therefore shalt thou not exalt them.

He that speaketh flattery to his friends, even the eyes of his children shall fail.

He hath made me also a by-word of the people: and aforetime I was as a tabret.

Mine eye also is dim by reason of sorrow, and all my members are as a shadow.

Upright men shall be astonished at this, and the innocent shall stir up himself against the hypocrite.

The righteous also shall hold on his way, and he that hath clean hands shall be stronger and stronger.

But as for you all, do ye return, and come now: for I cannot find one wise man among you.

My days are past, my purposes are broken off, even the thoughts of my heart.

They change the night into day: the light is short because of darkness.

If I wait, the grave is my house: I have made my bed in the darkness.

I have said to corruption, Thou art my father: to the worm, Thou art my mother, and my sister.

And where is now my hope? as for my hope, who shall see it?

They shall go down to the bars of the pit, when our rest together is in the dust.

❧

Then answered Bildad the Shuhite, and said,

How long will it be ere ye make an end of words? mark, and afterwards we will speak.

Wherefore are we counted as beasts, and reputed vile in your sight?

He teareth himself in his anger: shall the earth be forsaken for thee? and shall the rock be removed out of his place?

Yea, the light of the wicked shall be put out, and the spark of his fire shall not shine.

The light shall be dark in his tabernacle, and his candle shall be put out with him.

The steps of his strength shall be straitened, and his own counsel shall cast him down.

For he is cast into a net by his own feet, and he walketh upon a snare.

The gin shall take him by the heel, and the robber shall prevail against him.

The snare is laid for him in the ground, and a trap for him in the way.

Terrors shall make him afraid on every side, and shall drive him to his feet.

His strength shall be hunger-bitten, and destruction shall be ready at his side.

It shall devour the strength of his skin: even the first-born of death shall devour his strength.

His confidence shall be rooted out of his tabernacle, and it shall bring him to the king of terrors.

It shall dwell in his tabernacle, because it is none of his: brimstone shall be scattered upon his habitation.

His roots shall be dried up beneath, and above shall his branch be cut off.

His remembrance shall perish from the earth, and he shall have no name in the street.

He shall be driven from light into darkness, and chased out of the world.

He shall neither have son nor nephew among his people, nor any remaining in his dwellings.

They that come after him shall be astonished at his day, as they that went before were affrighted.

Surely such are the dwellings of the wicked, and this is the place of him that knoweth not God.

❧

Then Job answered and said,

How long will ye vex my soul, and break me in pieces with words?

These ten times have ye reproached me; ye are not ashamed that ye make yourselves strange to me.

And be it indeed that I have erred, mine error remaineth with myself.

If indeed ye will magnify yourselves against me, and plead against me my reproach:

Know now that God hath overthrown me, and hath compassed me with his net.

Behold I cry out of wrong, but I am not heard: I cry aloud, but there is no judgment.

He hath fenced up my way that I cannot pass, and he hath set darkness in my paths.

He hath stripped me of my glory, and taken the crown from my head.

He hath destroyed me on every side, and I am gone: and my hope hath he removed like a tree.

He hath also kindled his wrath against me, and he counteth me unto him as one of his enemies.

His troops come together, and raise up their way against me, and encamp round about my tabernacle.

He hath put my brethren far from me, and mine acquaintance are verily estranged from me.

My kinsfolk have failed, and my familiar friends have forgotten me.

They that dwell in my house, and my maids, count me for a stranger: I am an alien in their sight.

I called my servant, and he gave me no answer; I entreated him with my mouth.

My breath is strange to my wife, though I entreated for the children's sake of mine own body.

Yea, young children despised me; I arose, and they spake against me.

All my inward friends abhorred me: and they whom I loved are turned against me.

My bone cleaveth to my skin and to my flesh, and I am escaped with the skin of my teeth.

Have pity upon me, have pity upon me, O ye my friends; for the hand of God hath touched me.

Why do ye persecute me as God, and are not satisfied with my flesh?

O that my words were now written! O that they were printed in a book!

That they were graven with an iron pen and lead in the rock for ever!

For I know that my Redeemer liveth, and that he shall stand

at the latter day upon the earth:

And though after my skin worms destroy this body, yet in my flesh shall I see God:

Whom I shall see for myself, and mine eyes shall behold, and not another; though my reins be consumed within me.

But ye should say, Why persecute we him, seeing the root of the matter is found in me?

Be ye afraid of the sword: for wrath bringeth the punishments of the sword, that ye may know there is a judgment.

❧

Then answered Zophar the Naamathite, and said,

Therefore do my thoughts cause me to answer, and for this I make haste.

I have heard the check of my reproach, and the spirit of my understanding causeth me to answer.

Knowest thou not this of old, since man was placed upon earth,

That the triumphing of the wicked is short, and the joy of the hypocrite but for a moment?

Though his excellency mount up to the heavens, and his head reach unto the clouds;

Yet he shall perish for ever like his own dung: they which have seen him shall say, Where is he?

He shall fly away as a dream, and shall not be found: yea, he shall be chased away as a vision of the night.

The eye also which saw him shall see him no more; neither shall his place any more behold him.

His children shall seek to please the poor, and his hands shall restore their goods.

His bones are full of the sin of his youth, which shall lie down with him in the dust.

Though wickedness be sweet in his mouth, though he hide it under his tongue;

Though he spare it, and forsake it not; but keep it still within his mouth:

Yet his meat in his bowels is turned, it is the gall of asps within him.

He hath swallowed down riches, and he shall vomit them up again: God shall cast them out of his belly.

He shall suck the poison of asps: the viper's tongue shall slay him.

He shall not see the rivers, the floods, the brooks of honey and butter.

That which he laboured for shall he restore, and shall not swallow it down: according to his substance shall the restitution be, and he shall not rejoice therein.

Because he hath oppressed and hath forsaken the poor; because he hath violently taken away a house which he builded not;

Surely he shall not feel quietness in his belly, he shall not save of that which he desired.

There shall none of his meat be left; therefore shall no man look for his goods.

In the fulness of his sufficiency he shall be in straits: every hand of the wicked shall come upon him.

When he is about to fill his belly, God shall cast the fury of his wrath upon him, and shall rain it upon him while he is eating.

He shall flee from the iron weapon, and the bow of steel shall strike him through.

It is drawn, and cometh out of the body; yea, the glittering sword cometh out of his gall: terrors are upon him.

All darkness shall be hid in his secret places: a fire not blown shall consume him; it shall go ill with him that is left in his tabernacle.

The heaven shall reveal his iniquity; and the earth shall rise up against him.

The increase of his house shall depart, and his goods shall flow away in the day of his wrath.

This is the portion of a wicked man from God, and the heritage appointed unto him by God.

❧

But Job answered and said,

Hear diligently my speech, and let this be your consolations.

Suffer me that I may speak; and after that I have spoken, mock on.

As for me, is my complaint to man? and if it were so, why should not my spirit be troubled?

Mark me, and be astonished, and lay your hand upon your mouth.

Even when I remember I am afraid, and trembling taketh hold on my flesh.

Wherefore do the wicked live, become old, yea, are mighty in power?

Their seed is established in their sight with them, and their offspring before their eyes.

Their houses are safe from fear, neither is the rod of God upon them.

Their bull gendereth, and faileth not: their cow calveth, and casteth not her calf.

They send forth their little ones like a flock, and their children dance.

They take the timbrel and harp, and rejoice at the sound of the organ.

They spend their days in wealth, and in a moment go down to the grave.

Therefore they say unto God, Depart from us; for we desire not the knowledge of thy ways.

What is the Almighty, that we should serve him? and what profit should we have, if we pray unto him?

Lo, their good is not in their hand: the counsel of the wicked is far from me.

How oft is the candle of the wicked put out? and how oft cometh their destruction upon them? God distributeth sorrows in his anger.

They are as stubble before the wind, and as chaff that the storm carrieth away.

God layeth up his iniquity for his children: he rewardeth him, and he shall know it.

His eyes shall see his destruction, and he shall drink of the wrath of the Almighty.

For what pleasure hath he in his house after him, when the number of his months is cut off in the midst?

Shall any teach God knowledge? seeing he judgeth those that are high.

One dieth in his full strength, being wholly at ease and quiet.

His breasts are full of milk, and his bones are moistened with marrow.

And another dieth in the bitterness of his soul, and never eateth with pleasure.

They shall lie down alike in the dust, and the worms shall cover them.

Behold, I know your thoughts, and the devices which ye wrongfully imagine against me.

For ye say, Where is the house of the prince? and where are the dwelling-places of the wicked?

Have ye not asked them that go by the way? and do ye not know their tokens,

That the wicked is reserved to the day of destruction? they shall be brought forth to the day of wrath.

Who shall declare his way to his face? and who shall repay him what he hath done?

Yet shall he be brought to the grave, and shall remain in the tomb.

The clods of the valley shall be sweet unto him, and every man shall draw after him, as there are innumerable before him.

How then comfort ye me in vain, seeing in your answers there remaineth falsehood?

❧

Then Eliphaz the Temanite answered and said,

Can a man be profitable unto God, as he that is wise may be profitable unto himself?

Is it any pleasure to the Almighty, that thou art righteous? or is it gain to him, that thou makest thy ways perfect?

Will he reprove thee for fear of thee? will he enter with thee into judgment?

Is not thy wickedness great? and thine iniquities infinite?

For thou hast taken a pledge from thy brother for nought, and stripped the naked of their clothing.

Thou hast not given water to the weary to drink, and thou hast withholden bread from the hungry.

But as for the mighty man, he had the earth; and the honourable man dwelt in it.

Thou hast sent widows away empty, and the arms of the fatherless have been broken.

Therefore snares are round about thee, and sudden fear troubleth thee;

Or darkness, that thou canst not see; and abundance of waters cover thee.

Is not God in the height of heaven? and behold the height of the stars, how high they are!

And thou sayest, How doth God know? can he judge through the dark cloud?

Thick clouds are a covering to him, that he seeth not; and he walketh in the circuit of heaven.

Hast thou marked the old way which wicked men have trodden?

Which were cut down out of time, whose foundation was overflown with a flood:

Which said unto God, Depart from us: and what can the Almighty do for them?

Yet he filled their houses with good things: but the counsel of the wicked is far from me.

The righteous see it, and are glad: and the innocent laugh them to scorn.

Whereas our substance is not cut down, but the remnant of them the fire consumeth.

Acquaint now thyself with him, and be at peace: thereby good shall come unto thee.

Receive, I pray thee, the law from his mouth, and lay up his words in thy heart.

If thou return to the Almighty, thou shalt be built up, thou shalt put iniquity far from thy tabernacles.

Then shalt thou lay up gold as dust, and the gold of Ophir as the stones of the brooks.

Yea, the Almighty shall be thy defence, and thou shalt have plenty of silver.

For then shalt thou have thy delight in the almighty, and shalt lift up thy face unto God.

Thou shalt make thy prayer unto him, and he shall hear thee, and thou shalt pay thy vows.

Thou shalt also decree a thing, and it shall be established unto thee: and the light shall shine upon thy ways.

When men are cast down, then thou shalt say, There is lifting up; and he shall save the humble person.

He shall deliver the island of the innocent: and it is delivered by the pureness of thy hands.

❧

Then Job answered and said,

Even to-day is my complaint bitter: my stroke is heavier than my groaning.

Oh that I knew where I might find him! that I might come even to his seat!

I would order my cause before him, and fill my mouth with arguments.

I would know the words which he would answer me, and understand what he would say unto me.

Will he plead against me with his great power? No; but he would put strength in me.

There the righteous might dispute with him; so should I be delivered for ever from my judge.

Behold, I go forward, but he is not there; and backward, but I cannot perceive him:

On the left hand, where he doth work, but I cannot behold him: he hideth himself on the right hand, that I cannot see him:

But he knoweth the way that I take: when he hath tried me, I shall come forth as gold.

My foot hath held his steps, his way have I kept, and not declined.

Neither have I gone back from the commandment of his lips; I have esteemed the words of his mouth more than my necessary food.

But he is in one mind, and who can turn him? and what his soul desireth, even that he doeth.

For he performeth the thing that is appointed for me: and many such things are with him.

Therefore am I troubled at his presence: when I consider, I am afraid of him.

For God maketh my heart soft, and the Almighty troubleth me:

Because I was not cut off before the darkness, neither hath he covered the darkness from my face.

⸎

Why, seeing times are not hidden from the Almighty, do they that know him not see his days?

Some remove the landmarks; they violently take away flocks, and feed thereof.

They drive away the ass of the fatherless, they take the widow's ox for a pledge.

They turn the needy out of the way: the poor of the earth hide themselves together.

Behold, as wild asses in the desert, go they forth to their work; rising betimes for a prey: the wilderness yieldeth food for them and for their children.

They reap every one his corn in the field: and they gather the vintage of the wicked.

They cause the naked to lodge without clothing, that they have no covering in the cold.

They are wet with the showers of the mountains, and embrace the rock for want of a shelter.

They pluck the fatherless from the breast, and take a pledge of the poor.

They cause him to go naked without clothing, and they take away the sheaf from the hungry;

Which make oil within their walls, and tread their winepresses, and suffer thirst.

Men groan from out of the city, and the soul of the wounded crieth out: yet God layeth not folly to them.

They are of those that rebel against the light; they know not the ways thereof, nor abide in the paths thereof.

The murderer rising with the light killeth the poor and needy, and in the night is as a thief.

The eye also of the adulterer waiteth for the twilight, saying, No eye shall see me: and disguiseth his face.

In the dark they dig through houses, which they had marked for themselves in the day-time: they know not the light.

For the morning is to them even as the shadow of death: if one know them, they are in the terrors of the shadow of death.

He is swift as the waters; their portion is cursed in the

earth: he beholdeth not the way of the vineyards.

Drought and heat consume the snow-waters: so doth the grave those which have sinned.

The womb shall forget him; the worm shall feed sweetly on him; he shall be no more remembered; and wickedness shall be broken as a tree.

He evil-entreateth the barren that beareth not: and doeth not good to the widow.

He draweth also the mighty with his power: he riseth up, and no man is sure of life.

Though it be given him to be in safety, whereon he resteth; yet his eyes are upon their way.

They are exalted for a little while, but are gone and brought low; they are taken out of the way as all other and cut off as the tops of the ears of corn.

And if it be not so now, who will make me a liar, and make my speech nothing worth?

Then answered Bildad the Shuhite, and said,

Dominion and fear are with him, he maketh peace in his high places.

Is there any number of his armies? and upon whom doth not his light arise?

How then can man be justified with God? or how can he be clean that is born of a woman?

Behold even to the moon, and it shineth not; yea, the stars are not pure in his sight.

How much less man, that is a worm; and the son of man, which is a worm?

But Job answered and said,

How hast thou helped him that is without power? how savest thou the arm that hath no strength?

How hast thou counselled him that hath no wisdom? and how hast thou plentifully declared the thing as it is?

To whom hast thou uttered words? and whose spirit came from thee?

Dead things are formed from under the waters, and the inhabitants thereof.

Hell is naked before him, and destruction hath no covering.

He stretcheth out the north over the empty place, and hangeth the earth upon nothing.

He bindeth up the waters in his thick clouds; and the cloud is not rent under them.

He holdeth back the face of his throne, and spreadeth his cloud upon it.

He hath compassed the waters with bounds, until the day and night come to an end.

The pillars of heaven tremble, and are astonished at his reproof.

He divideth the sea with his power, and by his understanding he smiteth through the proud.

By his Spirit he hath garnished the heavens; his hand hath formed the crooked serpent.

Lo, these are parts of his ways; but how little a portion is heard of him? but the thunder of his power who can understand?

Moreover, Job continued his parable, and said,

As God liveth, who hath taken away my judgment; and the Almighty, who hath vexed my soul;

All the while my breath is in me, and the spirit of God is in my nostrils;

My lips shall not speak wickedness, nor my tongue utter deceit.

God forbid that I should justify you: till I die I will not remove mine integrity from me.

My righteousness I hold fast, and will not let it go: my heart shall not reproach me so long as I live.

Let mine enemy be as the wicked, and he that riseth up against me as the unrighteous.

For what is the hope of the hypocrite, though he hath gained, when God taketh away his soul?

Will God hear his cry when trouble cometh upon him?

Will he delight himself in the Almighty? will he always call upon God?

I will teach you by the hand of God: that which is with the Almighty will I not conceal.

Behold, all ye yourselves have seen it; why then are ye thus altogether vain?

This is the portion of a wicked man with God, and the heritage of oppressors, which they shall receive of the Almighty.

If his children be multiplied, it is for the sword: and his offspring shall not be satisfied with bread.

Those that remain of him shall be buried in death: and his widows shall not weep.

Though he heap up silver as the dust, and prepare raiment as the clay;

He may prepare it, but the just shall put it on, and the innocent shall divide the silver.

He buildeth his house as a moth, and as a booth that the keeper maketh.

The rich man shall lie down, but he shall not be gathered: he openeth his eyes, and he is not.

Terrors take hold on him as waters, a tempest stealeth him away in the night.

The east wind carrieth him away, and he departeth: and as a storm hurleth him out of his place.

For God shall cast upon him, and not spare: he would fain flee out of his hand.

Men shall clap their hands at him, and shall hiss him out of his place.

❧§❧

Surely there is a vein for the silver, and a place for gold where they fine it.

Iron is taken out of the earth, and brass is molten out of the stone.

He setteth an end to darkness, and searcheth out all perfection: the stones of darkness, and the shadow of death.

The flood breaketh out from the inhabitant; even the waters forgotten of the foot: they are dried up, they are gone away from men.

As for the earth, out of it cometh bread: and under it is turned up as it were fire.

The stones of it are the place of sapphires: and it hath dust of gold.

There is a path which no fowl knoweth, and which the vulture's eye hath not seen:

The lion's whelps have not trodden it, nor the fierce lion passed by it.

He putteth forth his hand upon the rock; he overturneth the mountains by the roots.

He cutteth out rivers among the rocks; and his eye seeth every precious thing.

He bindeth the floods from overflowing; and the thing that is hid bringeth he forth to light.

But where shall wisdom be found? and where is the place of understanding?

Man knoweth not the price thereof; neither is it found in the land of the living.

The depth saith, It is not in me: and the sea saith, It is not with me.

It cannot be gotten for gold, neither shall silver be weighed for the price thereof.

It cannot be valued with the gold of Ophir, with the precious onyx, or the sapphire.

The gold and the crystal cannot equal it: and the exchange

of it shalt not be for jewels of fine gold.

No mention shall be made of coral, or of pearls: for the price of wisdom is above rubies.

The topaz of Ethiopia shall not equal it, neither shall it be valued with pure gold.

Whence then cometh wisdom? and where is the place of understanding?

Seeing it is hid from the eyes of all living, and kept close from the fowls of the air.

Destruction and death say, We have heard the fame thereof with our ears.

God understandeth the way thereof, and he knoweth the place thereof.

For he looketh to the ends of the earth, and seeth under the whole heaven;

To make the weight for the winds; and he weigheth the waters by measure.

When he made a decree for the rain, and a way for the lightning of the thunder;

Then did he see it, and declare it; he prepared it, yea, and searched it out.

And unto man he said, Behold, the fear of the Lord, that is wisdom; and to depart from evil is understanding.

Moreover, Job continued his parable, and said,

Oh that I were as in months past, as in the days when God preserved me;

When his candle shined upon my head, and when by his light I walked through darkness;

As I was in the days of my youth, when the secret of God was upon my tabernacle;

When the Almighty was yet with me, when my children were about me;

When I washed my steps with butter, and the rock poured me out rivers of oil;

When I went out to the gate through the city, when I prepared my seat in the street!

The young men saw me, and hid themselves: and the aged arose, and stood up.

The princes refrained talking, and laid their hand on their mouth.

The nobles held their peace, and their tongue cleaved to the roof of their mouth.

When the ear heard me, then it blessed me; and when the eye saw me, it gave witness to me:

Because I delivered the poor that cried, and the fatherless, and him that had none to help him.

The blessing of him that was ready to perish came upon me: and I caused the widow's heart to sing for joy.

I put on righteousness, and it clothed me: my judgment was a robe and a diadem.

I was eyes to the blind, and feet was I to the lame.

I was a father to the poor: and the cause which I knew not I searched out.

And I brake the jaws of the wicked, and plucked the spoil out of his teeth.

Then I said, I shall die in my nest, and I shall multiply my days as the sand.

My root was spread out by the waters, and the dew lay all night upon my branch.

My glory was fresh in me, and my bow was renewed in my hand.

Unto me men gave ear, and waited, and kept silence at my counsel.

After my words they spake not again; and my speech dropped upon them.

And they waited for me as for the rain; and they opened their mouth wide as for the latter rain.

If I laughed on them, they believed it not; and the light of my countenance they cast not down.

I chose out their way, and sat chief, and dwelt as a king in the army, as one that comforteth the mourners.

❧

But now they that are younger than I have me in derision, whose fathers I would have disdained to have set with the dogs of my flock.

Yea, whereto might the strength of their hands profit me, in whom old age was perished?

For want and famine they were solitary: fleeing into the wilderness in former time desolate and waste.

Who cut up mallows by the bushes and juniper-roots for their meat.

They were driven forth from among men, (they cried after them as after a thief;)

To dwell in the cliffs of the valleys, in caves of the earth, and in the rocks.

Among the bushes they brayed; under the nettles they were gathered together.

They were children of fools, yea, children of base men: they were viler than the earth.

And now am I their song, yea, I am their by-word.

They abhor me, they flee far from me, and spare not to spit in my face.

Because he hath loosed my cord, and afflicted me, they have also let loose the bridle before me.

Upon my right hand rise the youth; they push away my feet, and they raise up against me the ways of their destruction.

They mar my path, they set forward my calamity, they have no helper.

They came upon me as a wide breaking in of waters: in

the desolation they rolled themselves upon me.

Terrors are turned upon me: they pursue my soul as the wind: and my welfare passeth away as a cloud.

And now my soul is poured out upon me; the days of affliction have taken hold upon me.

My bones are pierced in me in the night season: and my sinews take no rest.

By the great force of my disease is my garment changed: it bindeth me about as the collar of my coat.

He hath cast me into the mire, and I am become like dust and ashes.

I cry unto thee, and thou dost not hear me: I stand up, and thou regardest me not.

Thou art become cruel to me: with thy strong hand thou opposest thyself against me.

Thou liftest me up to the wind; thou causest me to ride upon it, and dissolvest my substance.

For I know that thou wilt bring me to death, and to the house appointed for all living.

Howbeit he will not stretch out his hand to the grave, though they cry in his destruction.

Did not I weep for him that was in trouble? was not my soul grieved for the poor?

When I looked for good, then evil came unto me: and when I waited for light, there came darkness.

My bowels boiled, and rested not: the days of affliction prevented me.

I went mourning without the sun: I stood up, and I cried in the congregation.

I am a brother to dragons, and a companion to owls.

My skin is black upon me, and my bones are burnt with heat.

My harp also is turned to mourning, and my organ into the voice of them that weep.

❧

I made a covenant with mine eyes; why then should I think upon a maid?

For what portion of God is there from above? and what inheritance of the Almighty from on high?

Is not destruction to the wicked? and a strange punishment to the workers of iniquity?

Doth not he see my ways, and count all my steps?

If I have walked with vanity, or if my foot hath hasted to deceit;

Let me be weighed in an even balance, that God may know mine integrity.

If my step hath turned out of the way, and my heart walked after mine eyes, and if any blot hath cleaved to my hands;

Then let me sow, and let another eat; yea, let my offspring be rooted out.

If my heart have been deceived by a woman, or if I have laid wait at my neighbour's door;

Then let my wife grind unto another, and let others bow down upon her.

For this is a heinous crime; yea, it is iniquity to be punished by the judges.

For it is a fire that consumeth to destruction, and would root out all mine increase.

If I did despise the cause of my man-servant or of my maid-servant, when they contended with me;

What then shall I do when God riseth up? and when he visiteth, what shall I answer him?

Did not he that made me in the womb make him? and did not one fashion us in the womb?

If I have withheld the poor from their desire, or have caused the eyes of the widow to fail;

Or have eaten my morsel myself alone, and the fatherless hath not eaten thereof;

(For from my youth he was brought up with me, as with a

father, and I have guided her from my mother's womb;)

If I have seen any perish for want of clothing, or any poor without covering;

If his loins have not blessed me, and if he were not warmed with the fleece of my sheep;

If I have lifted up my hand against the fatherless, when I saw my help in the gate:

Then let mine arm fall from my shoulder-blade, and mine arm be broken from the bone.

For destruction from God was a terror to me, and by reason of his highness I could not endure.

If I have made gold my hope, or have said to the fine gold, Thou art my confidence;

If I rejoiced because my wealth was great, and because my hand had gotten much;

If I beheld the sun when it shined, or the moon walking in brightness;

And my heart hath been secretly enticed, or my mouth hath kissed my hand:

This also were an iniquity to be punished by the judge: for I should have denied the God that is above.

If I rejoiced at the destruction of him that hated me, or lifted up myself when evil found him:

Neither have I suffered my mouth to sin by wishing a curse to his soul.

If the men of my tabernacle said not, Oh that we had of his flesh! we cannot be satisfied.

The stranger did not lodge in the street: but I opened my doors to the traveller.

If I covered my transgressions as Adam, by hiding mine iniquity in my bosom:

Did I fear a great multitude, or did the contempt of families terrify me, that I kept silence, and went not out of the door?

Oh that one would hear me! behold, my desire is, that the

Almighty would answer me, and that mine adversary had written a book.

Surely I would take it upon my shoulder, and bind it as a crown to me.

I would declare unto him the number of my steps; as a prince would I go near unto him.

If my land cry against me, or that the furrows likewise thereof complain;

If I have eaten the fruits thereof without money, or have caused the owners thereof to lose their life:

Let thistles grow instead of wheat, and cockle instead of barley. The words of Job are ended.

❧

So these three men ceased to answer Job, because he was righteous in his own eyes.

Then was kindled the wrath of Elihu the son of Barachel the Buzite, of the kindred of Ram: against Job was his wrath kindled, because he justified himself rather than God.

Also against his three friends was his wrath kindled, because they had found no answer, and yet had condemned Job.

Now Elihu had waited till Job had spoken, because they were elder than he.

When Elihu saw that there was no answer in the mouth of these three men, then his wrath was kindled.

And Elihu the son of Barachel the Buzite answered and said, I am young, and ye are very old; wherefore I was afraid, and durst not shew you mine opinion.

I said, Days should speak, and multitude of years should teach wisdom.

But there is a spirit in man: and the inspiration of the Almighty giveth them understanding.

Great men are not always wise; neither do the aged understand judgment.

Therefore I said, Hearken to me; I also will shew mine opinion.

Behold, I waited for your words; I gave ear to your reasons, whilst ye searched out what to say.

Yea, I attended unto you, and behold, there was none of you that convinced Job, or that answered his words:

Lest ye should say, We have found out wisdom: God thrusteth him down, not man.

Now he hath not directed his words against me: neither will I answer him with your speeches.

They were amazed, they answered no more: they left off speaking.

When I had waited, (for they spake not, but stood still, and answered no more;)

I said, I will answer also my part, I also will shew mine opinion.

For I am full of matter, the spirit within me constraineth me.

Behold, my belly is as wine which hath no vent; it is ready to burst like new bottles.

I will speak, that I may be refreshed: I will open my lips and answer.

Let me not, I pray you, accept any man's person, neither let me give flattering titles unto man.

For I know not to give flattering titles; in so doing my Maker would soon take me away.

❧

Wherefore, Job, I pray thee, hear my speeches, and hearken to all my words.

Behold, now I have opened my mouth, my tongue hath spoken in my mouth.

My words shall be of the uprightness of my heart: and my lips shall utter knowledge clearly.

The Spirit of God hath made me, and the breath of the Almighty hath given me life.

If thou canst answer me, set thy words in order before me, stand up.

Behold, I am according to thy wish in God's stead: I also am formed out of the clay.

Behold, my terror shall not make thee afraid, neither shall my hand be heavy upon thee.

Surely thou hast spoken in my hearing, and I have heard the voice of thy words, saying,

I am clean without transgression, I am innocent; neither is there iniquity in me.

Behold, he findeth occasions against me, he counteth me for his enemy.

He putteth my feet in the stocks, he marketh all my paths.

Behold, in this thou art not just: I will answer thee that God is greater than man.

Why dost thou strive against him? for he giveth not account of any of his matters.

For God speaketh once, yea twice, yet man perceiveth it not.

In a dream, in a vision of the night, when deep sleep falleth upon men, in slumberings upon the bed;

Then he openeth the ears of men, and sealeth their instruction,

That he may withdraw man from his purpose, and hide pride from man.

He keepeth back his soul from the pit, and his life from perishing by the sword.

He is chastened also with pain upon his bed, and the multitude of his bones with strong pain:

So that his life abhorreth bread, and his soul dainty meat.

His flesh is consumed away, that it cannot be seen; and his bones that were not seen, stick out.

Yes, his soul draweth near unto the grave, and his life to the destroyers.

If there be a messenger with him, an interpreter, one among a thousand, to shew unto man his uprightness:

Then he is gracious unto him, and saith, Deliver him from going down to the pit: I have found a ransom.

His flesh shall be fresher than a child's: he shall return to the days of his youth:

He shall pray unto God, and he will be favourable unto him: and he shall see his face with joy: for he will render unto man his righteousness.

He looketh upon men, and if any say, I have sinned, and perverted that which was right, and it profited me not;

He will deliver his soul from going into the pit, and his life shall see the light.

Lo, all these things worketh God oftentimes with man,

To bring back his soul from the pit, to be enlightened with the light of the living.

Mark well, O Job, hearken unto me: hold thy peace, and I will speak,

If thou hast any thing to say, answer me: speak, for I desire to justify thee.

If not, hearken unto me: hold thy peace, and I shall teach thee wisdom.

⁂

Furthermore Elihu answered and said,

Hear my words, O ye wise men; and give ear unto me, ye that have knowledge.

For the ear trieth words, as the mouth tasteth meat.

Let us choose to us judgment: let us know among ourselves what is good.

For Job hath said I am righteous: and God hath taken away my judgment.

Should I lie against my right? my wound is incurable without transgression.

What man is like Job, who drinketh up scorning like water;

Which goeth in company with the workers of iniquity, and walketh with wicked men?

For he hath said, It profiteth a man nothing that he should delight himself with God.

Therefore hearken unto me, ye men of understanding: far be it from God, that he should do wickedness; and from the Almighty, that he should commit iniquity.

For the work of a man shall he render unto him, and cause every man to find according to his ways.

Yea surely God will not do so wickedly, neither will the Almighty pervert judgment.

Who hath given him a charge over the earth? or who hath disposed the whole world?

If he set his heart upon man, if he gather unto himself his spirit and his breath;

All flesh shall perish together, and man shall turn again unto dust.

If now thou hast understanding, hear this: hearken to the voice of my words.

Shall even he that hateth right govern? and wilt thou condemn him that is most just?

Is it fit to say to a king, Thou art wicked? and to princes, Ye are ungodly?

How much less to him that accepteth not the persons of princes, nor regardeth the rich more than the poor? for they all are the work of his hands.

In a moment shall they die, and the people shall be troubled at midnight, and pass away: and the mighty shall be taken away without hand.

For his eyes are upon the ways of man, and he seeth all his goings.

There is no darkness, nor shadow of death, where the workers of iniquity may hide themselves.

For he will not lay upon man more than right; that he should enter into judgment with God.

He shall break in pieces mighty men without number, and set others in their stead.

Therefore he knoweth their works, and he overturneth them in the night, so that they are destroyed.

He striketh them as wicked men in the open sight of others;

Because they turned back from him, and would not consider any of his ways:

So that they cause the cry of the poor to come unto him and he heareth the cry of the afflicted.

When he giveth quietness, who then can make trouble? and when he hideth his face, who then can behold him? whether it be done against a nation, or against a man only:

That the hypocrite reign not, lest the people be ensnared.

Surely it is meet to be said unto God, I have done iniquity, I will do no more.

Should it be according to thy mind? he will recompense it, whether thou refuse, or whether thou choose; and not I: therefore speak what thou knowest.

Let men of understanding tell me, and let a wise man hearken unto me.

Job hath spoken without knowledge, and his words were without wisdom.

My desire is that Job may be tried unto the end, because of his answers for wicked men.

For he addeth rebellion unto his sin, he clappeth his hands among us, and multiplieth his words against God.

❧

Elihu spake moreover, and said,

Thinkest thou this to be right, that thou saidst, My righteousness is more than God's?

For thou saidst, What advantage will it be unto thee? and, What profit shall I have if I be cleansed from my sin?

I will answer thee, and thy companions with thee.

Look unto the heavens, and see, and behold the clouds which are higher than thou.

If thou sinnest, what dost thou against him? or if thy transgressions be multiplied, what dost thou unto him?

If thou be righteous, what givest thou him? or what receiveth he of thy hand?

Thy wickedness may hurt a man as thou art: and thy righteousness may profit the son of man.

By reason of the multitude of oppressions they make the oppressed to cry: they cry out by reason of the arm of the mighty.

But none saith, Where is God my maker, who giveth songs in the night;

Who teacheth us more than the beasts of the earth, and maketh us wiser than the fowls of heaven?

There they cry, but none giveth answer, because of the pride of evil men.

Surely God will not hear vanity, neither will the Almighty regard it.

Although thou sayest thou shalt not see him, yet judgment is before him; therefore trust thou in him.

But now, because it is not so, he hath visited in his anger; yet he knoweth it not in great extremity:

Therefore doth Job open his mouth in vain; he multiplieth words without knowledge.

❧

Elihu also proceeded and said,

Suffer me a little, and I will shew thee that I have yet to speak on God's behalf.

I will fetch my knowledge from afar, and will ascribe righteousness to my Maker.

For truly my words shall not be false: he that is perfect in knowledge is with thee.

Behold, God is mighty, and despiseth not any: he is mighty in strength and wisdom.

He preserveth not the life of the wicked: but giveth right to the poor.

He withdraweth not his eyes from the righteous: but with kings are they on the throne; yea, he doth establish them for ever, and they are exalted.

And if they be bound in fetters, and be holden in cords of affliction;

Then he sheweth them their work, and their transgressions that they have exceeded.

He openeth also their ear to discipline, and commandeth that they return from iniquity.

If they obey and serve him, they shall spend their days in prosperity, and their years in pleasures.

But if they obey not, they shall perish by the sword, and they shall die without knowledge.

But the hypocrites in heart heap up wrath: they cry not when he bindeth them.

They die in youth, and their life is among the unclean.

He delivereth the poor in his affliction, and openeth their ears in oppression.

Even so would he have removed thee out of the strait into a broad place, where there is no straitness; and that which should be set on thy table should be full of fatness.

But thou hast fulfilled the judgment of the wicked; judgment and justice take hold on thee.

Because there is wrath, beware lest he take thee away with his stroke: then a great ransom cannot deliver thee.

Will he esteem thy riches? no, not gold, nor all the forces of strength.

Desire not the night, when people are cut off in their place.

Take heed, regard not iniquity: for this hast thou chosen rather than affliction.

Behold, God exalteth by his power: who teacheth like him?

Who hath enjoined him his way? or who can say, Thou hast wrought iniquity?

Remember that thou magnify his work, which men behold.

Every man may see it; man may behold it afar off.

Behold, God is great, and we know him not, neither can the number of his years be searched out.

For he maketh small the drops of water: they pour down rain according to the vapour thereof;

Which the clouds do drop and distil upon man abundantly.

Also can any understand the spreadings of the clouds, or the noise of his tabernacle?

Behold, he spreadeth his light upon it, and covereth the bottom of the sea.

For by them judgeth he the people; he giveth meat in abundance.

With clouds he covereth the light, and commandeth it not to shine by the cloud that cometh betwixt.

The noise thereof sheweth concerning it, the cattle also concerning the vapour.

❧§❧

At this also my heart trembleth, and is moved out of his place.

Hear attentively the noise of his voice, and the sound that goeth out of his mouth.

He directeth it under the whole heaven, and his lightning unto the ends of the earth.

After it a voice roareth; he thundereth with the voice of his excellency: and he will not stay them when his voice is heard.

God thundereth marvellously with his voice; great things doeth he, which we cannot comprehend.

For he saith to the snow, Be thou on the earth; likewise to the small rain, and to the great rain of his strength.

He sealeth up the hand of every man; that all men may know his work.

Then the beasts go into dens, and remain in their places.

Out of the south cometh the whirlwind: and cold out of the north.

By the breath of God frost is given: and the breadth of the waters is straitened.

Also by watering he wearieth the thick cloud; he scattereth his bright cloud:

And it is turned round by his counsels: that they may do whatsoever he commandeth them upon the face of the world in the earth.

He causeth it to come, whether for correction, or for his land, or for mercy.

Hearken unto this, O, Job: stand still, and consider the wondrous works of God.

Dost thou know when God disposed them, and caused the light of his cloud to shine?

Dost thou know the balancings of the clouds, the wondrous works of him which is perfect in knowledge?

How thy garments are warm, when he quieteth the earth by the south wind?

Hast thou with him spread out the sky, which is strong, and as a molten looking-glass?

Teach us what we shall say unto him; for we cannot order our speech by reason of darkness.

Shall it be told him that I speak? if a man speak, surely he shall be swallowed up.

And now men see not the bright light which is in the clouds: but the wind passeth, and cleanseth them.

Fair weather cometh out of the north: with God is terrible majesty.

Touching the Almighty, we cannot find him out: he is excellent in power, and in judgment, and in plenty of justice: he will not afflict.

Men do therefore fear him: he respecteth not any that are wise of heart.

Then the Lord answered Job out of the whirlwind, and said,

Who is this that darkeneth counsel by words without knowledge?

Gird up now thy loins like a man; for I will demand of thee, and answer thou me.

Where wast thou when I laid the foundations of the earth? declare, if thou hast understanding.

Who hath laid the measures thereof, if thou knowest? or who hath stretched the line upon it?

Whereupon are the foundations thereof fastened? or who laid the corner-stone thereof:

When the morning stars sang together, and all the sons of God shouted for joy?

Or who shut up the sea with doors, when it brake forth, as if it had issued out of the womb?

When I made the cloud the garment thereof, and thick darkness a swaddling band for it,

And brake up for it my decreed place, and set bars and doors,

And said, Hitherto shalt thou come, but no further: and here shall thy proud waves be stayed?

Hast thou commanded the morning since thy days; and caused the day-spring to know his place;

That it might take hold of the ends of the earth, that the wicked might be shaken out of it?

It is turned as clay to the seal; and they stand as a garment.

And from the wicked their light is withholden, and the high arm shall be broken.

Hast thou entered into the springs of the sea? or hast thou walked in the search of the depth?

Have the gates of death been opened unto thee? or hast thou seen the doors of the shadow of death?

Hast thou perceived the breadth of the earth? declare if thou knowest it all.

Where is the way where light dwelleth? and as for darkness, where is the place thereof,

That thou shouldest take it to the bound thereof, and that thou shouldest know the paths to the house thereof?

Knowest thou it, because thou wast then born? or because the number of thy days is great?

Hast thou entered into the treasures of the snow? or hast thou seen the treasures of the hail,

Which I have reserved against the time of trouble, against the day of battle and war?

By what way is the light parted, which scattereth the east wind upon the earth?

Who hath divided a watercourse for the overflowing of waters, or a way for the lightning of thunder;

To cause it to rain on the earth, where no man is; on the wilderness, wherein there is no man;

To satisfy the desolate and waste ground; and to cause the bud of the tender herb to spring forth?

Hath the rain a father? or who hath begotten the drops of the dew?

Out of whose womb came the ice? and the hoary frost of heaven, who hath gendered it?

The waters are hid as with a stone, and the face of the deep is frozen.

Canst thou bind the sweet influences of Pleiades, or loose the bands of Orion?

Canst thou bring forth Mazzaroth in his season? or canst thou guide Arcturus with his sons?

Knowest thou the ordinances of heaven? canst thou set the dominion thereof in the earth?

Canst thou lift up thy voice to the clouds, that abundance of waters may cover thee?

Canst thou send lightnings, that they may go, and say unto thee, Here we are?

Who hath put wisdom in the inward parts? or who hath given understanding to the heart?

Who can number the clouds in wisdom? or who can stay the bottles of heaven,

When the dust groweth into hardness, and the clods cleave fast together?

Wilt thou hunt the prey for the lion? or fill the appetite of the young lions,

When they crouch in their dens, and abide in the covert to lie in wait?

Who provideth for the raven his food? when his young ones cry unto God, they wander for lack of meat.

❧§❧

Knowest thou the time when the wild goats of the rock bring forth? or canst thou mark when the hinds do calve?

Canst thou number the months that they fulfil? or knowest thou the time when they bring forth?

They bow themselves, they bring forth their young ones, they cast out their sorrows.

Their young ones are in good liking, they grow up with corn; they go forth, and return not unto them.

Who hath sent out the wild ass free? or who hath loosed the bands of the wild ass?

Whose house I have made the wilderness, and the barren land his dwellings.

He scorneth the multitude of the city, neither regardeth he the crying of the driver.

The range of the mountains is his pasture, and he searcheth after every green thing.

Will the unicorn be willing to serve thee, or abide by thy crib?

Canst thou bind the unicorn with his band in the furrow? or will he harrow the valleys after thee?

Wilt thou trust him, because his strength is great or wilt thou leave thy labour to him?

Wilt thou believe him, that he will bring home thy seed, and gather it into thy barn?

Gavest thou the goodly wings unto the peacocks? or wings and feathers unto the ostrich?

Which leaveth her eggs in the earth, and warmeth them in the dust,

And forgetteth that the foot may crush them, or that the wild beast may break them.

She is hardened against her young ones, as though they were not hers: her labour is in vain without fear;

Because God hath deprived her of wisdom, neither hath he imparted to her understanding.

What time she lifteth up herself on high, she scorneth the horse and his rider.

Hast thou given the horse strength? hast thou clothed his neck with thunder?

Canst thou make him afraid as a grasshopper? the glory of his nostrils is terrible.

He paweth in the valley, and rejoiceth in his strength: he goeth on to meet the armed men.

He mocketh at fear, and is not affrighted; neither turneth he back from the sword.

The quiver rattleth against him, the glittering spear and the shield.

He swalloweth the ground with fierceness and rage; neither believeth he that it is the sound of the trumpet.

He saith among the trumpets, Ha, ha! and he smelleth the battle afar off, the thunder of the captains, and the shouting.

Doth the hawk fly by thy wisdom, and stretch her wings toward the south?

Doth the eagle mount up at thy command, and make her nest on high?

She dwelleth and abideth on the rock, upon the crag of the rock, and the strong place.

From thence she seeketh the prey, and her eyes behold afar off.

Her young ones also suck up blood: and where the slain are, there is she.

§

Moreover, the Lord answered Job, and said,

Shall he that contendeth with the Almighty instruct him? he that reproveth God, let him answer it.

Then Job answered the Lord, and said,

Behold, I am vile; what shall I answer thee? I will lay my hand upon my mouth.

Once have I spoken; but I will not answer: yea, twice; but I will proceed no further.

Then answered the Lord unto Job out of the whirlwind, and said,

Gird up thy loins now like a man: I will demand of thee, and declare thou unto me.

Wilt thou also disannul my judgment? wilt thou condemn me, that thou mayest be righteous?

Hast thou an arm like God? or canst thou thunder with a voice like him?

Deck thyself now with majesty and excellency; and array thyself with glory and beauty.

Cast abroad the rage of thy wrath: and behold every one that is proud, and abase him.

Look on every one that is proud, and bring him low; and tread down the wicked in their place.

Hide them in the dust together; and bind their faces in secret.

Then will I also confess unto thee that thine own right hand can save thee.

Behold now behemoth, which I made with thee; he eateth grass as an ox.

Lo now, his strength is in his loins, and his force is in the navel of his belly.

He moveth his tail like a cedar; the sinews of his stones are wrapped together.

His bones are as strong pieces of brass; his bones are like bars of iron.

He is the chief of the ways of God: he that made him can make his sword to approach unto him.

Surely the mountains bring him forth food, where all the beasts of the field play.

He lieth under the shady trees, in the covert of the reed, and fens.

The shady trees cover him with their shadow; the willows of the brook compass him about.

Behold, he drinketh up a river, and hasteth not: he trusteth that he can draw up Jordan into his mouth.

He taketh it with his eyes: his nose pierceth through snares.

❧

Canst thou draw out leviathan with a hook? or his tongue with a cord which thou lettest down?

Canst thou put a hook into his nose? or bore his jaw through with a thorn?

Will he make many supplications unto thee? will he speak soft words unto thee?

Will he make a covenant with thee? wilt thou take him for a servant for ever?

Wilt thou play with him as with a bird? or wilt thou bind him for thy maidens?

Shall thy companions make a banquet of him? shall they part him among the merchants?

Canst thou fill his skin with barbed irons? or his head with fish-spears?

Lay thine hand upon him, remember the battle, do no more.

Behold, the hope of him is in vain: shall not one be cast down even at the sight of him?

None is so fierce that dare stir him up: who then is able to stand before me?

Who hath prevented me, that I should repay him? whatsoever is under the whole heaven is mine.

I will not conceal his parts, nor his power, nor his comely proportion.

Who can discover the face of his garment? or who can come to him with his double bridle?

Who can open the doors of his face? his teeth are terrible round about.

His scales are his pride, shut up together as with a close seal.

One is so near to another, that no air can come between them.

They are joined one to another, they stick together, that they cannot be sundered.

By his neesings a light doth shine, and his eyes are like the eyelids of morning.

Out of his mouth go burning lamps, and sparks of fire leap out.

Out of his nostrils goeth smoke, as out of a seething pot or caldron.

His breath kindleth coals, and a flame goeth out of his mouth.

In his neck remaineth strength, and sorrow is turned into joy before him.

The flakes of his flesh are joined together: they are firm in themselves; they cannot be moved.

His heart is firm as a stone; yea, as hard as a piece of the nether millstone.

When he raiseth up himself, the mighty are afraid; by reason of breakings they purify themselves.

The sword of him that layeth at him cannot hold: the spear, the dart, nor the habergeon.

He esteemeth iron as straw, and brass as rotten wood.

The arrow cannot make him flee: sling-stones are turned with him into stubble.

Darts are counted as stubble, he laugheth at the shaking of a spear.

Sharp stones are under him: he spreadeth sharp-pointed things upon the mire.

He maketh the deep to boil like a pot; he maketh the sea like a pot of ointment.

He maketh a path to shine after him; one would think the deep to be hoary.

Upon earth there is not his like, who is made without fear.

He beholdeth all high things: he is a king over all the children of pride.

⸙

Then Job answered the Lord, and said,

I know that thou canst do every thing, and that no thought can be withholden from thee.

Who is he that hideth counsel without knowledge? therefore have I uttered that I understood not; things too wonderful for me, which I knew not.

Hear, I beseech thee, and I will speak: I will demand of thee, and declare thou unto me.

I have heard of thee by the hearing of the ear: but now mine eye seeth thee:

Wherefore I abhor myself, and repent in dust and ashes.

And it was so, that after the Lord had spoken these words unto Job, the Lord said to Eliphaz the Temanite, My wrath is kindled against thee, and against thy two friends: for ye have not spoken of me the thing that is right, as my servant Job hath.

Therefore take unto you now seven bullocks and seven rams, and go to my servant Job, and offer up for yourselves a burnt-offering; and my servant Job shall pray for you: for him will I accept: lest I deal with you after your folly, in that ye have not spoken of me the thing which is right, like my servant Job.

So Eliphaz the Temanite and Bildad the Shuhite and Zophar the Naamathite went, and did according as the Lord commanded them: the Lord also accepted Job.

And the Lord turned the captivity of Job, when he prayed for his friends: also the Lord gave Job twice as much as he had before.

Then came there unto him all his brethren, and all his sisters, and all they that had been of his acquaintance before, and did eat bread with him in his house: and they bemoaned him, and comforted him over all the evil that the Lord had brought upon him: every man also gave him a piece of money, and every one an ear-ring of gold.

So the Lord blessed the latter end of Job more than his beginning: for he had fourteen thousand sheep, and six thousand camels, and a thousand yoke of oxen, and a thousand she-asses.

He had also seven sons, and three daughters.

And he called the name of the first, Jemima; and the name of the second, Kezia; and the name of the third, Keren-happuch.

And in all the land were no women found so fair as the daughters of Job: and their father gave them inheritance among their brethren.

After this lived Job a hundred and forty years, and saw his sons, and his sons' sons, even four generations.

So Job died, being old and full of days.

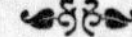

Poems of King David

BLESSED IS THE MAN that walketh not in the counsel of the ungodly, nor standeth in the way of sinners, nor sitteth in the seat of the scornful.

But his delight is in the law of the Lord; and in his law doth he meditate day and night.

And he shall be like a tree planted by the rivers of water, that bringeth forth his fruit in his season; his leaf also shall not wither; and whatsoever he doeth shall prosper.

The ungodly are not so: but are like the chaff which the wind driveth away.

Therefore the ungodly shall not stand in the judgment, nor sinners in the congregation of the righteous.

For the Lord knoweth the way of the righteous: but the way of the ungodly shall perish.

Psalms, i

Why standest thou afar off, O Lord? why hidest thou thyself in times of trouble?

The wicked in his pride doth persecute the poor: let them be taken in the devices that they have imagined.

For the wicked boasteth of his heart's desire, and blesseth the covetous, whom the Lord abhorreth.

The wicked, through the pride of his countenance, will not seek after God: God is not in all his thoughts.

His ways are always grievous; thy judgments are far above out of his sight: as for all his enemies, he puffeth at them.

He hath said in his heart, I shall not be moved: for I shall never be in adversity.

His mouth is full of cursing and deceit and fraud: under his tongue is mischief and vanity.

He sitteth in the lurking-places of the villages: in the secret places doth he murder the innocent: his eyes are privily set against the poor.

He lieth in wait secretly as a lion in his den: he lieth in wait to catch the poor: he doth catch the poor, when he draweth him into his net.

He croucheth, and humbleth himself, that the poor may fall by his strong ones.

He hath said in his heart, God hath forgotten: he hideth his face: he will never see it.

Arise, O Lord; O God, lift up thy hand: forget not the humble.

Wherefore doth the wicked contemn God? he hath said in his heart, thou wilt not require it.

Thou hast seen it; for thou beholdest mischief and spite, to requite it with thy hand: the poor committeth himself unto thee; thou art the helper of the fatherless.

Break thou the arm of the wicked and the evil man: seek out his wickedness till thou find none.

The Lord is King for ever and ever: the heathen are perished out of his land.

Lord, thou hast heard the desire of the humble: thou wilt prepare their heart, thou wilt cause thine ear to hear:

To judge the fatherless and the oppressed, that the man of the earth may no more oppress.

Psalms, x

In the Lord put I my trust: how say ye to my soul, Flee as a bird to your mountain?

For lo, the wicked bend their bow, they make ready their arrow upon the string, that they may privily shoot at the upright in heart.

If the foundations be destroyed, what can the righteous do?

The Lord is in his holy temple, the Lord's throne is in heaven: his eyes behold, his eyelids try the children of men.

The Lord trieth the righteous: but the wicked and him that loveth violence his soul hateth.

Upon the wicked he shall rain snares, fire and brimstone, and a horrible tempest: this shall be the portion of their cup.

For the righteous Lord loveth righteousness; his countenance doth behold the upright.

Psalms, xi

⁂

Help, Lord; for the godly man ceaseth; for the faithful fail from among the children of men.

They speak vanity every one with his neighbour: with flattering lips and with a double heart do they speak.

The Lord shall cut off all flattering lips, and the tongue that speaketh proud things:

Who have said, With our tongue will we prevail; our lips are our own: who is lord over us?

For the oppression of the poor, for the sighing of the needy, now will I arise, saith the Lord; I will set him in safety from him that puffeth at him.

The words of the Lord are pure words: as silver tried in a furnace of earth, purified seven times.

Thou shalt keep them, O Lord, thou shalt preserve them from this generation for ever.

The wicked walk on every side, when the vilest men are exalted.

Psalms, xii

⁂

How long wilt thou forget me, O Lord? for ever? how long wilt thou hide thy face from me?

How long shall I take counsel in my soul, having sorrow in

my heart daily? how long shall mine enemy be exalted over me?

Consider and hear me, O Lord my God: lighten mine eyes, lest I sleep the sleep of death.

Psalms, xiii

❧

Lord, who shall abide in thy tabernacle? who shall dwell in thy holy hill?

He that walketh uprightly, and worketh righteousness, and speaketh the truth in his heart.

He that backbiteth not with his tongue, nor doeth evil to his neighbour, nor taketh up a reproach against his neighbour.

In whose eyes a vile person is contemned; but he honoureth them that fear the Lord. He that sweareth to his own hurt, and changeth not.

He that putteth not out his money to usury, nor taketh reward against the innocent. He that doeth these things shall never be moved.

Psalms, xv

❧

My God, my God, why hast thou forsaken me? why art thou so far from helping me, and from the words of my roaring?

O my God, I cry in the day-time, but thou hearest not; and in the night season, and am not silent.

But thou art holy, O thou that inhabitest the praises of Israel.

Our fathers trusted in thee: they trusted, and thou didst deliver them.

They cried unto thee, and were delivered: they trusted in thee, and were not confounded.

But I am a worm, and no man; a reproach of men, and despised of the people.

All they that see me laugh me to scorn: they shoot out the lip, they shake the head, saying,

He trusted on the Lord that he would deliver him: let him deliver him, seeing he delighted in him.

But thou art he that took me out of the womb: thou didst make me hope when I was upon my mother's breasts.

I was cast upon thee from the womb: thou art my God from my mother's belly.

Be not far from me; for trouble is near; for there is none to help.

Psalms, xxii

❧

The Lord is my shepherd; I shall not want.

He maketh me to lie down in green pastures: he leadeth me beside the still waters.

He restoreth my soul: he leadeth me in the paths of righteousness for his name's sake.

Yea, though I walk through the valley of the shadow of death, I will fear no evil: for thou art with me; thy rod and thy staff they comfort me.

Thou preparest a table before me in the presence of mine enemies: thou anointest my head with oil; my cup runneth over.

Surely goodness and mercy shall follow me all the days of my life: and I will dwell in the house of the Lord for ever.

Psalms, xxiii

❧

The earth is the Lord's, and the fulness thereof; the world, and they that dwell therein.

For he hath founded it upon the seas, and established it upon the floods.

Who shall ascend into the hill of the Lord? and who shall stand in his holy place?

He that hath clean hands, and a pure heart; who hath not lifted up his soul unto vanity, nor sworn deceitfully.

He shall receive the blessing from the Lord, and righteousness from the God of his salvation.

This is the generation of them that seek him, that seek thy face. O Jacob. Selah.

Lift up your heads, O ye gates: and be ye lift up, ye everlasting doors; and the King of glory shall come in.

Who is this King of glory? the Lord strong and mighty, the Lord mighty in battle.

Lift up your heads, O ye gates; even lift them up, ye everlasting doors; and the King of glory shall come in.

Who is this King of glory? the Lord of hosts, he is the King of glory. Selah.

Psalms, xxiv

Unto thee, O Lord, do I lift up my soul.

O my God, I trust in thee: let me not be ashamed, let not mine enemies triumph over me.

Yea, let none that wait on thee be ashamed: let them be ashamed which transgress without cause.

Shew me thy ways, O Lord; teach me thy paths.

Lead me in thy truth, and teach me: for thou art the God of my salvation; on thee do I wait all the day.

Remember, O Lord, thy tender mercies and thy lovingkindnesses; for they have been ever of old.

Remember not the sins of my youth, nor my transgressions: according to thy mercy remember thou me for thy goodness' sake, O Lord.

Good and upright is the Lord: therefore will he teach sinners in the way.

The meek will he guide in judgment: and the meek will he teach his way.

All the paths of the Lord are mercy and truth unto such as keep his covenant and his testimonies.

For thy name's sake, O Lord, pardon mine iniquity; for it is great.

What man is he that feareth the Lord? him shall he teach in the way that he shall choose.

His soul shall dwell at ease; and his seed shall inherit the earth.

The secret of the Lord is with them that fear him; and he will shew them his covenant.

Mine eyes are ever toward the Lord; for he shall pluck my feet out of the net.

Turn thee unto me, and have mercy upon me; for I am desolate and afflicted.

The troubles of my heart are enlarged: O bring thou me out of my distresses.

Look upon mine affliction and my pain; and forgive all my sins.

Consider mine enemies; for they are many; and they hate me with cruel hatred.

O keep my soul, and deliver me: let me not be ashamed; for I put my trust in thee.

Let integrity and uprightness preserve me; for I wait on thee.

Redeem Israel, O God, out of all his troubles.

***Psalms*, XXV**

Judge me, O Lord; for I have walked in mine integrity: I have trusted also in the Lord; therefore I shall not slide.

Examine me, O Lord, and prove me; try my reins and my heart.

For thy loving-kindness is before mine eyes: and I have walked in thy truth.

I have not sat with vain persons, neither will I go in with dissemblers.

I have hated the congregation of evil doers; and will not sit with the wicked.

I will wash my hands in innocency: so will I compass thine altar, O Lord:

That I may publish with the voice of thanksgiving, and tell of all thy wondrous works.

Lord, I have loved the habitation of thy house, and the place where thine honour dwelleth.

Gather not my soul with sinners, nor my life with bloody men:

In whose hands is mischief, and their right hand is full of bribes.

But as for me, I will walk in mine integrity: redeem me, and be merciful unto me.

My foot standeth in an even place: in the congregations will I bless the Lord.

Psalms, xxvi

❧

The Lord is my light and my salvation; whom shall I fear? the Lord is the strength of my life; of whom shall I be afraid?

When the wicked, even mine enemies and my foes, came upon me to eat up my flesh, they stumbled and fell.

Though a host should encamp against me, my heart shall not fear: though war should rise against me, in this will I be confident.

One thing have I desired of the Lord, that will I seek after; that I may dwell in the house of the Lord all the days of my life, to behold the beauty of the Lord, and to inquire in his temple.

For in the time of trouble he shall hide me in his pavilion: in the secret of his tabernacle shall he hide me; he shall set me up upon a rock.

And now shall my head be lifted up above mine enemies round about me: therefore will I offer in his tabernacle sacrifices of joy; I will sing, yea, I will sing praises unto the Lord.

Hear, O Lord, when I cry with my voice: have mercy also upon me, and answer me.

When thou saidst, Seek ye my face; my heart said unto thee, Thy face, Lord, will I seek.

Hide not thy face far from me; put not thy servant away in anger: thou hast been my help; leave me not, neither forsake me, O God of my salvation.

When my father and my mother forsake me, then the Lord will take me up.

Teach me thy way, O Lord, and lead me in a plain path, because of mine enemies.

Deliver me not over unto the will of mine enemies: for false witnesses are risen up against me, and such as breathe out cruelty.

I had fainted, unless I had believed to see the goodness of the Lord in the land of the living.

Wait on the Lord: be of good courage, and he shall strengthen thy heart: wait, I say, on the Lord.

Psalms, xxvii

Fret not thyself because of evil doers, neither be thou envious against the workers of iniquity.

For they shall soon be cut down like the grass, and wither as the green herb.

Trust in the Lord, and do good; so shalt thou dwell in the land, and verily thou shalt be fed.

Delight thyself also in the Lord; and he shall give thee the desires of thy heart.

Commit thy way unto the Lord; trust also in him; and he shall bring it to pass.

And he shall bring forth thy righteousness as the light, and thy judgment as the noon-day.

Rest in the Lord, and wait patiently for him: fret not thyself because of him who prospereth in his way, because of the man who bringeth wicked devices to pass.

Cease from anger, and forsake wrath: fret not thyself in any wise to do evil.

For evil doers shall be cut off: but those that wait upon the Lord, they shall inherit the earth.

For yet a little while, and the wicked shall not be: yea, thou shalt diligently consider his place, and it shall not be.

But the meek shall inherit the earth; and shall delight

themselves in the abundance of peace.

The wicked plotteth against the just, and gnasheth upon him with his teeth.

The Lord shall laugh at him: for he seeth that his day is coming.

The wicked have drawn out the sword, and have bent their bow, to cast down the poor and needy, and to slay such as be of upright conversation.

Their sword shall enter into their own heart, and their bows shall be broken.

A little that a righteous man hath is better than the riches of many wicked.

For the arms of the wicked shall be broken: but the Lord upholdeth the righteous.

The Lord knoweth the days of the upright: and their inheritance shall be for ever.

They shall not be ashamed in the evil time: and in the days of famine they shall be satisfied.

But the wicked shall perish, and the enemies of the Lord shall be as the fat of lambs: they shall consume; into smoke shall they consume away.

The wicked borroweth, and payeth not again: but the righteous sheweth mercy, and giveth.

For such as be blessed of him shall inherit the earth; and they that be cursed of him shall be cut off.

The steps of a good man are ordered by the Lord: and he delighteth in his way.

Though he fall, he shall not be utterly cast down: for the Lord upholdeth him with his hand.

I have been young, and now am old; yet have I not seen the righteous forsaken, nor his seed begging bread.

He is ever merciful, and lendeth; and his seed is blessed.

Depart from evil, and do good; and dwell for evermore.

For the Lord loveth judgment, and forsaketh not his saints;

they are preserved for ever: but the seed of the wicked shall be cut off.

The righteous shall inherit the land, and dwell therein for ever.

The mouth of the righteous speaketh wisdom, and his tongue talketh of judgment.

The law of his God is in his heart; none of his steps shall slide.

The wicked watcheth the righteous, and seeketh to slay him.

The Lord will not leave him in his hand, nor condemn him when he is judged.

Wait on the Lord, and keep his way, and he shall exalt thee to inherit the land: when the wicked are cut off, thou shalt see it.

I have seen the wicked in great power, and spreading himself like a green bay-tree.

Yet he passed away, and lo, he was not: yea, I sought him, but he could not be found.

Mark the perfect man, and behold the upright: for the end of that man is peace.

But the transgressors shall be destroyed together: the end of the wicked shall be cut off.

But the salvation of the righteous is of the Lord: he is their strength in the time of trouble.

And the Lord shall help them, and deliver them: he shall deliver them from the wicked, and save them, because they trust in him.

Psalms, xxxvii

O God, thou art my God; early will I seek thee: my soul thirsteth for thee, my flesh longeth for thee in a dry and thirsty land, where no water is;

To see thy power and thy glory, so as I have seen thee in the sanctuary.

Because thy loving-kindness is better than life, my lips shall praise thee.

Thus will I bless thee while I live: I will lift up my hands in thy name.

My soul shall be satisfied as with marrow and fatness; and my mouth shall praise thee with joyful lips:

When I remember thee upon my bed, and meditate on thee in the night watches.

Because thou hast been my help, therefore in the shadow of thy wings will I rejoice.

My soul followeth hard after thee: thy right hand upholdeth me.

Psalms, lxiii

Lord, thou hast been our dwelling-place in all generations.

Before the mountains were brought forth, or ever thou hadst formed the earth and the world, even from everlasting to everlasting, thou art God.

Thou turnest man to destruction; and sayest, Return, ye children of men.

For a thousand years in thy sight are but as yesterday when it is past, and as a watch in the night.

Thou carriest them away as with a flood; they are as a sleep; in the morning they are like grass which groweth up.

In the morning it flourisheth, and groweth up; in the evening it is cut down, and withereth.

For we are consumed by thine anger, and by thy wrath are we troubled.

Thou hast set our iniquities before thee, our secret sins in the light of thy countenance.

For all our days are passed away in thy wrath: we spend our years, as a tale that is told.

The days of our years are threescore years and ten; and if by reason of strength they be fourscore years, yet is their strength labour and sorrow; for it is soon cut off, and we fly away.

Who knoweth the power of thine anger? even according to thy fear, so is thy wrath.

So teach us to number our days, that we may apply our hearts unto wisdom.

Return, O Lord, how long? and let it repent thee concerning thy servants.

O satisfy us early with thy mercy; that we may rejoice and be glad all our days.

Make us glad according to the days wherein thou hast afflicted us, and the years wherein we have seen evil.

Let thy work appear unto thy servants, and thy glory unto their children.

And let the beauty of the Lord our God be upon us: and establish thou the work of our hands upon us; yea, the work of our hands establish thou it.

Psalms, xc

Hear my prayer, O Lord, and let my cry come unto thee.

Hide not thy face from me in the day when I am in trouble; incline thine ear unto me: in the day when I call, answer me speedily.

For my days are consumed like smoke, and my bones are burned as a hearth.

My heart is smitten, and withered like grass; so that I forget to eat my bread.

By reason of the voice of my groaning my bones cleave to my skin.

I am like a pelican of the wilderness: I am like an owl of the desert.

I watch, and am as a sparrow alone upon the housetop. Mine enemies reproach me all the day; and they that are mad against me are sworn against me.

For I have eaten ashes like bread, and mingled my drink with weeping,

Because of thine indignation and thy wrath: for thou hast lifted me up, and cast me down.

My days are like a shadow that declineth; and I am withered like grass.

But thou, O Lord, shalt endure for ever; and thy remembrance unto all generations.

Thou shalt arise, and have mercy upon Zion: for the time to favour her, yea, the set time, is come.

Psalms, cii

❧

And David lamented with this lamentation over Saul and over Jonathan his son:

The beauty of Israel is slain upon thy high places: How are the mighty fallen!

Tell it not in Gath. Publish it not in the streets of Askelon; lest the daughters of the Philistines rejoice, lest the daughters of the uncircumcised triumph.

Ye mountains of Gilboa, let there be no dew, neither let there be rain, upon you, nor fields of offerings: For there the shield of the mighty is vilely cast away, the shield of Saul, as though he had not been anointed with oil.

From the blood of the slain, from the fat of the mighty, the bow of Jonathan turned not back, and the sword of Saul returned not empty.

Saul and Jonathan were lovely and pleasant in their lives, and in their death they were not divided. They were swifter than eagles; they were stronger than lions.

Ye daughters of Israel, weep over Saul, who clothed you in scarlet, with other delights; who put ornaments of gold upon your apparel.

How are the mighty fallen in the midst of the battle! O Jonathan, thou wast slain in thine high places.

I am distressed for thee, my brother Jonathan: Very pleasant hast thou been unto me: Thy love to me was wonderful, passing the love of women.

How are the mighty fallen, and the weapons of war perished!

Samuel 2, i

Parables of King Solomon

THE PROVERBS OF SOLOMON the son of David, king of Israel;

To know wisdom and instruction; to perceive the words of understanding;

To receive the instruction of wisdom, justice, and judgment, and equity;

To give subtilty to the simple, to the young man knowledge and discretion.

A wise man will hear, and will increase learning; and a man of understanding shall attain unto wise counsels:

To understand a proverb, and the interpretation: the words of the wise, and their dark sayings.

The fear of the Lord is the beginning of knowledge: but fools despise wisdom and instruction.

My son, hear the instruction of thy father, and forsake not the law of thy mother:

For they shall be an ornament of grace unto thy head, and chains about thy neck.

My son, if sinners entice thee, consent thou not.

If they say, Come with us, let us lay wait for blood, let us lurk privily for the innocent without cause:

Let us swallow them up alive as the grave; and whole, as those that go down into the pit:

We shall find all precious substance, we shall fill our houses with spoil:

Cast in thy lot among us; let us all have one purse:

My son walk not thou in the way with them; refrain thy foot from their path:

For their feet run to evil, and make haste to shed blood:

Surely in vain the net is spread in the sight of any bird.

And they lay wait for their own blood; they lurk privily for their own lives.

So are the ways of every one that is greedy of gain; which taketh away the life of the owners thereof.

Wisdom crieth without; she uttereth her voice in the streets:

She crieth in the chief place of concourse, in the openings of the gates: in the city she uttereth her words, saying,

How long, ye simple ones, will ye love simplicity? and the scorners delight in their scorning, and fools hate knowledge?

Turn you at my reproof: behold, I will pour out my spirit unto you, I will make known my words unto you.

Because I have called and ye refused; I have stretched out my hand, and no man regarded;

But ye have set at nought all my counsel, and would none of my reproof:

I also will laugh at your calamity: I will mock when your fear cometh;

When your fear cometh as desolation, and your destruction cometh as a whirlwind; when distress and anguish cometh upon you.

Then shall they call upon me, but I will not answer; they shall seek me early, but they shall not find me;

For that they hated knowledge, and did not choose the fear of the Lord:

They would none of my counsel; they despised all my reproof.

Therefore shall they eat of the fruit of their own way, and be filled with their own devices.

For the turning away of the simple shall slay them, and the prosperity of fools shall destroy them.

But whoso hearkeneth unto me shall dwell safely, and shall be quiet from fear of evil.

My son, if thou wilt receive my words, and hide my commandments with thee;

So that thou incline thine ear unto wisdom, and apply thy heart to understanding;

Yea, if thou criest after knowledge, and liftest up thy voice for understanding;

If thou seekest her as silver, and searchest for her as for hid treasures;

Then shalt thou understand the fear of the Lord, and find the knowledge of God.

For the Lord giveth wisdom: out of his mouth cometh knowledge and understanding.

He layeth up sound wisdom for the righteous: he is a buckler to them that walk uprightly.

He keepeth the paths of judgment, and preserveth the way of his saints.

Then shalt thou understand righteousness, and judgment, and equity; yea, every good path.

When wisdom entereth into thy heart, and knowledge is pleasant unto thy soul;

Discretion shall preserve thee, understanding shall keep thee:

To deliver thee from the way of the evil man, from the man that speaketh froward things;

Who leave the paths of uprightness, to walk in the ways of darkness;

Who rejoice to do evil, and delight in the frowardness of the wicked;

Whose ways are crooked, and they froward in their paths:

To deliver thee from the strange woman, even from the stranger which flattereth with her words;

Which forsaketh the guide of her youth, and forgetteth the covenant of her God.

For her house inclineth unto death, and her paths unto the dead.

None that go unto her return again, neither take they hold of the paths of life.

That thou mayest walk in the way of good men, and keep the paths of the righteous.

For the upright shall dwell in the land, and the perfect shall remain in it.

But the wicked shall be cut off from the earth, and the transgressors shall be rooted out of it.

⁂

My son, forget not my law; but let thy heart keep my commandments:

For length of days, and long life, and peace shall they add to thee.

Let not mercy and truth forsake thee; bind them about thy neck; write them upon the table of thy heart;

So shalt thou find favour and good understanding in the sight of God and man.

Trust in the Lord with all thy heart; and lean not unto thine own understanding.

In all thy ways acknowledge him, and he shall direct thy paths.

Be not wise in thine own eyes: fear the Lord, and depart from evil.

It shall be health to thy navel, and marrow to thy bones.

Honour the Lord with thy substance, and with the first-fruits of all thine increase:

So shall thy barns be filled with plenty, and thy presses shall burst out with new wine.

My son, despise not the chastening of the Lord; neither be weary of his correction:

For whom the Lord loveth he correcteth; even as a father the son in whom he delighteth.

Happy is the man that findeth wisdom, and the man that getteth understanding.

For the merchandise of it is better than the merchandise of silver, and the gain thereof than fine gold.

She is more precious than rubies: and all the things thou canst desire are not to be compared unto her.

Length of days is in her right hand; and in her left hand riches and honour.

Her ways are ways of pleasantness, and all her paths are peace.

She is a tree of life to them that lay hold upon her: and happy is every one that retaineth her.

The Lord by wisdom hath founded the earth; by understanding hath he established the heavens.

By his knowledge the depths are broken up, and the clouds drop down the dew.

My son, let not them depart from thine eyes: keep sound wisdom and discretion:

So shall they be life unto thy soul, and grace to thy neck.

Then shalt thou walk in thy way safely, and thy foot shall not stumble.

When thou liest down, thou shalt not be afraid: yea, thou shalt lie down, and thy sleep shall be sweet.

Be not afraid of sudden fear, neither of the desolation of the wicked, when it cometh.

For the Lord shall be thy confidence, and shall keep thy foot from being taken.

Withhold not good from them to whom it is due, when it is in the power of thy hand to do it.

Say not unto thy neighbour, Go, and come again, and to-morrow I will give, when thou hast it by thee.

Devise not evil against thy neighbour, seeing he dwelleth securely by thee.

Strive not with a man without cause, if he have done thee no harm.

Envy thou not the oppressor, and choose none of his ways.

For the froward is abomination to the Lord: but his secret is with the righteous.

The curse of the Lord is in the house of the wicked: but he blesseth the habitation of the just.

Surely he scorneth the scorners: but he giveth grace unto the lowly.

The wise shall inherit glory: but shame shall be the promotion of fools.

❧

Hear, ye children, the instruction of a father, and attend to know understanding.

For I give you good doctrine, forsake ye not my law.

For I was my father's son, tender and only beloved in the sight of my mother.

He taught me also, and said unto me, Let thy heart retain my words: keep my commandments, and live.

Get wisdom, get understanding: forget it not; neither decline from the words of my mouth.

Forsake her not, and she shall preserve thee: love her, and she shall keep thee.

Wisdom is the principal thing; therefore get wisdom: and with all thy getting get understanding.

Exalt her, and she shall promote thee: she shall bring thee to honour, when thou dost embrace her.

She shall give to thy head an ornament of grace: a crown of glory shall she deliver to thee.

Hear, O my son, and receive my sayings; and the years of thy life shall be many.

I have taught thee in the way of wisdom; I have led thee in right paths.

When thou goest, thy steps shall not be straitened; and when thou runnest, thou shalt not stumble.

Take fast hold of instruction; let her not go: keep her, for she is thy life.

Enter not into the path of the wicked, and go not in the way of evil men.

Avoid it, pass not by it, turn from it, and pass away.

For they sleep not, except they have done mischief; and their sleep is taken away, unless they cause some to fall.

For they eat the bread of wickedness, and drink the wine of violence.

But the path of the just is as the shining light, that shineth more and more unto the perfect day.

The way of the wicked is as darkness: they know not at what they stumble.

My son, attend to my words; incline thine ear unto my sayings.

Let them not depart from thine eyes; keep them in the midst of thy heart.

For they are life unto those that find them, and health to all their flesh.

Keep thy heart with all diligence; for out of it are the issues of life.

Put away from thee a froward mouth, and perverse lips put far from thee.

Let thine eyes look right on, and let thine eye-lids look straight before thee.

Ponder the path of thy feet, and let all thy ways be established.

Turn not to the right hand nor to the left: remove thy foot from evil.

❧

My son, attend unto my wisdom, and bow thine ear to my understanding:

That thou mayest regard discretion, and that thy lips may keep knowledge.

For the lips of a strange woman drop as a honey-comb, and her mouth is smoother than oil:

But her end is bitter as wormwood, sharp as a two-edged sword.

Her feet go down to death; her steps take hold on hell.

Lest thou shouldest ponder the path of life, her ways are moveable, that thou canst not know them.

Hear me now therefore, O ye children, and depart not from the words of my mouth.

Remove thy way far from her, and come not nigh the door of her house:

Lest thou give thine honour unto others, and thy years unto the cruel:

Lest strangers be filled with thy wealth; and thy labours be in the house of a stranger:

And thou mourn at the last, when thy flesh and thy body are consumed,

And say, How have I hated instruction, and my heart despised reproof;

And have not obeyed the voice of my teachers, nor inclined mine ear to them that instructed me!

I was almost in all evil in the midst of the congregation and assembly.

Drink waters out of thine own cistern, and running waters out of thine own well.

Let thy fountains be dispersed abroad, and rivers of waters in the streets.

Let them be only thine own, and not strangers' with thee.

Let thy fountain be blessed: and rejoice with the wife of thy youth.

Let her be as the loving hind and pleasant roe; let her breasts satisfy thee at all times; and be thou ravished always with her love.

And why wilt thou, my son, be ravished with a strange woman, and embrace the bosom of a stranger?

For the ways of man are before the eyes of the Lord, and he pondereth all his goings.

His own iniquities shall take the wicked himself, and he shall be holden with the cords of his sins.

He shall die without instruction; and in the greatness of his folly he shall go astray.

❧

My son, if thou be surety for thy friend, if thou hast stricken thy hand with a stranger,

Thou art snared with the words of thy mouth, thou art taken with the words of thy mouth.

Do this now, my son, and deliver thyself, when thou art come into the hand of thy friend; go, humble thyself, and make sure thy friend.

Give not sleep to thine eyes, nor slumber to thine eyelids.

Deliver thyself as a roe from the hand of the hunter, and as a bird from the hand of the fowler.

Go to the ant, thou sluggard; consider her ways, and be wise:

Which having no guide, overseer, or ruler,

Provideth her meat in the summer, and gathereth her food in the harvest.

How long wilt thou sleep, O sluggard? when wilt thou arise out of thy sleep?

Yet a little sleep, a little slumber, a little folding of the hands to sleep:

So shall thy poverty come as one that travelleth, and thy want as an armed man.

A naughty person, a wicked man, walketh with a froward mouth.

He winketh with his eyes, he speaketh with his feet, he teacheth with his fingers;

Frowardness is in his heart, he deviseth mischief continually; he soweth discord.

Therefore shall his calamity come suddenly; suddenly shall he be broken without remedy.

These six things doth the Lord hate; yea, seven are an abomination unto him:

A proud look, a lying tongue, and hands that shed innocent blood,

A heart that deviseth wicked imaginations, feet that be swift in running to mischief,

A false witness that speaketh lies, and him that soweth discord among brethren.

My son, keep thy father's commandment, and forsake not the law of thy mother:

Bind them continually upon thy heart, and tie them about thy neck.

When thou goest, it shall lead thee; when thou sleepest, it shall keep thee; and when thou awakest, it shall talk with thee.

For the commandment is a lamp; and the law is light; and reproofs of instruction are the way of life:

To keep thee from the evil woman, from the flattery of the tongue of a strange woman.

Lust not after her beauty in thy heart; neither let her take thee with her eyelids.

For by means of a whorish women a man is brought to a piece of bread: and the adulteress will hunt for the precious life.

Can a man take fire in his bosom, and his clothes not be burned?

Can one go upon hot coals, and his feet not be burned?

So he that goeth in to his neighbour's wife; whosoever toucheth her shall not be innocent.

Men do not despise a thief, if he steal to satisfy his soul when he is hungry;

But if he be found, he shall restore seven-fold; he shall give all the substance of his house.

But whoso committeth adultery with a woman, lacketh understanding: he that doeth it, destroyeth his own soul.

A wound and dishonour shall he get; and his reproach shall not be wiped away,

For jealousy is the rage of a man: therefore he will not spare in the day of vengeance.

He will not regard any ransom; neither will he rest content, though thou givest many gifts.

❧

My son, keep my words, and lay up my commandments with thee.

Keep my commandments, and live; and my law as the apple of thine eye.

Bind them upon thy fingers, write them upon the table of thy heart.

Say unto wisdom, Thou art my sister, and call understanding thy kinswoman:

That they may keep thee from the strange woman, from the stranger which flattereth with her words.

For at the window of my house I looked through my casement,

And beheld among the simple ones, I discerned among the youths, a young man void of understanding,

Passing through the street near her corner; and he went the way to her house.

In the twilight, in the evening, in the black and dark night:

And behold, there met him a woman with the attire of a harlot, and subtile of heart.

(She is loud and stubborn; her feet abide not in her house:

Now is she without, now in the streets, and lieth in wait at every corner.)

So she caught him, and kissed him, and with an impudent face said unto him,

I have peace-offerings with me; this day have I paid my vows.

Therefore came I forth to meet thee, diligently to seek thy face, and I have found thee.

I have decked my bed with coverings of tapestry, with carved works, with fine linen of Egypt.

I have perfumed my bed with myrrh, aloes, and cinnamon.

Come, let us take our fill of love until the morning: let us solace ourselves with loves.

For the good-man is not at home, he is gone a long journey:

He hath taken a bag of money with him, and will come home at the day appointed.

With her much fair speech she caused him to yield, with the flattering of her lips she forced him.

He goeth after her straightway, as an ox goeth to slaughter, or as a fool to the correction of the stocks;

Till a dart strike through his liver, as a bird hasteth to the snare, and knoweth not that it is for his life.

Hearken unto me now therefore, O ye children, and attend to the words of my mouth.

Let not thy heart decline to her ways, go not astray in her paths.

For she hath cast down many wounded: yea, many strong men have been slain by her.

Her house is the way to hell, going down to the chambers of death.

❧

Doth not wisdom cry? and understanding put forth her voice?

She standeth in the top of high places, by the way in the places of the paths.

She crieth at the gates, at the entry of the city, at the coming in at the doors:

Unto you, O men, I call; and my voice is to the sons of man.

O ye simple, understand wisdom; and ye fools, be ye of an understanding heart.

Hear: for I will speak of excellent things; and the opening of my lips shall be right things.

For my mouth shall speak truth: and wickedness is an abomination to my lips.

All the words of my mouth are in righteousness; there is nothing froward or perverse in them.

They are all plain to him that understandeth, and right to them that find knowledge.

Receive my instruction, and not silver; and knowledge rather than choice gold.

For wisdom is better than rubies; and all the things that may be desired are not to be compared to it.

I Wisdom dwell with prudence, and find out knowledge of witty inventions.

The fear of the Lord is to hate evil; pride, and arrogancy, and the evil way, and the froward mouth, do I hate.

Counsel is mine, and sound wisdom: I am understanding; I have strength.

By me kings reign, and princes decree justice.

By me princes rule, and nobles, even all the judges of the earth.

I love them that love me; and those that seek me early shall find me.

Riches and honour are with me; yea, durable riches and righteousness.

My fruit is better than gold, yea, than fine gold; and my revenue than choice silver.

I lead in the way of righteousness, in the midst of the paths of judgment:

That I may cause those that love me to inherit substance; and I will find their treasures.

The Lord possessed me in the beginning of his way, before his works of old.

I was set up from everlasting, from the beginning, or ever the earth was.

When there were no depths, I was brought forth; when there were no fountains abounding with water.

Before the mountains were settled, before the hills was I brought forth.

While as yet he had not made the earth, nor the fields, nor the highest part of the dust of the world.

When he prepared the heavens, I was there: when he set a compass upon the face of the depth:

When he established the clouds above: when he strengthened the fountains of the deep:

When he gave to the sea his decree, that the waters should not pass his commandment; when he appointed the foundations of the earth:

Then I was by him, as one brought up with him: and I was daily his delight, rejoicing always before him;

Rejoicing in the habitable part of his earth; and my delights were with the sons of men.

Now therefore hearken unto me, O ye children: for blessed are they that keep my ways.

Hear instruction, and be wise, and refuse it not.

Blessed is the man that heareth me, watching daily at my gates, waiting at the posts of my doors.

For whoso findeth me findeth life, and shall obtain favour of the Lord.

But he that sinneth against me wrongeth his own soul; all they that hate me love death.

❧

Wisdom hath builded her house, she hath hewn out her seven pillars:

She hath killed her beasts; she hath mingled her wine; she hath also furnished her table.

She hath sent forth her maidens: she crieth upon the highest places of the city,

Whoso is simple, let him turn in hither: as for him that wanteth understanding, she saith to him,

Come, eat of my bread, and drink of the wine which I have mingled.

Forsake the foolish, and live; and go in the way of understanding.

He that reproveth a scorner getteth to himself shame; and he that rebuketh a wicked man getteth himself a blot.

Reprove not a scorner, lest he hate thee: rebuke a wise man, and he will love thee.

Give instruction to a wise man, and he will be yet wiser: teach a just man, and he will increase in learning.

The fear of the Lord is the beginning of wisdom: and the knowledge of the holy is understanding.

For by me thy days shall be multiplied, and the years of thy life shall be increased.

If thou be wise, thou shalt be wise for thyself: but if thou scornest, thou alone shalt bear it.

A foolish woman is clamorous: she is simple, and knoweth nothing.

For she sitteth at the door of her house, on a seat in the high places of the city,

To call passengers who go right on their ways:

Whoso is simple, let him turn in hither: and as for him that wanteth understanding, she saith to him,

Stolen waters are sweet, and bread eaten in secret is pleasant.

But he knoweth not that the dead are there; and that her guests are in the depths of hell.

❧

The proverbs of Solomon. A wise son maketh a glad father: but a foolish son is the heaviness of his mother.

Treasures of wickedness profit nothing: but righteousness delivereth from death.

The Lord will not suffer the soul of the righteous to famish: but he casteth away the substance of the wicked.

He becometh poor that dealeth with a slack hand: but the hand of the diligent maketh rich.

He that gathereth in summer is a wise son: but he that sleepeth in harvest is a son that causeth shame.

Blessings are upon the head of the just: but violence covereth the mouth of the wicked.

The memory of the just is blessed: but the name of the wicked shall rot.

The wise in heart will receive commandments: but a prating fool shall fall.

He that walketh uprightly walketh surely: but he that perverteth his ways shall be known.

He that winketh with the eye causeth sorrow: but a prating fool shall fall.

The mouth of a righteous man is a well of life: but violence covereth the mouth of the wicked.

Hatred stirreth up strifes: but love covereth all sins.

In the lips of him that hath understanding wisdom is found: but a rod is for the back of him that is void of understanding.

Wise men lay up knowledge: but the mouth of the foolish is near destruction.

The rich man's wealth is his strong city: the destruction of the poor is their poverty.

The labour of the righteous tendeth to life: the fruit of the wicked to sin.

He is in the way of life that keepeth instruction: but he that refuseth reproof erreth.

He that hideth hatred with lying lips, and he that uttereth a slander, is a fool.

In the multitude of words there wanteth not sin: but he that refraineth his lips is wise.

The tongue of the just is as choice silver: the heart of the wicked is little worth.

The lips of the righteous feed many: but fools die for want of wisdom.

The blessing of the Lord, it maketh rich, and he addeth no sorrow with it.

It is as sport to a fool to do mischief: but a man of understanding hath wisdom.

The fear of the wicked, it shall come upon him: but the desire of the righteous shall be granted.

As the whirlwind passeth, so is the wicked no more: but the righteous is an everlasting foundation.

As vinegar to the teeth, and as smoke to the eyes, so is the sluggard to them that send him.

The fear of the Lord prolongeth days: but the years of the wicked shall be shortened.

The hope of the righteous shall be gladness: but the expectation of the wicked shall perish.

The way of the Lord is strength to the upright: but destruction shall be to the workers of iniquity.

The righteous shall never be removed: but the wicked shall not inhabit the earth.

The mouth of the just bringeth forth wisdom: but the froward tongue shall be cut out.

The lips of the righteous know what is acceptable: but the mouth of the wicked speaketh frowardness.

❧

A false balance is abomination to the Lord: but a just weight is his delight.

When pride cometh, then cometh shame: but with the lowly is wisdom.

The integrity of the upright shall guide them: but the

perverseness of transgressors shall destroy them.

Riches profit not in the day of wrath: but righteousness delivereth from death.

The righteousness of the perfect shall direct his way: but the wicked shall fall by his own wickedness.

The righteousness of the upright shall deliver them: but transgressors shall be taken in their own naughtiness.

When a wicked man dieth, his expectation shall perish: and the hope of unjust men perisheth.

The righteous is delivered out of trouble, and the wicked cometh in his stead.

A hypocrite with his mouth destroyeth his neighbour: but through knowledge shall the just be delivered.

When it goeth well with the righteous the city rejoiceth: and when the wicked perish, there is shouting.

By the blessing of the upright the city is exalted: but it is overthrown by the mouth of the wicked.

He that is void of wisdom despiseth his neighbour: but a man of understanding holdeth his peace.

A tale-bearer revealeth secrets: but he that is of a faithful spirit concealeth the matter.

Where no counsel is, the people fall: but in the multitude of counsellors there is safety.

He that is surety for a stranger shall smart for it: and he that hateth suretiship is sure.

A gracious woman retaineth honour: and strong men retain riches.

The merciful man doeth good to his own soul: but he that is cruel troubleth his own flesh.

The wicked worketh a deceitful work: but to him that soweth righteousness shall be a sure reward.

As righteousness tendeth to life: so he that pursueth evil pursueth it to his own death.

They that are of a froward heart are abomination to the Lord: but such as are upright in their way are his delight.

Though hand join in hand, the wicked shall not be unpunished: but the seed of the righteous shall be delivered.

As a jewel of gold in a swine's snout, so is a fair woman which is without discretion.

The desire of the righteous is only good: but the expectation of the wicked is wrath.

There is that scattereth, and yet increaseth; and there is that withholdeth more than is meet, but it tendeth to poverty.

The liberal soul shall be made fat; and he that watereth shall be watered also himself.

He that withholdeth corn, the people shall curse him: but blessing shall be upon the head of him that selleth it.

He that diligently seeketh good procureth favour: but he that seeketh mischief, it shall come unto him.

He that trusteth in his riches shall fall: but the righteous shall flourish as a branch.

He that troubleth his own house shall inherit the wind: and a fool shall be servant to the wise of heart.

The fruit of the righteous is a tree of life; and he that winneth souls is wise.

Behold, the righteous shall be recompensed in the earth: much more the wicked and the sinner.

❧

Whoso loveth instruction loveth knowledge: but he that hateth reproof is brutish.

A good man obtaineth favour of the Lord: but a man of wicked devices will he condemn.

A man shall not be established by wickedness: but the root of the righteous shall not be moved.

A virtuous woman is a crown to her husband: but she that maketh ashamed is as rottenness in his bones.

The thoughts of the righteous are right: but the counsels of the wicked are deceit.

The words of the wicked are to lie in wait for blood: but the mouth of the upright shall deliver them.

The wicked are overthrown, and are not: but the house of the righteous shall stand.

A man shall be commended according to his wisdom: but he that is of a perverse heart shall be despised.

He that is despised, and hath a servant, is better than he that honoureth himself, and lacketh bread.

A righteous man regardeth the life of his beast: but the tender mercies of the wicked are cruel.

He that tilleth his land shall be satisfied with bread: but he that followeth vain persons is void of understanding.

The wicked desireth the net of evil men: but the root of the righteous yieldeth fruit.

The wicked is snared by the transgression of his lips: but the just shall come out of trouble.

A man shall be satisfied with good by the fruit of his mouth: and the recompense of a man's hands shall be rendered unto him.

The way of a fool is right in his own eyes: but he that hearkeneth unto counsel is wise.

A fool's wrath is presently known: but a prudent man covereth shame.

He that speaketh truth sheweth forth righteousness: but a false witness deceit.

There is that speaketh like the piercings of a sword: but the tongue of the wise is health.

The lip of truth shall be established for ever: but a lying tongue is but for a moment.

Deceit is in the heart of them that imagine evil: but to the counsellors of peace is joy.

There shall no evil happen to the just: but the wicked shall be filled with mischief.

Lying lips are abomination to the Lord: but they that deal truly are his delight.

A prudent man concealeth knowledge: but the heart of fools proclaimeth foolishness.

The hand of the diligent shall bear rule: but the slothful shall be under tribute.

Heaviness in the heart of man maketh it stoop: but a good word maketh it glad.

The righteous is more excellent than his neighbour: but the way of the wicked seduceth them.

The slothful man roasteth not that which he took in hunting: but the substance of a diligent man is precious.

In the way of righteousness is life; and in the pathway thereof there is no death.

❧

A wise son heareth his father's instruction: but a scorner heareth not rebuke.

A man shall eat good by the fruit of his mouth: but the soul of the transgressors shall eat violence.

He that keepeth his mouth keepeth his life: but he that openeth wide his lips shall have destruction.

The soul of the sluggard desireth, and hath nothing: but the soul of the diligent shall be made fat.

A righteous man hateth lying: but a wicked man is loathsome, and cometh to shame.

Righteousness keepeth him that is upright in the way: but wickedness overthroweth the sinner.

There is that maketh himself rich, yet hath nothing: there is that maketh himself poor, yet hath great riches.

The ransom of a man's life are his riches: but the poor heareth not rebuke.

The light of the righteous rejoiceth: but the lamp of the wicked shall be put out.

Only by pride cometh contention: but with the well-advised is wisdom.

Wealth gotten by vanity shall be diminished: but he that

gathereth by labour shall increase.

Hope deferred maketh the heart sick: but when the desire cometh, it is a tree of life.

Whoso despiseth the word shall be destroyed: but he that feareth the commandment shall be rewarded.

The law of the wise is a fountain of life, to depart from the snares of death.

Good understanding giveth favour: but the way of transgressors is hard.

Every prudent man dealeth with knowledge: but a fool layeth open his folly.

A wicked messenger falleth into mischief: but a faithful ambassador is health.

Poverty and shame shall be to him that refuseth instruction: but he that regardeth reproof shall be honoured.

The desire accomplished is sweet to the soul: but it is abomination to fools to depart from evil.

He that walketh with wise men shall be wise: but a companion of fools shall be destroyed.

Evil pursueth sinners: but to the righteous, good shall be repaid.

A good man leaveth an inheritance to his children's children: and the wealth of the sinner is laid up for the just.

Much food is in the tillage of the poor: but there is that is destroyed for want of judgment.

He that spareth his rod hateth his son: but he that loveth him chasteneth him betimes.

The righteous eateth to the satisfying of his soul: but the belly of the wicked shall want.

Every wise woman buildeth her house: but the foolish plucketh it down with her hands.

He that walketh in his uprightness feareth the Lord: but he that is perverse in his ways, despiseth him.

In the mouth of the foolish is a rod of pride: but the lips of the wise shall preserve them.

Where no oxen are, the crib is clean: but much increase is by the strength of the ox.

A faithful witness will not lie: but a false witness will utter lies.

A scorner seeketh wisdom, and findeth it not: but knowledge is easy unto him that understandeth.

Go from the presence of a foolish man, when thou perceivest not in him the lips of knowledge.

The wisdom of the prudent is to understand his way: but the folly of fools is deceit.

Fools make a mock at sin: but among the righteous there is favour.

The heart knoweth his own bitterness; and a stranger doth not intermeddle with his joy.

The house of the wicked shall be overthrown: but the tabernacle of the upright shall flourish.

There is a way which seemeth right unto a man, but the end thereof are the ways of death.

Even in laughter the heart is sorrowful; and the end of that mirth is heaviness.

The backslider in heart shall be filled with his own ways: and a good man shall be satisfied from himself.

The simple believeth every word: but the prudent man looketh well to his going.

A wise man feareth, and departeth from evil: but the fool rageth, and is confident.

He that is soon angry dealeth foolishly: and a man of wicked devices is hated.

The simple inherit folly: but the prudent are crowned with knowledge.

The evil bow before the good; and the wicked at the gates of the righteous.

The poor is hated even of his own neighbour: but the rich

hath many friends.

He that despiseth his neighbour sinneth: but he that hath mercy on the poor, happy is he.

Do they not err that devise evil? but mercy and truth shall be to them that devise good.

In all labour there is profit: but the talk of the lips tendeth only to penury.

The crown of the wise is their riches: but the foolishness of fools is folly.

A true witness delivereth souls: but a deceitful witness speaketh lies.

In the fear of the Lord is strong confidence: and his children shall have a place of refuge.

The fear of the Lord is a fountain of life, to depart from the snares of death.

In the multitude of people is the king's honour: but in the want of people is the destruction of the prince.

He that is slow to wrath is of great understanding: but he that is hasty of spirit exalteth folly.

A sound heart is the life of the flesh: but envy the rottenness of the bones.

He that oppresseth the poor reproacheth his Maker: but he that honoureth him hath mercy on the poor.

The wicked is driven away in his wickedness: but the righteous hath hope in his death.

Wisdom resteth in the heart of him that hath understanding: but that which is in the midst of fools is made known.

Righteousness exalteth a nation: but sin is a reproach to any people.

The king's favour is toward a wise servant: but his wrath is against him that causeth shame.

❧

A soft answer turneth away wrath: but grievous words stir up anger.

The tongue of the wise useth knowledge aright: but the mouth of fools poureth out foolishness.

The eyes of the Lord are in every place, beholding the evil and the good.

A wholesome tongue is a tree of life: but perverseness therein is a breach in the spirit.

A fool despiseth his father's instruction: but he that regardeth reproof is prudent.

In the house of the righteous is much treasure: but in the revenues of the wicked is trouble.

The lips of the wise disperse knowledge: but the heart of the foolish doeth not so.

The sacrifice of the wicked is an abomination to the Lord: but the prayer of the upright is his delight.

The way of the wicked is an abomination unto the Lord; but he loveth him that followeth after righteousness.

Correction is grievous unto him that forsaketh the way: and he that hateth reproof shall die.

Hell and destruction are before the Lord: how much more then the hearts of the children of men?

A scorner loveth not one that reproveth him: neither will he go unto the wise.

A merry heart maketh a cheerful countenance: but by sorrow of the heart the spirit is broken.

The heart of him that hath understanding seeketh knowledge: but the mouth of fools feedeth on foolishness.

All the days of the afflicted are evil: but he that is of a merry heart hath a continual feast.

Better is little with the fear of the Lord, than great treasure and trouble therewith.

Better is a dinner of herbs where love is, than a stalled ox and hatred therewith.

A wrathful man stirreth up strife: but he that is slow to anger appeaseth strife.

The way of the slothful man is as a hedge of thorns: but

the way of the righteous is made plain.

A wise son maketh a glad father: but a foolish man despiseth his mother.

Folly is joy to him that is destitute of wisdom: but a man of understanding walketh uprightly.

Without counsel purposes are disappointed: but in the multitude of counsellors they are established.

A man hath joy by the answer of his mouth: and a word spoken in due season, how good is it!

The way of life is above to the wise, that he may depart from hell beneath.

The Lord will destroy the house of the proud: but he will establish the border of the widow.

The thoughts of the wicked are an abomination to the Lord: but the words of the pure are pleasant words.

He that is greedy of gain troubleth his own house; but he that hateth gifts shall live.

The heart of the righteous studieth to answer: but the mouth of the wicked poureth out evil things.

The Lord is far from the wicked: but he heareth the prayer of the righteous.

The light of the eyes rejoiceth the heart: and a good report maketh the bones fat.

The ear that heareth the reproof of life abideth among the wise.

He that refuseth instruction despiseth his own soul, but he that heareth reproof getteth understanding.

The fear of the Lord is the instruction of wisdom; and before honour is humility.

❧

The preparations of the heart in man, and the answer of the tongue, is from the Lord.

All the ways of a man are clean in his own eyes; but the Lord weigheth the spirits.

Commit thy works unto the Lord, and thy thoughts shall be established.

The Lord hath made all things for himself: yea, even the wicked for the day of evil.

Every one that is proud in heart is an abomination to the Lord: though hand join in hand, he shall not be unpunished.

By mercy and truth iniquity is purged: and by the fear of the Lord men depart from evil.

When a man's ways please the Lord, he maketh even his enemies to be at peace with him.

Better is a little with righteousness, than great revenues without right.

A man's heart deviseth his way: but the Lord directeth his steps.

A divine sentence is in the lips of the king: his mouth transgresseth not in judgment.

A just weight and balance are the Lord's: all the weights of the bag are his work.

It is an abomination to kings to commit wickedness: for the throne is established by righteousness.

Righteous lips are the delight of kings; and they love him that speaketh right.

The wrath of a king is as messengers of death: but a wise man will pacify it.

In the light of the king's countenance is life, and his favour is as a cloud of the latter rain.

How much better is it to get wisdom than gold? and to get understanding rather to be chosen than silver?

The highway of the upright is to depart from evil: he that keepeth his way preserveth his soul.

Pride goeth before destruction, and a haughty spirit before a fall.

Better it is to be of an humble spirit with the lowly, than to divide the spoil with the proud.

He that handleth a matter wisely shall find good: and

whoso trusteth in the Lord, happy is he.

The wise in heart shall be called prudent: and the sweetness of the lips increaseth learning.

Understanding is a well-spring of life unto him that hath it: but the instruction of fools is folly.

The heart of the wise teacheth his mouth and addeth learning to his lips.

Pleasant words are as a honey-comb, sweet to the soul, and health to the bones.

There is a way that seemeth right unto a man, but the end thereof are the ways of death.

He that laboureth, laboureth for himself, for his mouth craveth it of him.

An ungodly man diggeth up evil; and in his lips there is as a burning fire.

A froward man soweth strife: and a whisperer separateth chief friends.

A violent man enticeth his neighbour, and leadeth him into the way that is not good.

He shutteth his eyes to devise froward things: moving his lips he bringeth evil to pass.

The hoary head is a crown of glory, if it be found in the way of righteousness.

He that is slow to anger is better than the mighty; and he that ruleth his spirit, than he that taketh a city.

The lot is cast into the lap; but the whole disposing thereof is of the Lord.

❧

Better is a dry morsel, and quietness therewith, than a house full of sacrifices with strife.

A wise servant shall have rule over a son that causeth shame, and shall have part of the inheritance among the brethren.

The fining-pot is for silver, and the furnace for gold: but

the Lord trieth the hearts.

A wicked doer giveth heed to false lips; and a liar giveth ear to a naughty tongue.

Whoso mocketh the poor reproacheth his Maker: and he that is glad of calamities shall not be unpunished.

Children's children are the crown of old men; and the glory of children are their fathers.

Excellent speech becometh not a fool: much less do lying lips a prince.

A gift is as a precious stone in the eyes of him that hath it: whithersoever it turneth, it prospereth.

He that covereth a transgression seeketh love; but he that repeateth a matter, separateth very friends.

A reproof entereth more into a wise man than a hundred stripes into a fool.

An evil man seeketh only rebellion: therefore a cruel messenger shall be sent against him.

Let a bear robbed of her whelps meet a man, rather than a fool in his folly.

Whoso rewardeth evil for good, evil shall not depart from his house.

The beginning of strife is as when one letteth out water: therefore leave off contention, before it be meddled with.

He that justifieth the wicked, and he that condemneth the just, even they both are abomination to the Lord.

Wherefore is there a price in the hand of a fool to get wisdom, seeing he hath no heart to it?

A friend loveth at all times, and a brother is born for adversity.

A man void of understanding striketh hands, and becometh surety in the presence of his friend.

He loveth transgression that loveth strife: and he that exalteth his gate seeketh destruction.

He that hath a froward heart findeth no good: and he that hath a perverse tongue falleth into mischief.

He that begetteth a fool doeth it to his sorrow: and the father of a fool hath no joy.

A merry heart doeth good like a medicine: but a broken spirit drieth the bones.

A wicked man taketh a gift out of the bosom to pervert the ways of judgment.

Wisdom is before him that hath understanding; but the eyes of a fool are in the ends of the earth.

A foolish son is a grief to his father, and bitterness to her that bare him.

Also to punish the just is not good, nor to strike princes for equity.

He that hath knowledge spareth his words: and a man of understanding is of an excellent spirit.

Even a fool, when he holdeth his peace, is counted wise: and he that shutteth his lips is esteemed a man of understanding.

❧

Through desire, a man, having separated himself, seeketh and intermeddleth with all wisdom.

A fool hath no delight in understanding, but that his heart may discover itself.

When the wicked cometh, then cometh also contempt, and with ignominy reproach.

The words of a man's mouth are as deep waters, and the well-spring of wisdom as a flowing brook.

It is not good to accept the person of the wicked, to overthrow the righteous in judgment.

A fool's lips enter into contention, and his mouth calleth for strokes.

A fool's mouth is his destruction, and his lips are the snare of his soul.

The words of a tale-bearer are as wounds, and they go down into the innermost parts of the belly.

He also that is slothful in his work is brother to him that is a great waster.

The name of the Lord is a strong tower: the righteous runneth into it, and is safe.

The rich man's wealth is his strong city, and as a high wall in his own conceit.

Before destruction the heart of man is haughty, and before honour is humility.

He that answereth a matter before he heareth it, it is folly and shame unto him.

The spirit of a man will sustain his infirmity; but a wounded spirit who can bear?

The heart of the prudent getteth knowledge; and the ear of the wise seeketh knowledge.

A man's gift maketh room for him, and bringeth him before great men.

He that is first in his own cause seemeth just; but his neighbour cometh and searcheth him.

The lot causeth contentions to cease, and parteth between the mighty.

A brother offended is harder to be won than a strong city; and their contentions are like the bars of a castle.

A man's belly shall be satisfied with the fruit of his mouth; and with the increase of his lips shall he be filled.

Death and life are in the power of the tongue: and they that love it shall eat the fruit thereof.

Whoso findeth a wife, findeth a good thing, and obtaineth favour of the Lord.

The poor useth entreaties; but the rich answereth roughly.

A man that hath friends must shew himself friendly: and there is a friend that sticketh closer than a brother.

❧

Better is the poor that walketh in his integrity, than he that is perverse in his lips, and is a fool.

Also, that the soul be without knowledge, it is not good; and he that hasteth with his feet sinneth.

The foolishness of man perverteth his way: and his heart fretteth against the Lord.

Wealth maketh many friends; but the poor is separated from his neighbour.

A false witness shall not be unpunished, and he that speaketh lies shall not escape.

Many will entreat the favour of the prince: and every man is a friend to him that giveth gifts.

All the brethren of the poor do hate him: how much more do his friends go far from him? he pursueth them with words, yet they are wanting to him.

He that getteth wisdom loveth his own soul: he that keepeth understanding shall find good.

A false witness shall not be unpunished, and he that speaketh lies shall perish.

Delight is not seemly for a fool; much less for a servant to have rule over princes.

The discretion of a man deferreth his anger; and it is his glory to pass over a transgression.

The king's wrath is as the roaring of a lion; but his favour is as dew upon the grass.

A foolish son is the calamity of his father: and the contentions of a wife are a continual dropping.

House and riches are the inheritance of fathers: and a prudent wife is from the Lord.

Slothfulness casteth into a deep sleep; and an idle soul shall suffer hunger.

He that keepeth the commandment keepeth his own soul: but he that despiseth his ways shall die.

He that hath pity upon the poor, lendeth unto the Lord; and that which he hath given will he pay him again.

Chasten thy son while there is hope, and let not thy soul spare for his crying.

A man of great wrath shall suffer punishment: for if thou deliver him, yet thou must do it again.

Hear counsel, and receive instruction, that thou mayest be wise in thy latter end.

There are many devices in a man's heart; nevertheless the counsel of the Lord, that shall stand.

The desire of a man is his kindness: and a poor man is better than a liar.

The fear of the Lord tendeth to life: and he that hath it shall abide satisfied; he shall not be visited with evil.

A slothful man hideth his hand in his bosom, and will not so much as bring it to his mouth again.

Smite a scorner, and the simple will beware: and reprove one that hath understanding, and he will understand knowledge.

He that wasteth his father, and chaseth away his mother, is a son that causeth shame, and bringeth reproach.

Cease, my son, to hear the instruction that causeth to err from the words of knowledge.

An ungodly witness scorneth judgment: and the mouth of the wicked devoureth iniquity.

Judgments are prepared for scorners, and stripes for the back of fools.

❧

Wine is a mocker, strong drink is raging: and whosoever is deceived thereby is not wise.

The fear of a king is as the roaring of a lion: whoso provoketh him to anger sinneth against his own soul.

It is an honour for a man to cease from strife: but every fool will be meddling.

The sluggard will not plough by reason of the cold; therefore shall he beg in harvest, and have nothing.

Counsel in the heart of man is like deep water; but a man of understanding will draw it out.

Most men will proclaim every one his own goodness; but a faithful man who can find?

The just man walketh in his integrity: his children are blessed after him.

A king that sitteth in the throne of judgment, scattereth away all evil with his eyes.

Who can say, I have made my heart clean, I am pure from my sin?

Divers weights, and divers measures, both of them are alike abomination to the Lord.

Even a child is known by his doings, whether his work be pure, and whether it be right.

The hearing ear, and the seeing eye, the Lord hath made even both of them.

Love not sleep, lest thou come to poverty; open thine eyes, and thou shalt be satisfied with bread.

It is naught, it is naught, saith the buyer: but when he is gone his way, then he boasteth.

There is gold, and a multitude of rubies: but the lips of knowledge are a precious jewel.

Take his garment that is surety for a stranger: and take a pledge of him for a strange woman.

Bread of deceit is sweet to a man; but afterwards his mouth shall be filled with gravel.

Every purpose is established by counsel: and with good advice make war.

He that goeth about as a tale-bearer revealeth secrets: therefore meddle not with him that flattereth with his lips.

Whoso curseth his father or his mother, his lamp shall be put out in obscure darkness.

An inheritance may be gotten hastily at the beginning; but the end thereof shall not be blessed.

Say not thou, I will recompense evil; but wait on the Lord, and he shall save thee.

Divers weights are an abomination unto the Lord; and a

false balance is not good.

Man's goings are of the Lord; how can a man then understand his own way?

It is a snare to the man who devoureth that which is holy, and after vows to make inquiry.

A wise king scattereth the wicked, and bringeth the wheel over them.

The spirit of man is the candle of the Lord, searching all the inward parts of the belly.

Mercy and truth preserve the king: and his throne is upholden by mercy.

The glory of young men is their strength: and the beauty of old men is the gray head.

The blueness of a wound cleanseth away evil: so do stripes the inward parts of the belly.

❧§❧

The king's heart is in the hand of the Lord, as the rivers of water: he turneth it whithersoever he will.

Every way of a man is right in his own eyes: but the Lord pondereth the hearts.

To do justice and judgment is more acceptable to the Lord than sacrifice.

A high look, and a proud heart, and the ploughing of the wicked, is sin.

The thoughts of the diligent tend only to plenteousness; but of every one that is hasty, only to want.

The getting of treasures by a lying tongue is a vanity tossed to and fro of them that seek death.

The robbery of the wicked shall destroy them; because they refuse to do judgment.

The way of man is froward and strange: but as for the pure, his work is right.

It is better to dwell in a corner of the house-top, than with a brawling woman in a wide house.

The soul of the wicked desireth evil: his neighbour findeth no favour in his eyes.

When the scorner is punished, the simple is made wise: and when the wise is instructed, he receiveth knowledge.

The righteous man wisely considereth the house of the wicked: but God overthroweth the wicked for their wickedness.

Whoso stoppeth his ears at the cry of the poor, he also shall cry himself, but shall not be heard.

A gift in secret pacifieth anger: and a reward in the bosom, strong wrath.

It is joy to the just to do judgment: but destruction shall be to the workers of iniquity.

The man that wandereth out of the way of understanding shall remain in the congregation of the dead.

He that loveth pleasure shall be a poor man: he that loveth wine and oil shall not be rich.

The wicked shall be a ransom for the righteous and the transgressor for the upright.

It is better to dwell in the wilderness, than with a contentious and an angry woman.

There is treasure to be desired, and oil in the dwelling of the wise; but a foolish man spendeth it up.

He that followeth after righteousness and mercy, findeth life, righteousness, and honour.

A wise man scaleth the city of the mighty, and casteth down the strength of the confidence thereof.

Whoso keepeth his mouth and his tongue, keepeth his soul from troubles.

Proud and haughty scorner is his name, who dealeth in proud wrath.

The desire of the slothful killeth him; for his hands refuse to labour.

He coveteth greedily all the day long: but the righteous giveth and spareth not.

The sacrifice of the wicked is abomination: how much more, when he bringeth it with a wicked mind?

A false witness shall perish: but the man that heareth, speaketh constantly.

A wicked man hardeneth his face: but as for the upright, he directeth his way.

There is no wisdom nor understanding nor counsel against the Lord.

The horse is prepared against the day of battle: but safety is of the Lord.

❧

A good name is rather to be chosen than great riches, and loving favour than silver and gold.

The rich and poor meet together: the Lord is the maker of them all.

A prudent man foreseeth the evil, and hideth himself: but the simple pass on, and are punished.

By humility and the fear of the Lord are riches, and honour, and life.

Thorns and snares are in the way of the froward: he that doth keep his soul shall be far from them.

Train up a child in the way he should go: and when he is old, he will not depart from it.

The rich ruleth over the poor, and the borrower is servant to the lender.

He that soweth iniquity shall reap vanity: and the rod of his anger shall fail.

He that hath a bountiful eye shall be blessed; for he giveth of his bread to the poor.

Cast out the scorner, and contention shall go out; yea, strife and reproach shall cease.

He that loveth pureness of heart, for the grace of his lips the king shall be his friend.

The eyes of the Lord preserve knowledge, and he overthroweth the words of the transgressor.

The slothful man saith, There is a lion without, I shall be slain in the streets.

The mouth of strange women is a deep pit: he that is abhorred of the Lord shall fall therein.

Foolishness is bound in the heart of a child; but the rod of correction shall drive it far from him.

He that oppresseth the poor to increase his riches, and he that giveth to the rich, shall surely come to want.

Bow down thine ear, and hear the words of the wise, and apply thy heart unto my knowledge.

For it is a pleasant thing if thou keep them within thee; they shall withal be fitted in thy lips.

That thy trust may be in the Lord, I have made known to thee this day, even to thee.

Have not I written to thee excellent things in counsels and knowledge,

That I might make thee know the certainty of the words of truth; that thou mightest answer the words of truth to them that send unto thee?

Rob not the poor, because he is poor: neither oppress the afflicted in the gate:

For the Lord will plead their cause, and spoil the soul of those that spoiled them.

Make no friendship with an angry man; and with a furious man thou shalt not go:

Lest thou learn his way, and get a snare to thy soul.

Be not thou one of them that strike hands, or of them that are sureties for debts.

If thou hast nothing to pay, why should he take away thy bed from under thee?

Remove not the ancient landmark, which thy fathers have set.

Seest thou a man diligent in his business? he shall stand before kings; he shall not stand before mean men.

❧

When thou sittest to eat with a ruler, consider diligently what is before thee:

And put a knife to thy throat, if thou be a man given to appetite.

Be not desirous of his dainties: for they are deceitful meat.

Labour not to be rich: cease from thine own wisdom.

Wilt thou set thine eyes upon that which is not? for riches certainly make themselves wings; they fly away as an eagle toward heaven.

Eat thou not the bread of him that hath an evil eye, neither desire thou his dainty meats:

For as he thinketh in his heart, so is he: Eat and drink, saith he to thee; but his heart is not with thee.

The morsel which thou hast eaten shalt thou vomit up, and lose thy sweet words.

Speak not in the ears of a fool: for he will despise the wisdom of thy words.

Remove not the old landmark; and enter not into the fields of the fatherless:

For their Redeemer is mighty; he shall plead their cause with thee.

Apply thy heart unto instruction, and thine ears to the words of knowledge.

Withhold not correction from the child: for if thou beatest him with the rod, he shall not die.

Thou shalt beat him with the rod, and shalt deliver his soul from hell.

My son, if thy heart be wise, my heart shall rejoice, even mine.

Yea, my reins shall rejoice, when thy lips speak right things.

Let not thy heart envy sinners: but be thou in the fear of the Lord all the day long.

For surely there is an end; and thine expectation shall not be cut off.

Hear thou, my son, and be wise, and guide thy heart in the way.

Be not among wine-bibbers; among riotous eaters of flesh:

For the drunkard and the glutton shall come to poverty: and drowsiness shall clothe a man with rags.

Hearken unto thy father that begat thee, and despise not thy mother when she is old.

Buy the truth, and sell it not; also wisdom, and instruction, and understanding.

The father of the righteous shall greatly rejoice: and he that begetteth a wise child shall have joy of him.

Thy father and thy mother shall be glad, and she that bare thee shall rejoice.

My son, give me thy heart, and let thine eyes observe my ways.

For a whore is a deep ditch; and a strange woman is a narrow pit.

She also lieth in wait as for a prey, and increaseth the transgressors among men.

Who hath wo? who hath sorrow? who hath contentions? who hath babbling? who hath wounds without cause? who hath redness of eyes?

They that tarry long at the wine; they that go to seek mixed wine.

Look not thou upon the wine when it is red, when it giveth his colour in the cup, when it moveth itself aright.

At the last it biteth like a serpent, and stingeth like an adder.

Thine eyes shall behold strange women, and thy heart shall utter perverse things.

Yea, thou shalt be as he that lieth down in the midst of

the sea, or as he that lieth upon the top of a mast.

They have stricken me, shalt thou say, and I was not sick; they have beaten me, and I felt it not: when shall I awake? I will seek it yet again.

❧

Be not thou envious against evil men, neither desire to be with them:

For their heart studieth destruction, and their lips talk of mischief.

Through wisdom is a house builded; and by understanding it is established:

And by knowledge shall the chambers be filled with all precious and pleasant riches.

A wise man is strong; yea, a man of knowledge increaseth strength.

For by wise counsel thou shalt make thy war: and in multitude of counsellors there is safety.

Wisdom is too high for a fool: he openeth not his mouth in the gate.

He that deviseth to do evil shall be called a mischievous person.

The thought of foolishness is sin: and the scorner is an abomination to men.

If thou faint in the day of adversity, thy strength is small.

If thou forbear to deliver them that are drawn unto death, and those that are ready to be slain;

If thou sayest, Behold, we knew it not; doth not he that pondereth the heart consider it? and he that keepeth thy soul, doth not he know it? and shall not he render to every man according to his works?

My son, eat thou honey, because it is good; and the honeycomb, which is sweet to thy taste:

So shall the knowledge of wisdom be unto thy soul: when thou hast found it, then there shall be a reward, and thy expectation shall not be cut off.

Lay not wait, O wicked man, against the dwelling of the righteous; spoil not his resting-place:

For a just man falleth seven times, and riseth up again: but the wicked shall fall into mischief.

Rejoice not when thine enemy falleth, and let not thy heart be glad when he stumbleth.

Lest the Lord see it, and it displease him, and he turn away his wrath from him.

Fret not thyself because of evil men, neither be thou envious at the wicked;

For there shall be no reward to the evil man; the candle of the wicked shall be put out.

My son, fear thou the Lord and the king: and meddle not with them that are given to change:

For their calamity shall rise suddenly; and who knoweth the ruin of them both?

These things also belong to the wise. It is not good to have respect of persons in judgment.

He that saith unto the wicked, Thou art righteous; him shall the people curse, nations shall abhor him:

But to them that rebuke him shall be delight, and a good blessing shall come upon them.

Every man shall kiss his lips that giveth a right answer.

Prepare thy work without, and make it fit for thyself in the field; and afterwards build thy house.

Be not a witness against thy neighbour without cause; and deceive not with thy lips.

Say not, I will do so to him as he hath done to me: I will render to the man according to his work.

I went by the field of the slothful, and by the vineyard of the man void of understanding;

And lo, it was all grown over with thorns, and nettles had covered the face thereof, and the stone wall thereof was broken down.

Then I saw, and considered it well: I looked upon it, and

received instruction.

Yet a little sleep, a little slumber, a little folding of the hands to sleep:

So shall thy poverty come as one that travelleth; and thy want as an armed man.

❧§❧

These are also the proverbs of Solomon, which men of Hezekiah king of Judah copied out.

It is the glory of God to conceal a thing: but the honour of kings is to search out a matter.

The heaven for height, and the earth for depth, and the heart of kings is unsearchable.

Take away the dross from the silver, and there shall come forth a vessel for the finer.

Take away the wicked from before the king, and his throne shall be established in righteousness.

Put not forth thyself in the presence of the king, and stand not in the place of great men.

For better it is that it be said unto thee, Come up hither; than that thou shouldest be put lower in the presence of the prince whom thine eyes have seen.

Go not forth hastily to strive, lest thou know not what to do in the end thereof, when thy neighbour hath put thee to shame.

Debate thy cause with thy neighbour himself; and discover not a secret to another:

Lest he that heareth it put thee to shame, and thine infamy turn not away.

A word fitly spoken is like apples of gold in pictures of silver.

As an ear-ring of gold, and an ornament of fine gold, so is a wise reprover upon an obedient ear.

As the cold of snow in the time of harvest, so is a faithful messenger to them that send him: for he refresheth the soul of his masters.

Whoso boasteth himself of a false gift is like clouds and wind without rain.

By long forbearing is a prince persuaded, and a soft tongue breaketh the bone.

Hast thou found honey? eat so much as is sufficient for thee, lest thou be filled therewith, and vomit it.

Withdraw thy foot from thy neighbour's house; lest he be weary of thee, and so hate thee.

A man that beareth false witness against his neighbour is a maul, and a sword, and a sharp arrow.

Confidence in an unfaithful man in time of trouble is like a broken tooth, and a foot out of joint.

As he that taketh away a garment in cold weather, and as vinegar upon nitre: so is he that singeth songs to a heavy heart.

If thine enemy be hungry, give him bread to eat; and if he be thirsty, give him water to drink:

For thou shalt heap coals of fire upon his head, and the Lord shall reward thee.

The north wind driveth away rain: so doth an angry countenance a backbiting tongue.

It is better to dwell in a corner of the house-top, than with a brawling woman and in a wide house.

As cold waters to a thirsty soul, so is good news from a far country.

A righteous man falling down before the wicked is as a troubled fountain, and a corrupt spring.

It is not good to eat much honey: so for men to search their own glory is not glory.

He that hath no rule over his own spirit is like a city that is broken down, and without walls.

❧

As snow in summer, and as rain in harvest; so honour is not seemly for a fool.

As the bird by wandering, as the swallow by flying, so the curse causeless shall not come.

A whip for the horse, a bridle for the ass, and a rod for the fool's back.

Answer not a fool according to his folly, lest thou also be like unto him.

Answer a fool according to his folly, lest he be wise in his own conceit.

He that sendeth a message by the hand of a fool cutteth off the feet, and drinketh damage.

The legs of the lame are not equal: so is a parable in the mouth of fools.

As he that bindeth a stone in a sling, so is he that giveth honour to a fool.

As a thorn goeth up into the hand of a drunkard, so is a parable in the mouth of fools.

The great God that formed all things both rewardeth the fool, and rewardeth transgressors.

As a dog returneth to his vomit, so a fool returneth to his folly.

Seest thou a man wise in his own conceit? there is more hope of a fool than of him.

The slothful man saith, There is a lion in the way; a lion is in the streets.

As the door turneth upon his hinges, so doth the slothful upon his bed.

The slothful hideth his hand in his bosom; it grieveth him to bring it again to his mouth.

The sluggard is wiser in his own conceit than seven men that can render a reason.

He that passeth by, and meddleth with strife belonging not to him, is like one that taketh a dog by the ears.

As a mad man, who casteth firebrands, arrows, and death,

So is the man that deceiveth his neighbour, and saith, Am not I in sport?

Where no wood is, there the fire goeth out: so where there is no tale-bearer, the strife ceaseth.

As coals are to burning coals, and wood to fire; so is a contentious man to kindle strife.

The words of a tale-bearer are as wounds, and they go down into the innermost parts of the belly.

Burning lips and a wicked heart are like a potsherd covered with silver dross.

He that hateth, dissembleth with his lips, and layeth up deceit within him;

When he speaketh fair, believe him not: for there are seven abominations in his heart.

Whose hatred is covered by deceit, his wickedness shall be shewed before the whole congregation.

Whoso diggeth a pit shall fall therein: and he that rolleth a stone, it will return upon him.

A lying tongue hateth those that are afflicted by it; and a flattering mouth worketh ruin.

⁂

Boast not thyself of to-morrow; for thou knowest not what a day may bring forth.

Let another man praise thee, and not thine own mouth; a stranger, and not thine own lips.

A stone is heavy, and the sand weighty; but a fool's wrath is heavier than them both.

Wrath is cruel, and anger is outrageous; but who is able to stand before envy?

Open rebuke is better than secret love.

Faithful are the wounds of a friend; but the kisses of an enemy are deceitful.

The full soul loatheth a honey-comb; but to the hungry soul every bitter thing is sweet.

As a bird that wandereth from her nest, so is a man that wandereth from his place.

Ointment and perfume rejoice the heart: so doth the sweetness of a man's friend by hearty counsel.

Thine own friend, and thy father's friend, forsake not; neither go into thy brother's house in the day of thy calamity: for better is a neighbour that is near, than a brother far off.

My son, be wise, and make my heart glad, that I may answer him that reproacheth me.

A prudent man forseeth the evil, and hideth himself; but the simple pass on, and are punished.

Take his garment that is surety for a stranger, and take a pledge of him for a strange woman.

He that blesseth his friend with a loud voice, rising early in the morning, it shall be counted a curse to him.

A continual dropping in a very rainy day and a contentious woman are alike.

Whosoever hideth her, hideth the wind, and the ointment of his right hand which bewrayeth itself.

Iron sharpeneth iron; so a man sharpeneth the countenance of his friend.

Whoso keepeth the fig-tree shall eat the fruit thereof: so he that waiteth on his master shall be honoured.

As in water face answereth to face, so the heart of man to man.

Hell and destruction are never full; so the eyes of man are never satisfied.

As the fining-pot for silver, and the furnace for gold; so is a man to his praise.

Though thou shouldest bray a fool in a mortar among wheat with a pestle, yet will not his foolishness depart from him.

Be thou diligent to know the state of thy flocks, and look well to thy herds:

For riches are not for ever: and doth the crown endure to every generation?

The hay appeareth, and the tender grass sheweth itself, and

herbs of the mountains are gathered.

The lambs are for thy clothing, and the goats are the price of the field.

And thou shalt have goats' milk enough for thy food, for the food of thy household, and for the maintenance for thy maidens.

❧

The wicked flee when no man pursueth: but the righteous are bold as a lion.

For the transgression of a land many are the princes thereof: but by a man of understanding and knowledge the state thereof shall be prolonged.

A poor man that oppresseth the poor is like a sweeping rain which leaveth no food.

They that forsake the law praise the wicked: but such as keep the law contend with them.

Evil men understand not judgment: but they that seek the Lord understand all things.

Better is the poor that walketh in his uprightness, than he that is perverse in his ways, though he be rich.

Whoso keepeth the law is a wise son: but he that is a companion of riotous men shameth his father.

He that by usury and unjust gain increaseth his substance, he shall gather it for him that will pity the poor.

He that turneth away his ear from hearing the law, even his prayer shall be abomination.

Whoso causeth the righteous to go astray in an evil way, he shall fall himself into his own pit: but the upright shall have good things in possession.

The rich man is wise in his own conceit; but the poor that hath understanding searcheth him out.

When righteous men do rejoice, there is great glory: but when the wicked rise, a man is hidden.

He that covereth his sins shall not prosper: but whoso confesseth and forsaketh them shall have mercy.

Happy is the man that feareth always: but he that hardeneth his heart shall fall into mischief.

As a roaring lion, and a ranging bear; so is a wicked ruler over the poor people.

The prince that wanteth understanding is also a great oppressor: but he that hateth covetousness shall prolong his days.

A man that doeth violence to the blood of any person shall flee to the pit; let no man stay him.

Whoso walketh uprightly shall be saved; but he that is perverse in his ways shall fall at once.

He that tilleth his land shall have plenty of bread but he that followeth after vain persons shall have poverty enough.

A faithful man shall abound with blessings: but he that maketh haste to be rich shall not be innocent.

To have respect of persons is not good: for, for a piece of bread that man will transgress.

He that hasteth to be rich hath an evil eye, and considereth not that poverty shall come upon him.

He that rebuketh a man, afterwards shall find more favour than he that flattereth with the tongue.

Whoso robbeth his father or his mother, and saith, It is no transgression; the same is the companion of a destroyer.

He that is of a proud heart stirreth up strife: but he that putteth his trust in the Lord shall be made fat.

He that trusteth in his own heart is a fool: but whoso walketh wisely, he shall be delivered.

He that giveth unto the poor shall not lack: but he that hideth his eyes shall have many a curse.

When the wicked rise, men hide themselves: but when they perish, the righteous increase.

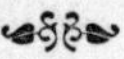

He that, being often reproved, hardeneth his neck, shall suddenly be destroyed, and that without remedy.

When the righteous are in authority, the people rejoice: but when the wicked beareth rule, the people mourn.

Whoso loveth wisdom rejoiceth his father: but he that keepeth company with harlots spendeth his substance.

The king by judgment establisheth the land: but he that receiveth gifts overthroweth it.

A man that flattereth his neighbour spreadeth a net for his feet.

In the transgression of an evil man there is a snare: but the righteous doth sing and rejoice.

The righteous considereth the cause of the poor; but the wicked regardeth not to know it.

Scornful men bring a city into a snare: but wise men turn away wrath.

If a wise man contendeth with a foolish man, whether he rage or laugh, there is no rest.

The blood-thirsty hate the upright: but the just seek his soul.

A fool uttereth all his mind: but a wise man keepeth it in till afterwards.

If a ruler hearken to lies, all his servants are wicked.

The poor and the deceitful man meet together: the Lord lighteneth both their eyes.

The king that faithfully judgeth the poor, his throne shall be established for ever.

The rod and reproof give wisdom: but a child left to himself bringeth his mother to shame.

When the wicked are multiplied, transgression increaseth: but the righteous shall see their fall.

Correct thy son, and he shall give thee rest; yea, he shall give delight unto thy soul.

Where there is no vision, the people perish: but he that keepeth the law, happy is he.

A servant will not be corrected by words: for though he understand he will not answer.

Seest thou a man that is hasty in his words? there is more hope of a fool than of him.

He that delicately bringeth up his servant from a child shall have him become his son at the length.

An angry man stirreth up strife, and a furious man aboundeth in transgression.

A man's pride shall bring him low: but honour shall uphold the humble in spirit.

Whoso is partner with a thief, hateth his own soul: he heareth cursing, and bewrayeth it not.

The fear of man bringeth a snare: but whoso putteth his trust in the Lord shall be safe.

Many seek the ruler's favour; but every man's judgment cometh from the Lord.

An unjust man is an abomination to the just; and he that is upright in the way is abomination to the wicked.

⁂

The words of Agur the son of Jakeh, even the prophecy: the man spake unto Ithiel, even unto Ithiel and Ucal,

Surely I am more brutish than any man, and have not the understanding of a man.

I neither learned wisdom, nor have the knowledge of the holy.

Who hath ascended up into heaven, or descended? who hath gathered the wind in his fists? who hath bound the waters in a garment? who hath established all the ends of the earth? what is his name, and what is his son's name, if thou canst tell?

Every word of God is pure: he is a shield unto them that put their trust in him.

Add thou not unto his words, lest he reprove thee, and thou be found a liar.

Two things have I required of thee; deny me them not before I die:

Remove far from me vanity and lies; give me neither poverty nor riches; feed me with food convenient for me:

Lest I be full, and deny thee, and say, Who is the Lord? or lest I be poor, and steal, and take the name of my God in vain.

Accuse not a servant unto his master, lest he curse thee, and thou be found guilty.

There is a generation that curseth their father, and doth not bless their mother.

There is a generation that are pure in their own eyes, and yet is not washed from their filthiness.

There is a generation, O how lofty are their eyes! and their eyelids are lifted up.

There is a generation, whose teeth are as swords, and their jaw-teeth as knives, to devour the poor from off the earth, and the needy from among men.

The horse-leech hath two daughters, crying, Give, give. There are three things that are never satisfied, yea, four things say not, It is enough:

The grave; and the barren womb; the earth that is not filled with water; and the fire that saith not, It is enough.

The eye that mocketh at his father, and despiseth to obey his mother, the ravens of the valley shall pick it out, and the young eagles shall eat it.

There be three things which are too wonderful for me, yea, four which I know not:

The way of an eagle in the air; the way of a serpent upon a rock; the way of a ship in the midst of the sea; and the way of a man with a maid.

Such is the way of an adulterous woman; she eateth, and wipeth her mouth, and saith, I have done no wickedness.

For three things the earth is disquieted, and for four which it cannot bear:

For a servant when he reigneth; and a fool when he is filled with meat;

For an odious woman when she is married; and a handmaid that is heir to her mistress.

There be four things which are little upon the earth, but they are exceeding wise:

The ants are a people not strong, yet they prepare their meat in the summer;

The conies are but a feeble folk, yet make they their houses in the rocks;

The locusts have no king, yet go they forth all of them by bands;

The spider taketh hold with her hands, and is in kings' palaces.

There be three things which go well, yea, four are comely in going.

A lion, which is strongest among beasts, and turneth not away for any;

A greyhound; a he-goat also; and a king, against whom there is no rising up.

If thou hast done foolishly in lifting up thyself, or if thou hast thought evil, lay thy hand upon thy mouth.

Surely the churning of milk bringeth forth butter, and the wringing of the nose bringeth forth blood: so the forcing of wrath bringeth forth strife.

The words of king Lemuel, the prophecy that his mother taught him.

What, my son? and what, the son of my womb? and what, the son of my vows?

Give not thy strength unto women, nor thy ways to that which destroyeth kings.

It is not for kings, O Lemuel, it is not for kings to drink wine; nor for princes strong drink:

Lest they drink, and forget the law, and pervert the judgment of any of the afflicted.

Give strong drink unto him that is ready to perish, and wine to those that be of heavy hearts.

Let him drink, and forget his poverty, and remember his misery no more.

Open thy mouth for the dumb in the cause of all such as are appointed to destruction.

Open thy mouth, judge righteously, and plead the cause of the poor and needy.

Who can find a virtuous woman? for her price is far above rubies.

The heart of her husband doth safely trust in her, so that he shall have no need of spoil.

She will do him good and not evil all the days of her life.

She seeketh wool, and flax, and worketh willingly with her hands.

She is like the merchants' ships; she bringeth her food from afar.

She riseth also while it is yet night, and giveth meat to her household, and a portion to her maidens.

She considereth a field, and buyeth it: with the fruit of her hands she planteth a vineyard.

She girdeth her loins with strength, and strengtheneth her arms.

She perceiveth that her merchandise is good: her candle goeth not out by night.

She layeth her hands to the spindle, and her hands hold the distaff.

She stretcheth out her hand to the poor; yea, she reacheth forth her hands to the needy.

She is not afraid of the snow for her household: for all her household are clothed with scarlet.

She maketh herself coverings of tapestry; her clothing is silk and purple.

Her husband is known in the gates, when he sitteth among the elders of the land.

She maketh fine linen, and selleth it; and delivereth girdles unto the merchant.

Strength and honour are her clothing; and she shall rejoice in time to come.

She openeth her mouth with wisdom; and in her tongue is the law of kindness.

She looketh well to the ways of her household, and eateth not the bread of idleness.

Her children arise up, and call her blessed; her husband also, and he praiseth her.

Many daughters have done virtuously, but thou excellest them all.

Favour is deceitful, and beauty is vain: but a woman that feareth the Lord, she shall be praised.

Give her of the fruit of her hands; and let her own works praise her in the gates.

Solomon's Elegy on Vanity

THE WORDS OF THE PREACHER, the son of David, king of Jerusalem.

Vanity of vanities, saith the Preacher, vanity of vanities; all is vanity.

What profit hath a man of all his labour which he taketh under the sun?

One generation passeth away, and another generation cometh: but the earth abideth for ever.

The sun also ariseth, and the sun goeth down, and hasteth to his place where he arose.

The wind goeth toward the south, and turneth about unto the north; it whirleth about continually, and the wind returneth again according to his circuits.

All the rivers run into the sea; yet the sea is not full: unto the place from whence the rivers come, thither they return again.

All things are full of labour; man cannot utter it: the eye is not satisfied with seeing, nor the ear filled with hearing.

The thing that hath been, it is that which shall be; and that which is done is that which shall be done: and there is no new thing under the sun.

Is there any thing whereof it may be said, See, this is new? it hath been already of old time, which was before us.

There is no remembrance of former things; neither shall there be any remembrance of things that are to come with those that shall come after.

I the Preacher was king over Israel in Jerusalem.

And I gave my heart to seek and search out by wisdom

concerning all things that are done under heaven: this sore travail hath God given to the sons of man to be exercised therewith.

I have seen all the works that are done under the sun; and behold, all is vanity and vexation of spirit.

That which is crooked cannot be made straight: and that which is wanting cannot be numbered.

I communed with mine own heart, saying, Lo, I am come to great estate, and have gotten more wisdom than all they that have been before me in Jerusalem: yea, my heart had great experience of wisdom and knowledge.

And I gave my heart to know wisdom, and to know madness and folly: I perceived that this also is vexation of spirit.

For in much wisdom is much grief: and he that increaseth knowledge increaseth sorrow.

❧

I said in my heart, Go to now, I will prove thee with mirth; therefore enjoy pleasure: and behold, this also is vanity.

I said of laughter, It is mad: and of mirth, What doeth it?

I sought in my heart to give myself unto wine, yet acquainting my heart with wisdom; and to lay hold on folly, till I might see what was that good for the sons of men, which they should do under the heaven all the days of their life.

I made me great works; I builded me houses; I planted me vineyards:

I made me gardens and orchards, and I planted trees in them of all kind of fruits:

I made me pools of water, to water therewith the wood that bringeth forth trees:

I got me servants and maidens, and had servants born in my house; also I had great possessions of great and small cattle above all that were in Jerusalem before me;

I gathered me also silver and gold, and the peculiar treasure of kings, and of the provinces: I gat me men-singers and women-singers, and the delights of the sons of men, as musical instruments, and that of all sorts.

So I was great, and increased more than all that were before me in Jerusalem: also my wisdom remained with me.

And whatsoever mine eyes desired I kept not from them, I withheld not my heart from any joy; for my heart rejoiced in all my labour: and this was my portion of all my labour.

Then I looked on all the works that my hands had wrought, and on the labour that I had laboured to do: and behold, all was vanity and vexation of spirit, and there was no profit under the sun.

And I turned myself to behold wisdom, and madness, and folly: for what can the man do that cometh after the king? even that which hath been already done.

Then I saw that wisdom excelleth folly, as far as light excelleth darkness.

The wise man's eyes are in his head; but the fool walketh in darkness: and I myself perceived also that one event happeneth to them all.

Then said I in my heart, As it happeneth to the fool, so it happeneth even to me; and why was I then more wise? Then I said in my heart, that this also is vanity.

For there is no remembrance of the wise more than of the fool for ever; seeing that which now is in the days to come shall all be forgotten. And how dieth the wise man? as the fool.

Therefore I hated life; because the work that is wrought under the sun is grievous unto me: for all is vanity and vexation of spirit.

Yea, I hated all my labour which I had taken under the sun: because I should leave it unto the man that shall be after me.

And who knoweth whether he shall be a wise man or a fool? yet shall he have rule over all my labour wherein I have laboured, and wherein I have shewed myself wise under the sun. This is also vanity.

Therefore I went about to cause my heart to despair of all the labour which I took under the sun.

For there is a man whose labour is in wisdom, and in knowledge, and in equity; yet to a man that hath not laboured therein shall he leave it for his portion. This also is vanity and a great evil.

For what hath man of all his labour, and of the vexation of his heart, wherein he hath laboured under the sun?

For all his days are sorrows, and his travail grief; yea, his heart taketh not rest in the night. This is also vanity.

There is nothing better for a man than that he should eat and drink, and that he should make his soul enjoy good in his labour. This also I saw, that it was from the hand of God.

For who can eat, or who else can hasten hereunto more than I?

For God giveth to a man that is good in his sight, wisdom, and knowledge, and joy: but to the sinner he giveth travail, to gather and to heap up, that he may give to him that is good before God. This also is vanity and vexation of spirit.

❧

To every thing there is a season, and a time to every purpose under the heaven:

A time to be born, and a time to die; a time to plant, and a time to pluck up that which is planted;

A time to kill, and a time to heal; a time to break down, and a time to build up;

A time to weep, and a time to laugh; a time to mourn, and a time to dance;

A time to cast away stones, and a time to gather stones together; a time to embrace, and a time to refrain from embracing;

A time to get, and a time to lose; a time to keep, and a time to cast away;

A time to rend, and a time to sew; a time to keep silence, and a time to speak;

A time to love, and a time to hate; a time of war, and a time of peace.

What profit hath he that worketh in that wherein he laboureth?

I have seen the travail, which God hath given to the sons of men to be exercised in it.

He hath made every thing beautiful in his time: also he hath set the world in their heart, so that no man can find out the work that God maketh from the beginning to the end.

I know that there is no good in them, but for a man to rejoice, and to do good in his life.

And also that every man should eat and drink, and enjoy the good of all his labour; it is the gift of God.

I know that, whatsoever God doeth, it shall be for ever: nothing can be put to it, nor any thing taken from it: and God doeth it, that men should fear before him.

That which hath been is now; and that which is to be hath already been; and God requireth that which is past.

And moreover I saw under the sun the place of judgment, that wickedness was there; and the place of righteousness, that iniquity was there.

I said in my heart, God shall judge the righteous and the wicked: for there is a time there for every purpose and for every work.

I said in my heart concerning the estate of the sons of men, that God might manifest them, and that they might see that they themselves are beasts.

For that which befalleth the sons of men befalleth beasts; even one thing befalleth them: as the one dieth, so dieth the other; yea, they have all one breath; so that a man hath no pre-eminence above a beast: for all is vanity.

All go unto one place; all are of the dust, and all turn to dust again.

Who knoweth the spirit of man that goeth upward, and the spirit of the beast that goeth downward to the earth?

Wherefore I perceive that there is nothing better, than that a man should rejoice in his own works; for that is his portion: for who shall bring him to see what shall be after him?

❧

So I returned and considered all the oppressions that are done under the sun: and behold the tears of such as were oppressed, and they had no comforter; and on the side of their oppressors there was power; but they had no comforter.

Wherefore I praised the dead which are already dead more than the living which are yet alive.

Yea, better is he than both they, which hath not yet been, who hath not seen the evil work that is done under the sun.

Again, I considered all travail, and every right work, that for this a man is envied of his neighbour. This is also vanity and vexation of spirit.

The fool foldeth his hands together, and eateth his own flesh.

Better is a handful with quietness, than both the hands full with travail and vexation of spirit.

Then I returned, and I saw vanity under the sun.

There is one alone, and there is not a second; yea, he hath neither child nor brother: yet is there no end of all his labour; neither is his eye satisfied with riches: neither saith he, For whom do I labour, and bereave my soul of good? This is also vanity, yea, it is a sore travail.

Two are better than one; because they have a good reward for their labour.

For if they fall, the one will lift up his fellow: but wo to him that is alone when he falleth: for he hath not another to help him up.

Again, if two lie together, then they have heat: but how can one be warm alone?

And if one prevail against him, two shall withstand him; and a threefold cord is not quickly broken.

Better is a poor and a wise child, than an old and foolish king, who will no more be admonished.

For out of prison he cometh to reign; whereas also he that is born in his kingdom becometh poor.

I considered all the living which walk under the sun, with the second child that shall stand up in his stead.

There is no end of all the people, even of all that have been before them: they also that come after shall not rejoice in him. Surely this also is vanity and vexation of spirit.

❧

Keep thy foot when thou goest to the house of God, and be more ready to hear, than to give the sacrifice of fools: for they consider not that they do evil.

Be not rash with thy mouth, and let not thy heart be hasty to utter any thing before God: for God is in heaven, and thou upon earth: therefore let thy words be few.

For a dream cometh through the multitude of business; and a fool's voice is known by multitude of words.

When thou vowest a vow unto God, defer not to pay it; for he hath no pleasure in fools: pay that which thou hast vowed.

Better is it that thou shouldest not vow, than that thou shouldest vow and not pay.

Suffer not thy mouth to cause thy flesh to sin; neither say thou before the angel, that it was an error: wherefore should God be angry at thy voice, and destroy the work of thy hands?

For in the multitude of dreams and many words there are also divers vanities: but fear thou God.

If thou seest the oppression of the poor, and violent perverting of judgment and justice in a province, marvel not at the matter: for he that is higher than the highest regardeth; and there be higher than they.

Moreover, the profit of the earth is for all: the king himself is served by the field.

He that loveth silver shall not be satisfied with silver; nor he that loveth abundance with increase: this is also vanity.

When goods increase, they are increased that eat them: and what good is there to the owners thereof, saving the beholding of them with their eyes?

The sleep of a labouring man is sweet, whether he eat little or much: but the abundance of the rich will not suffer him to sleep.

There is a sore evil which I have seen under the sun, namely, riches kept for the owners thereof to their hurt.

But those riches perish by evil travail: and he begetteth a son, and there is nothing in his hand.

As he came forth of his mother's womb, naked shall he return to go as he came, and shall take nothing of his labour, which he may carry away in his hand.

And this also is a sore evil, that in all points as he came, so shall he go: and what profit hath he that hath laboured for the wind?

All his days also he eateth in darkness, and he hath much sorrow and wrath with his sickness.

Behold that which I have seen: it is good and comely for one to eat and to drink, and to enjoy the good of all his labour that he taketh under the sun all the days of his life, which God giveth him: for it is his portion.

Every man also to whom God hath given riches and wealth, and hath given him power to eat thereof, and to take his portion, and to rejoice in his labour; this is the gift of God.

For he shall not much remember the days of his life; because God answereth him in the joy of his heart.

There is an evil which I have seen under the sun, and it is common among men:

A man to whom God hath given riches, wealth, and honour, so that he wanteth nothing for his soul of all that he desireth, yet God giveth him not power to eat thereof, but a stranger eateth it: this is vanity, and it is an evil disease.

If a man beget a hundred children, and live many years, so that the days of his years be many, and his soul be not filled with good, and also that he have no burial; I say, that an untimely birth is better than he.

For he cometh in with vanity, and departeth in darkness, and his name shall be covered with darkness.

Moreover he hath not seen the sun, nor known any thing: this hath more rest than the other.

Yea, though he live a thousand years twice told, yet hath he seen no good: do not all go to one place?

All the labour of man is for his mouth, and yet the appetite is not filled.

For what hath the wise more than the fool? what hath the poor, that knoweth to walk before the living?

Better is the sight of the eyes than the wandering of the desire: this is also vanity and vexation of spirit.

That which hath been is named already, and it is known that it is man: neither may he contend with him that is mightier than he.

Seeing there be many things that increase vanity, what is man the better?

For who knoweth what is good for man in this life, all the days of his vain life which he spendeth as a shadow? for who can tell a man what shall be after him under the sun?

❧

A good name is better than precious ointment; and the day of death than the day of one's birth.

It is better to go to the house of mourning, than to go to

the house of feasting: for that is the end of all men; and the living will lay it to his heart.

Sorrow is better than laughter: for by the sadness of the countenance the heart is made better.

The heart of the wise is in the house of mourning; but the heart of fools is in the house of mirth.

It is better to hear the rebuke of the wise, than for a man to hear the song of fools:

For as the crackling of thorns under a pot, so is the laughter of the fool: this also is vanity.

Surely oppression maketh a wise man mad; and a gift destroyeth the heart.

Better is the end of a thing than the beginning thereof: and the patient in spirit is better than the proud in spirit.

Be not hasty in thy spirit to be angry: for anger resteth in the bosom of fools.

Say not thou, What is the cause that the former days were better than these? for thou dost not inquire wisely concerning this.

Wisdom is good with an inheritance: and by it there is profit to them that see the sun.

For wisdom is a defence, and money is a defence: but the excellency of knowledge is, that wisdom giveth life to them that have it.

Consider the work of God: for who can make that straight, which he hath made crooked?

In the day of prosperity be joyful, but in the day of adversity consider: God also hath set the one over against the other, to the end that man should find nothing after him.

All things have I seen in the days of my vanity: there is a just man that perisheth in his righteousness, and there is a wicked man that prolongeth his life in his wickedness.

Be not righteous over much; neither make thyself over wise: why shouldest thou destroy thyself?

Be not over much wicked, neither be thou foolish: why

shouldest thou die before thy time?

It is good that thou shouldest take hold of this; yea, also from this withdraw not thy hand: for he that feareth God shall come forth of them all.

Wisdom strengtheneth the wise more than ten mighty men which are in the city.

For there is not a just man upon the earth, that doeth good, and sinneth not.

Also take no heed unto all words that are spoken lest thou hear thy servant curse thee:

For oftentimes also thine own heart knoweth that thou thyself likewise hast cursed others.

All this have I proved by wisdom: I said, I will be wise; but it was far from me.

That which is far off, and exceeding deep who can find it out?

I applied my heart to know, and to search, and to seek out wisdom, and the reason of things, and to know the wickedness of folly, even of foolishness and madness:

And I find more bitter than death the woman whose heart is snares and nets, and her hands as bands: whoso pleaseth God shall escape from her; but the sinner shall be taken by her.

Behold, this have I found, saith the Preacher, counting one by one, to find out the account;

Which yet my soul seeketh, but I find not: one man among a thousand have I found; but a woman among all those have I not found.

Lo, this only have I found, that God hath made man upright; but they have sought out many inventions.

❧

Who is as the wise man? and who knoweth the interpretation of a thing? a man's wisdom maketh his face to shine, and the boldness of his face shall be changed.

I counsel thee to keep the king's commandment, and that in regard of the oath of God.

Be not hasty to go out of his sight: stand not in an evil thing; for he doeth whatsoever pleaseth him.

Where the word of a king is, there is power: and who may say unto him, What doest thou?

Whoso keepeth the commandment shall feel no evil thing: and a wise man's heart discerneth both time and judgment.

Because to every purpose there is time and judgment, therefore the misery of man is great upon him.

For he knoweth not that which shall be: for who can tell him when it shall be?

There is no man that hath power over the spirit to retain the spirit: neither hath he power in the day of death: and there is no discharge in that war; neither shall wickedness deliver those that are given to it.

All this have I seen, and applied my heart unto every work that is done under the sun: there is a time wherein one man ruleth over another to his own hurt.

And so I saw the wicked buried, who had come and gone from the place of the holy, and they were forgotten in the city where they had so done: this is also vanity.

Because sentence against an evil work is not executed speedily, therefore the heart of the sons of men is fully set in them to do evil.

Though a sinner do evil a hundred times, and his days be prolonged, yet surely I know that it shall be well with them that fear God, which fear before him:

But it shall not be well with the wicked, neither shall he prolong his days, which are as a shadow; because he feareth not before God.

There is a vanity which is done upon the earth; that there be just men, unto whom it happeneth according to the work of the wicked: again, there be wicked men to whom it happeneth according to the work of the righteous: I said that this also is vanity.

Then I commended mirth, because a man hath no better thing under the sun, than to eat, and to drink, and to be merry: for that shall abide with him of his labour the days of his life, which God giveth him under the sun.

When I applied my heart to know wisdom, and to see the business that is done upon the earth: (for also there is that neither day nor night seeth sleep with his eyes:)

Then I beheld all the work of God, that a man cannot find out the work that is done under the sun: because though a man labour to seek it out, yet he shall not find it; yea further; though a wise man think to know it, yet shall he not be able to find it.

❧

For all this I considered in my heart even to declare all this, that the righteous, and the wise, and their works, are in the hand of God: no man knoweth either love or hatred by all that is before them.

All things come alike to all: there is one event to the righteous and to the wicked; to the good, and to the clean, and to the unclean; to him that sacrificeth, and to him that sacrificeth not: as is the good, so is the sinner; and he that sweareth, as he that feareth an oath.

This is an evil among all things that are done under the sun, that there is one event unto all: yea, also the heart of the sons of men is full of evil, and madness is in their heart while they live, and after that they go to the dead.

For to him that is joined to all the living there is hope: for a living dog is better than a dead lion.

For the living know that they shall die: but the dead know not any thing, neither have they any more a reward; for the memory of them is forgotten.

Also their love, and their hatred, and their envy, is now perished; neither have they any more a portion for ever in any thing that is done under the sun.

Go thy way, eat thy bread with joy, and drink thy wine with a merry heart; for God now accepteth thy works.

Let thy garments be always white; and let thy head lack no ointment.

Live joyfully with the wife whom thou lovest all the days of the life of thy vanity, which he hath given thee under the sun, all the days of thy vanity: for that is thy portion in this life, and in thy labour which thou takest under the sun.

Whatsoever thy hand findeth to do, do it with thy might; for there is no work, nor device, nor knowledge, nor wisdom, in the grave, whither thou goest.

I returned, and saw under the sun, that the race is not to the swift, nor the battle to the strong, neither yet bread to the wise, nor yet riches to men of understanding, nor yet favour to men of skill; but time and chance happeneth to them all.

For man also knoweth not his time: as the fishes that are taken in an evil net, and as the birds that are caught in the snare; so are the sons of men snared in an evil time, when it falleth suddenly upon them.

This wisdom have I seen also under the sun, and it seemed great unto me:

There was a little city, and a few men within it; and there came a great king against it, and besieged it, and built great bulwarks against it:

Now there was found in it a poor wise man, and he by his wisdom delivered the city; yet no man remembered that same poor man.

Then said I, Wisdom is better than strength: nevertheless the poor man's wisdom is despised, and his words are not heard.

The words of wise men are heard in quiet more than the cry of him that ruleth among fools.

Wisdom is better than weapons of war: but one sinner destroyeth much good.

❧§☙

Dead flies cause the ointment of the apothecary to send forth a stinking savour: so doth a little folly him that is in reputation for wisdom and honour.

A wise man's heart is at his right hand; but a fool's heart is at his left.

Yea also, when he that is a fool walketh by the way, his wisdom faileth him, and he saith to every one that he is a fool.

If the spirit of the ruler rise up against thee, leave not thy place; for yielding pacifieth great offences.

There is an evil which I have seen under the sun, as an error which proceedeth from the ruler:

Folly is set in great dignity, and the rich sit in low place.

I have seen servants upon horses, and princes walking as servants upon the earth.

He that diggeth a pit shall fall into it; and whoso breaketh a hedge, a serpent shall bite him.

Whoso removeth stones shall be hurt therewith: and he that cleaveth wood shall be endangered thereby.

If the iron be blunt, and he do not whet the edge, then must he put to more strength: but wisdom is profitable to direct.

Surely the serpent will bite without enchantment; and a babbler is no better.

The words of a wise man's mouth are gracious; but the lips of a fool will swallow up himself.

The beginning of the words of his mouth is foolishness: and the end of his talk is mischievous madness.

A fool also is full of words, a man cannot tell what shall be; and what shall be after him, who can tell him?

The labour of the foolish wearieth every one of them,

because he knoweth not how to go to the city.

Wo to thee, O land, when thy king is a child, and thy princes eat in the morning!

Blessed art thou, O land, when thy king is the son of nobles, and thy princes eat in due season, for strength, and not for drunkenness!

By much slothfulness the building decayeth; and through idleness of the hands the house droppeth through.

A feast is made for laughter, and wine maketh merry: but money answereth all things.

Curse not the king, no, not in thy thought; and curse not the rich in thy bed-chamber: for a bird of the air shall carry the voice, and that which hath wings shall tell the matter.

Cast thy bread upon the waters: for thou shalt find it after many days.

Give a portion to seven, and also to eight; for thou knowest not what evil shall be upon the earth.

If the clouds be full of rain, they empty themselves upon the earth: and if the tree fall toward the south, or toward the north, in the place where the tree falleth, there it shall be.

He that observeth the wind shall not sow; and he that regardeth the clouds shall not reap.

As thou knowest not what is the way of the spirit, nor how the bones do grow in the womb of her that is with child: even so thou knowest not the works of God who maketh all.

In the morning sow thy seed, and in the evening withhold not thy hand: for thou knowest not whether shall prosper, either this or that, or whether they both shall be alike good.

Truly the light is sweet, and a pleasant thing it is for the eyes to behold the sun:

But if a man live many years, and rejoice in them all; yet let him remember the days of darkness; for they shall be many. All that cometh is vanity.

Rejoice, O young man, in thy youth; and let thy heart cheer thee in the days of thy youth, and walk in the ways of thy heart, and in the sight of thine eyes: but know thou, that for all these things God will bring thee into judgment.

Therefore remove sorrow from thy heart, and put away evil from thy flesh: for childhood and youth are vanity.

❧

Remember now thy Creator in the days of thy youth, while the evil days come not, nor the years draw nigh, when thou shalt say, I have no pleasure in them;

While the sun, or the light, or the moon, or the stars, be not darkened, nor the clouds return after the rain:

In the day when the keepers of the house shall tremble, and the strong men shall bow themselves, and the grinders cease because they are few, and those that look out of the windows darkened,

And the doors shall be shut in the streets, when the sound of the grinding is low, and he shall rise up at the voice of the bird, and all the daughters of music shall be brought low;

Also when they shall be afraid of that which is high, and fears shall be in the way, and the almond-tree shall flourish, and the grasshopper shall be a burden, and desire shall fail: because man goeth to his long home, and the mourners go about the streets:

Or ever the silver cord be loosed, or the golden bowl be broken, or the pitcher be broken at the fountain, or the wheel broken at the cistern.

Then shall the dust return to the earth as it was: and the spirit shall return unto God who gave it.

Vanity of vanities, saith the Preacher; all is vanity.

And moreover, because the Preacher was wise, he still taught the people knowledge: yea, he gave good heed, and sought out, and set in order many proverbs.

The Preacher sought to find out acceptable words: and that which was written, was upright, even words of truth.

The words of the wise are as goads, and as nails fastened by the masters of assemblies, which are given from one shepherd.

And further, by these, my son, be admonished: of making many books there is no end; and much study is a weariness of the flesh.

Let us hear the conclusion of the whole matter: Fear God, and keep his commandments: for this is the whole duty of man.

For God shall bring every work into judgment with every secret thing, whether it be good, or whether it be evil.

The Vision of Isaiah

THE VISION OF ISAIAH the son of Amoz, which he saw concerning Judah and Jerusalem in the days of Uzziah, Jotham, Ahaz, and Hezekiah, kings of Judah.

Hear, O heavens, and give ear, O earth: for the Lord hath spoken, I have nourished and brought up children, and they have rebelled against me.

The ox knoweth his owner, and the ass his master's crib: but Israel doth not know, my people doth not consider.

Ah sinful nation, a people laden with iniquity, a seed of evil-doers, children that are corrupters! they have forsaken the Lord, they have provoked the Holy One of Israel unto anger, they are gone away backward.

Why should ye be stricken any more? ye will revolt more and more: the whole head is sick, and the whole heart faint.

From the sole of the foot even unto the head there is no soundness in it; but wounds, and bruises, and putrefying sores: they have not been closed, neither bound up, neither mollified with ointment.

Your country is desolate, your cities are burnt with fire: your land, strangers devour it in your presence, and it is desolate, as overthrown by strangers.

And the daughter of Zion is left as a cottage in a vineyard, as a lodge in a garden of cucumbers, as a besieged city.

Except the Lord of hosts had left unto us a very small remnant, we should have been as Sodom, and we should have been like unto Gomorrah.

Hear the word of the Lord, ye rulers of Sodom: give ear unto the law of our God, ye people of Gomorrah.

To what purpose is the multitude of your sacrifices unto me? saith the Lord: I am full of the burnt-offerings of rams, and the fat of fed beasts; and I delight not in the blood of bullocks, or of lambs, or of he-goats.

When ye come to appear before me, who hath required this at your hand, to tread my courts?

Bring no more vain oblations: incense is an abomination unto me; the new-moons and sabbaths, the calling of assemblies, I cannot away with; it is iniquity, even the solemn meeting.

Your new-moons and your appointed feasts my soul hateth: they are a trouble unto me; I am weary to bear them.

And when ye spread forth your hands, I will hide mine eyes from you; yea, when ye make many prayers, I will not hear: your hands are full of blood.

Wash you, make you clean: put away the evil of your doings from before mine eyes; cease to evil;

Learn to do well; seek judgment, relieve the oppressed, judge the fatherless, plead for the widow.

Come now, and let us reason together, saith the Lord: though your sins be as scarlet, they shall be as white as snow; though they be red like crimson, they shall be as wool.

If ye be willing and obedient, ye shall eat the good of the land:

But if ye refuse and rebel, ye shall be devoured with the sword: for the mouth of the Lord hath spoken it.

Isaiah, i

(Isaiah foretells the captivity)

THE VOICE OF HIM that crieth in the wilderness, prepare ye the way of the Lord, make straight in the desert a highway for our God.

Every valley shall be exalted, and every mountain and hill shall be made low: and the crooked shall be made straight, and the rough places plain:

And the glory of the Lord shall be revealed, and all flesh shall see it together: for the mouth of the Lord hath spoken it.

The voice said, cry. And he said, what shall I cry? All flesh is grass, and all the goodliness thereof is as the flower of the field.

The grass withereth, the flower fadeth: because the spirit of the Lord bloweth upon it: surely the people is grass.

The grass withereth, the flower fadeth: but the word of our God shall stand for ever.

O Zion, that bringest good tidings, get thee up into the high mountain; O Jerusalem, that bringest good tidings, lift up thy voice with strength; lift it up, be not afraid; say unto the cities of Judah, behold your God!

Behold, the Lord God will come with strong hand, and his arm shall rule for him: behold, his reward is with him, and his work before him.

He shall feed his flock like a shepherd: he shall gather the lambs with his arm, and carry them in his bosom, and shall gently lead those that are with young.

Who hath measured the waters in the hollow of his hand, meted out heaven with the span, and comprehended the dust of the earth in a measure, and weighed the mountains in scales, and the hills in a balance?

Who hath directed the spirit of the Lord, or being his counsellor hath taught him?

With whom took he counsel, and who instructed him, and taught him in the path of judgment, and taught him knowledge, and shewed to him the way of understanding?

Behold, the nations are as a drop of a bucket, and are counted as the small dust of the balance: behold, he taketh up the isles as a very little thing.

And Lebanon is not sufficient to burn, nor the beasts thereof sufficient for a burnt offering.

All nations before him are as nothing; and they are counted to him less than nothing, and vanity.

To whom then will ye liken God? or what likeness will ye compare unto him?

The workman melteth a graven image, and the goldsmith spreadeth it over with gold, and casteth silver chains.

He that is so impoverished that he hath no oblation chooseth a tree that will not rot; he seeketh unto him a cunning workman to prepare a graven image, that shall not be moved.

Have ye not known? Have ye not heard? Hath it not been told you from the beginning? Have ye not understood from the foundations of the earth?

It is he that sitteth upon the circle of the earth, and the inhabitants thereof are as grasshoppers; that stretcheth out the heavens as a curtain, and spreadeth them out as a tent to dwell in:

That bringeth the princes to nothing; he maketh the judges of the earth as vanity.

Yea, they shall not be planted; yea, they shall not be sown: yea, their stock shall not take root in the earth: and he shall also blow upon them, and they shall wither, and the whirlwind shall take them away as stubble.

To whom then will ye liken me, or shall I be equal? saith the Holy One.

Lift up your eyes on high, and behold who hath created these things, that bringeth out their host by number: he calleth them all by names by the greatness of his might, for that he is strong in power; not one faileth.

Why sayest thou, O Jacob, and speakest, O Israel, my way is hid from the Lord, and my judgment is passed over from my God?

Hast thou not known? Hast thou not heard, that the everlasting God, the Lord, the creator of the ends of the earth, fainteth not, neither is weary? There is no searching of his understanding.

He giveth power to the faint; and to them that have no might he increaseth strength.

Even the youths shall faint and be weary, and the young men shall utterly fall:

But they that wait upon the Lord shall renew their strength; they shall mount up with wings as eagles; they shall run, and not be weary; and they shall walk, and not faint.

Isaiah, xl

The Lament of Jeremiah

HOW doth the city sit solitary, that was full of people! how is she become as a widow! she that was great among the nations, and princess among the provinces, how is she become tributary!

She weepeth sore in the night, and her tears are on her cheeks: among all her lovers she hath none to comfort her: all her friends have dealt treacherously with her, they are become her enemies.

Judah is gone into captivity because of affliction, and because of great servitude: she dwelleth among the heathen, she findeth no rest: all her persecutors overtook her between the straits.

The ways of Zion do mourn, because none come to the solemn feasts: all her gates are desolate: her priests sigh, her virgins are afflicted, and she is in bitterness.

Her adversaries are the chief, her enemies prosper; for the Lord hath afflicted her for the multitude of her transgressions: her children are gone into captivity before the enemy.

And from the daughter of Zion all her beauty is departed: her princes are become like harts that find no pasture, and they are gone without strength before the pursuer.

Jerusalem remembered in the days of her affliction and of her miseries all her pleasant things that she had in the days of old, when her people fell into the hand of the enemy, and none did help her: the adversaries saw her, and did mock at her sabbaths.

Jerusalem hath grievously sinned; therefore she is removed: all that honored her despise her, because they have seen her nakedness: yea, she sigheth, and turneth backward.

Her filthiness is in her skirts; she remembereth not her last end; therefore she came down wonderfully: she had no comforter. O Lord, behold my affliction: for the enemy hath magnified himself.

The adversary hath spread out his hand upon all her pleasant things: for she hath seen that the heathen entered into her sanctuary, whom thou didst command that they should not enter into thy congregation.

All her people sigh, they seek bread; they have given their pleasant things for meat to relieve the soul: see, O Lord, and consider; for I am become vile.

Is it nothing to you, all ye that pass by? behold, and see if there be any sorrow like unto my sorrow, which is done unto me, wherewith the Lord hath afflicted me in the day of his fierce anger.

From above hath he sent fire into my bones, and it prevaileth against them: he hath spread a net for my feet, he hath turned me back: he hath made me desolate and faint all the day.

The yoke of my transgressions is bound by his hand: they are wreathed, and come up upon my neck: he hath made my strength to fall, the Lord hath delivered me into their hands, from whom I am not able to rise up.

The Lord hath trodden under foot all my mighty men in the midst of me: he hath called an assembly against me to crush my young men: the Lord hath trodden the virgin, the daughter of Judah, as in a wine-press.

For these things I weep; mine eye, mine eye runneth down with water, because the comforter that should relieve my soul is far from me: my children are desolate, because the enemy prevailed.

Zion spreadeth forth her hands, and there is none to comfort her: the Lord hath commanded concerning Jacob, that his adversaries should be round about him: Jerusalem is as a menstruous woman among them.

The Lord is righteous; for I have rebelled against his commandment: hear, I pray you, all people, and behold my sorrow: my virgins and my young men are gone into captivity.

I called for my lovers, but they deceived me: my priests and mine elders gave up the ghost in the city, while they sought their meat to relieve their souls.

Behold, O Lord; for I am in distress: my bowels are troubled; my heart is turned within me; for I have grievously rebelled: abroad the sword bereaveth, at home there is as death.

They have heard that I sigh: there is none to comfort me: all mine enemies have heard of my trouble; they are glad that thou hast done it: thou wilt bring the day that thou hast called, and they shall be like unto me.

Let all their wickedness come before thee, and do unto them, as thou hast done unto me for all my transgressions: for my sighs are many, and my heart is faint.

❧

How hath the Lord covered the daughter of Zion with a cloud in his anger, and cast down from heaven unto the earth the beauty of Israel, and remembered not his footstool in the day of his anger!

The Lord hath swallowed up all the habitations of Jacob, and hath not pitied: he hath thrown down in his wrath the strong holds of the daughter of Judah; he hath brought them down to the ground: he hath polluted the kingdom and the princes thereof.

He hath cut off in his fierce anger all the horn of Israel: he hath drawn back his right hand from before the enemy, and he burned against Jacob like a flaming fire, which devoureth round about.

He hath bent his bow like an enemy: he stood with his right hand as an adversary and slew all that were pleasant to the eye in the tabernacle of the daughter of Zion: he poured out his fury like fire.

The Lord was as an enemy: he hath swallowed up Israel, he hath swallowed up all her palaces: he hath destroyed his strong holds, and hath increased in the daughter of Judah mourning and lamentation.

And he hath violently taken away his tabernacle, as if it were of a garden: he hath destroyed his places of the assembly: the Lord hath caused the solemn feasts and sabbaths to be forgotten in Zion, and hath despised in the indignation of his anger the king and the priest.

The Lord hath cast off his altar, he hath abhorred his sanctuary, he hath given up into the hand of the enemy the walls of her palaces; they have made a noise in the house of the Lord, as in the day of a solemn feast.

The Lord hath purposed to destroy the wall of the daughter of Zion: he hath stretched out a line, he hath not withdrawn his hand from destroying: therefore he made the rampart and the wall to lament; they languished together.

Her gates are sunk into the ground; he hath destroyed and broken her bars; her king and her princes are among the Gentiles: the law is no more: her prophets also find no vision from the Lord.

The elders of the daughter of Zion sit upon the ground, and keep silence; they have cast up dust upon their heads: they have girded themselves with sack-cloth: the virgins of Jerusalem hang down their heads to the ground.

Mine eyes do fail with tears, my bowels are troubled, my liver is poured upon the earth, for the destruction of the daughter of my people; because the children and the sucklings swoon in the streets of the city.

They say to their mothers, Where is corn and wine? when they swooned as the wounded in the streets of the city, when their soul was poured out into their mothers' bosom.

What thing shall I take to witness for thee? what thing

shall I liken to thee, O daughter of Jerusalem? What shall I equal to thee, that I may comfort thee, O virgin daughter of Zion? for thy breach is great like the sea: who can heal thee?

Thy prophets have seen vain and foolish things for thee: and they have not discovered thine iniquity, to turn away thy captivity; but have seen for the false burdens and causes of banishment.

All that pass by, clap their hands at thee; they hiss and wag their head at the daughter of Jerusalem, saying, Is this the city that men call the Perfection of beauty, the Joy of the whole earth?

All thine enemies have opened their mouth against thee: they hiss and gnash the teeth: they say, We have swallowed her up: certainly this is the day that we looked for; we have found, we have seen it.

The Lord hath done that which he had devised; he hath fulfilled his word that he had commanded in the days of old: he hath thrown down, and hath not pitied: and he hath caused thine enemy to rejoice over thee, he hath set up the horn of thine adversaries.

Their heart cried unto the Lord, O wall of the daughter of Zion, Let tears run down like a river day and night: give thyself no rest; let not the apple of thine eye cease.

Arise, cry out in the night: in the beginning of the watches pour out thy heart like water before the face of the Lord: lift up thy hands toward him for the life of thy young children, that faint for hunger in the top of every street.

Behold, O Lord, and consider to whom thou hast done this. Shall the women eat their fruit, and children of a span long? shall the priest and the prophet be slain in the sanctuary of the Lord?

The young and the old lie on the ground in the streets; my virgins and my young men are fallen by the sword; thou hast slain them in the day of thine anger; thou hast killed, and not pitied.

Thou hast called as in a solemn day my terrors round about, so that in the day of the Lord's anger none escaped or remained: those that I have swaddled and brought up, hath mine enemy consumed.

❧

I am the man that hath seen affliction by the rod of his wrath.

He hath led me, and brought me into darkness, but not into light.

Surely against me is he turned; he turneth his hand against me all the day.

My flesh and my skin hath he made old; he hath broken my bones.

He hath builded against me, and compassed me with gall and travail.

He hath set me in dark places, as they that be dead of old.

He hath hedged me about, that I cannot get out: he hath made my chain heavy.

Also when I cry and shout, he shutteth out my prayer.

He hath enclosed my ways with hewn stone, he hath made my paths crooked.

He was unto me as a bear lying in wait, and as a lion in secret places.

He hath turned aside my ways, and pulled me in pieces: he hath made me desolate.

He hath bent his bow, and set me as a mark for the arrow.

He hath caused the arrows of his quiver to enter into my reins.

I was a derision to all my people; and their song all the day.

He hath filled me with bitterness, he hath made me drunken with wormwood.

He hath also broken my teeth with gravel-stones, he hath covered me with ashes.

And thou hast removed my soul far off from peace, I forgat prosperity.

And I said, My strength and my hope is perished from the Lord:

Remembering mine affliction and my misery, the wormwood and the gall.

My soul hath them still in remembrance, and is humbled in me.

This I recall to my mind, therefore have I hope.

It is of the Lord's mercies that we are not consumed, because his compassions fail not.

They are new every morning: great is thy faithfulness.

The Lord is my portion, saith my soul; therefore will I hope in him.

The Lord is good unto them that wait for him, to the soul that seeketh him.

It is good that a man should both hope and quietly wait for the salvation of the Lord.

It is good for a man that he bear the yoke in his youth.

He sitteth alone, and keepeth silence, because he hath borne it upon him.

He putteth his mouth in the dust; if so be there may be hope.

He giveth his cheek to him that smiteth him: he is filled full with reproach.

For the Lord will not cast off for ever:

But though he cause grief, yet will he have compassion according to the multitude of his mercies.

For he doth not afflict willingly, nor grieve the children of men.

To crush under his feet all the prisoners of the earth,

To turn aside the right of a man before the face of the Most High,

To subvert a man in his cause, the Lord approveth not.

Who is he that saith, and it cometh to pass, when the Lord commandeth it not?

Out of the mouth of the Most High proceedeth not evil and good?

Wherefore doth a living man complain, a man for the punishment of his sins?

Let us search and try our ways, and turn again to the Lord.

Let us lift up our heart with our hands unto God in the heavens.

We have transgressed and have rebelled: thou hast not pardoned.

Thou hast covered with anger, and persecuted us: thou hast slain, thou hast not pitied.

Thou hast covered thyself with a cloud, that our prayer should not pass through.

Thou hast made us as the off-scouring and refuse in the midst of the people.

All our enemies have opened their mouths against us.

Fear and a snare is come upon us, desolation and destruction.

Mine eye runneth down with rivers of water for the destruction of the daughter of my people.

Mine eye trickleth down, and ceaseth not, without any intermission,

Till the Lord look down, and behold from heaven.

Mine eye affecteth my heart because of all the daughters of my city.

Mine enemies chased me sore, like a bird, without cause.

They have cut off my life in the dungeon, and cast a stone upon me.

Waters flowed over my head; then I said, I am cut off.

I called upon thy name, O Lord, out of the low dungeon.

Thou hast heard my voice: hide not thine ear at my breathing, at my cry.

Thou drewest near in the day that I called upon thee: thou saidst, Fear not.

O Lord, thou hast pleaded the causes of my soul: thou hast redeemed my life.

O Lord, thou hast seen my wrong: judge thou my cause.

Thou hast seen all their vengeance and all their imaginations against me.

Thou hast heard their reproach, O Lord, and all their imaginations against me;

The lips of those that rose up against me, and their device against me all the day.

Behold their sitting down, and their rising up; I am their music.

Render unto them a recompense, O Lord, according to the work of their hands.

Give them sorrow of heart, thy curse unto them.

Persecute and destroy them in anger from under the heavens of the Lord.

❧

How is the gold become dim! how is the most fine gold changed! the stones of the sanctuary are poured out in the top of every street.

The precious sons of Zion, comparable to fine gold, how are they esteemed as earthen pitchers, the work of the hands of the potter!

Even the sea-monsters draw out the breast, they give suck to their young ones: the daughter of my people is become cruel, like the ostriches in the wilderness.

The tongue of the sucking child cleaveth to the roof of his mouth for thirst: the young children ask bread, and no man breaketh it unto them.

They that did feed delicately are desolate in the streets: they that were brought up in scarlet embrace dunghills.

For the punishment of the iniquity of the daughter of my people is greater than the punishment of the sin of Sodom, that was overthrown as in a moment, and no hands stayed on her.

Her Nazarites were purer than snow, they were whiter than milk, they were more ruddy in body than rubies, their polishing was of sapphire:

Their visage is blacker than a coal; they are not known in the streets: their skin cleaveth to their bones; it is withered, it is become like a stick.

They that be slain with the sword are better than they that be slain with hunger: for these pine away, stricken through for want of the fruits of the field.

The hands of the pitiful women have sodden their own children: they were their meat in the destruction of the daughter of my people.

The Lord hath accomplished his fury; he hath poured out his fierce anger, and hath kindled a fire in Zion, and it hath devoured the foundations thereof.

The kings of the earth, and all the inhabitants of the world, would not have believed that the adversary and the enemy should have entered into the gates of Jerusalem.

For the sins of her prophets, and the iniquities of her priests, that have shed the blood of the just in the midst of her,

They have wandered as blind men in the streets, they have polluted themselves with blood, so that men could not touch their garments.

They cried unto them, Depart ye; it is unclean, depart, depart, touch not: when they fled away and wandered, they said among the heathen, They shall no more sojourn there.

The anger of the Lord hath divided them; he will no more regard them: they respected not the persons of the priests, they favoured not the elders.

As for us, our eyes as yet failed for our vain help: in our watching we have watched for a nation that could not save us.

They hunt our steps, that we cannot go in our streets: our end is near, our days are fulfilled; for our end is come.

Our persecutors are swifter than the eagles of the heaven: they pursued us upon the mountains, they laid wait for us in the wilderness.

The breath of our nostrils, the anointed of the Lord, was taken in their pits, of whom we said, Under his shadow we shall live among the heathen.

Rejoice and be glad, O daughter of Edom, that dwellest in the land of Uz; the cup also shall pass through unto thee: thou shalt be drunken, and shalt make thyself naked.

The punishment of thine iniquity is accomplished, O daughter of Zion; he will no more carry thee away into captivity: he will visit thine iniquity, O daughter of Edom; he will discover thy sins.

❧

Remember, O Lord, what is come upon us: consider and behold our reproach.

Our inheritance is turned to strangers, our houses to aliens.

We are orphans and fatherless, our mothers are as widows.

We have drunken our water for money; our wood is sold unto us.

Our necks are under persecution: we labour, and have no rest.

We have given the hand to the Egyptians, and to the Assyrians, to be satisfied with bread.

Our fathers have sinned, and are not; and we have borne their iniquities.

Servants have ruled over us: there is none that doth deliver us out of their hand.

We gat our bread with the peril of our lives because of the sword of the wilderness.

Our skin was black like an oven because of the terrible famine.

They ravished the women in Zion, and the maids in the cities of Judah.

Princes are hanged up by their hand: the faces of elders were not honoured.

They took the young men to grind, and the children fell under the wood.

The elders have ceased from the gate, the young men from their music.

The joy of our heart is ceased; our dance is turned into mourning.

The crown is fallen from our head: wo unto us, that we have sinned!

For this our heart is faint; for these things our eyes are dim.

Because of the mountain of Zion, which is desolate, the foxes walk upon it.

Thou, O Lord, remainest for ever; thy throne from generation to generation.

Wherefore dost thou forget us for ever, and forsake us so long time?

Turn thou us unto thee, O Lord, and we shall be turned; renew our days as of old.

But thou hast utterly rejected us; thou art very wroth against us.

Ethics of King Solomon

LOVE RIGHTEOUSNESS, ye that be judges of the earth: think of the Lord with a good (heart,) and in simplicity of heart seek him.

For he will be found of them that tempt him not; and sheweth himself unto such as do not distrust him.

For froward thoughts separate from God: and his power, when it is tried, reproveth the unwise.

For into a malicious soul wisdom shall not enter; nor dwell in the body that is subject unto sin.

For the holy spirit of discipline will flee deceit, and remove from thoughts that are without understanding, and will not abide when unrighteousness cometh in.

For wisdom is a loving spirit; and will not acquit a blasphemer of his words: for God is witness of his reins, and a true beholder of his heart, and a hearer of his tongue.

For the Spirit of the Lord filleth the world: and that which containeth all things, hath knowledge of the voice.

Therefore he that speaketh unrighteous things cannot be hid: neither shall vengeance, when it punisheth, pass by him.

For inquisition shall be made into the counsels of the ungodly: and the sound of his words shall come unto the Lord for the manifestation of his wicked deeds.

For the ear of jealousy heareth all things: and the noise of murmurings is not hid.

Therefore beware of murmuring, which is unprofitable; and refrain your tongue from backbiting: for there is no word so secret, that shall go for nought: and the mouth that belieth, slayeth the soul.

Seek not death in the error of your life: and pull not upon yourselves destruction with the works of your hands.

For God made not death: neither hath he pleasure in the destruction of the living.

For he created all things, that they might have their being: and the generations of the world were healthful; and there is no poison of destruction in them, nor the kingdom of death upon the earth:

(For righteousness is immortal:)

But ungodly men with their works and words called it to them: for when they thought to have it their friend, they consumed to nought, and made a covenant with it, because they are worthy to take part with it.

For the ungodly said, reasoning with themselves, but not aright, Our life is short and tedious, and in the death of a man there is no remedy: neither was there any man known to have returned from the grave.

For we are born at all adventure: and we shall be hereafter, as though we had never been: for the breath in our nostrils is as smoke, and a little spark in the moving of our heart:

Which being extinguished, our body shall be turned into ashes, and our spirit shall vanish as the soft air,

And our name shall be forgotten in time, and no man shall have our works in remembrance, and our life shall pass away as the trace of a cloud, and shall be dispersed as the mist that is driven away with the beams of the sun, and overcome with the heat thereof.

For our time is a very shadow that passeth away; and after our end there is no returning: for it is fast sealed, so that no man cometh again.

Come on therefore, let us enjoy the good things that are present: and let us speedily use the creatures like as in youth.

Let us fill ourselves with costly wine and ointments: and let no flower of the spring pass by us:

Let us crown ourselves with rose-buds, before they be withered.

Let none of us go without his part of our voluptuousness: let us leave tokens of our joyfulness in every place: for this is our portion, and our lot is this.

Let us oppress the poor righteous man, let us not spare the widow, nor reverence the ancient gray hairs of the aged.

Let our strength be the law of justice: for that which is feeble is found to be nothing worth.

Therefore, let us lie in wait for the righteous; because he is not for our turn, and he is clean contrary to our doings: he upbraideth us with our offending the law, and objecteth to our infamy the transgressions of our education.

He professeth to have the knowledge of God: and he calleth himself the child of the Lord.

He was made to reprove our thoughts.

He is grievous unto us even to behold: for his life is not like other men's, his ways are of another fashion.

We are esteemed of him as counterfeits, he abstaineth from our ways as from filthiness: he pronounceth the end of the just to be blessed, and maketh his boast that God is his father.

Let us see if his words be true: and let us prove what shall happen in the end of him.

For if the just man be the son of God, he will help him, and deliver him from the hand of his enemies.

Let us examine him with despitefulness and torture, that we may know his meekness, and prove his patience.

Let us condemn him with a shameful death: for by his own saying he shall be respected.

Such things they did imagine, and were deceived: for their own wickedness hath blinded them.

As for the mysteries of God, they knew them not: neither hoped they for the wages of righteousness, nor discerned a reward for blameless souls.

For God created man to be immortal, and made him to be an image of his own eternity.

Nevertheless, through envy of the devil came death into the world: and they that do hold of his side do find it.

Wisdom, ii

❧

But the souls of the righteous are in the hand of God, and there shall no torment touch them.

In the sight of the unwise they seemed to die: and their departure is taken for misery,

And their going from us to be utter destruction: but they are in peace.

For though they be punished in ths sight of men, yet is their hope full of immortality.

And having been a little chastised, they shall be greatly rewarded: for God proved them, and found them worthy for himself.

As gold in the furnace hath he tried them, and received them as a burnt-offering.

And in the time of their visitation, they shall shine, and run to and fro like sparks among the stubble.

They shall judge the nations, and have dominion over the people, and their Lord shall reign for ever.

They that put their trust in him shall understand the truth: and such as be faithful in love shall abide with him: for grace and mercy is to his saints, and he hath care for his elect.

But the ungodly shall be punished according to their own imaginations, which have neglected the righteous, and forsaken the Lord.

For whoso despiseth wisdom and nurture, he is miserable, and their hope is vain, their labours unfruitful, and their works unprofitable:

Their wives are foolish, and their children wicked:

Their offspring is cursed. Wherefore blessed is the barren

that is undefiled, which hath not known the sinful bed: she shall have fruit in the visitation of souls.

And blessed is the eunuch, which with his hands hath wrought no iniquity, nor imagined wicked things against God: for unto him shall be given the special gift of faith, and an inheritance in the temple of the Lord more acceptable to his mind.

For glorious is the fruit of good labours: and the root of wisdom shall never fall away.

As for the children of adulterers, they shall not come to their perfection, and the seed of an unrighteous bed shall be rooted out.

For though they live long, yet shall they be nothing regarded: and their last age shall be without honour:

Or, if they die quickly, they have no hope, neither comfort in the day of trial.

For horrible is the end of the unrighteous generation.

Wisdom, iii

❧

Better it is to have no children, and to have virtue: for the memorial thereof is immortal: because it is known with God, and with men.

When it is present, men take example at it; and when it is gone, they desire it: it weareth a crown, and triumpheth for ever, having gotten the victory, striving for undefiled rewards.

But the multiplying brood of the ungodly shall not thrive, nor take deep rooting from bastard slips, nor lay any fast foundation.

For though they flourish in branches for a time; yet standing not fast, they shall be shaken with the wind, and through the force of winds they shall be rooted out.

The imperfect branches shall be broken off, their fruit unprofitable, not ripe to eat, yea, meet for nothing.

For children begotten of unlawful beds, are witnesses of wickedness against their parents in their trial.

But though the righteous be prevented with death, yet shall he be at rest.

For honourable age is not that which standeth in length of time, nor that is measured by number of years.

But wisdom is the gray hair unto men, and an unspotted life is old age.

He pleased God, and was beloved of him: so that living among sinners he was translated.

Yea, speedily was he taken away, lest that wickedness should alter his understanding, or deceit beguile his soul.

For the bewitching of naughtiness doth obscure things that are honest; and the wandering of concupiscence doth undermine the simple mind.

He, being made perfect in a short time, fulfilled a long time:

For his soul pleased the Lord: therefore hasted he to take him away from among the wicked.

This the people saw, and understood it not, neither laid they up this in their minds, That his grace and mercy is with his saints, and that he hath respect unto his chosen.

Thus the righteous that is dead shall condemn the ungodly which are living; and youth that is soon perfected, the many years and old age of the unrighteous.

For they shall see the end of the wise, and shall not understand what God in his counsel hath decreed of him, and to what end the Lord hath set him in safety.

They shall see him, and despise him; but God shall laugh them to scorn: and they shall hereafter be a vile carcass, and a reproach among the dead for evermore.

For he shall rend them, and cast them down headlong, that they shall be speechless; and he shall shake them from the foundation; and they shall be utterly laid waste, and be in sorrow; and their memorial shall perish.

And when they cast up the accounts of their sins, they shall come with fear: and their own iniquities shall convince them to their face.

Wisdom, iv

❧§❧

Then shall the righteous man stand in great boldness before the face of such as have afflicted him, and make no account of his labours.

When they see it, they shall be troubled with terrible fear and shall be amazed at the strangeness of his salvation, so far beyond all that they looked for.

And they repenting and groaning for anguish of spirit shall say within themselves, This was he, whom we had sometimes in derision, and a proverb of reproach:

We fools accounted his life madness, and his end to be without honour:

How is he numbered among the children of God, and his lot is among the saints!

Therefore have we erred from the way of truth, and the light of righteousness hath not shined unto us, and the sun of righteousness rose not upon us.

We wearied ourselves in the way of wickedness and destruction: yea, we have gone through deserts, where there lay no way: but as for the way of the Lord, we have not known it.

What hath pride profited us? or what good hath riches with our vaunting brought us?

All those things are passed away like a shadow, and as a post that hasteth by;

And as a ship that passeth over the waves of the water, which, when it is gone by the trace thereof cannot be found, neither the pathway of the keel in the waves.

Or as when a bird hath flown through the air there is no token of her way to be found, but the light air being beaten with the stroke of her wings, and parted with the violent noise and motion of them, is passed through, and therein afterward no sign where she went is to be found;

Or like as when an arrow is shot at a mark, it parteth the air, which immediately cometh together again, so that a man cannot know where it went through:

Even so we in like manner, as soon as we were born, began to draw to our end, and had no sign of virtue to shew; but were consumed in our own wickedness.

For the hope of the ungodly is like dust that is blown away with the wind; like a thin froth that is driven away with the storm; like as the smoke which is dispersed here and there with a tempest, and passeth away as the remembrance of a guest that tarrieth but a day.

But the righteous live for evermore; their reward also is with the Lord, and the care of them is with the Most High.

Therefore shall they receive a glorious kingdom, and a beautiful crown from the Lord's hand: for with his right hand shall he cover them, and with his arm shall he protect them.

He shall take to him his jealousy for complete armour, and make the creature his weapon for the revenge of his enemies.

He shall put on righteousness as a breast-plate, and true judgment instead of a helmet.

He shall take holiness for an invincible shield.

His severe wrath shall he sharpen for a sword, and the world shall fight with him against the unwise.

Then shall the right-aiming thunderbolts go abroad, and from the clouds, as from a well-drawn bow, shall they fly to the mark.

And hailstones full of wrath shall be cast as out of a stone-bow, and the water of the sea shall rage against them, and the floods shall cruelly drown them.

Yea, a mighty wind shall stand up against them, and like a storm shall blow them away: thus iniquity shall lay waste the whole earth, and ill-dealing shall overthrow the thrones of the mighty.

***Wisdom*, v**

Hear therefore O ye kings, and understand; learn, ye that be judges of the ends of the earth.

Give ear, ye that rule the people, and glory in the multitude of nations.

For power is given you of the Lord, and sovereignty from the Highest, who shall try your works, and search out your counsels.

Because, being ministers of his kingdom, ye have not judged aright, nor kept the law, nor walked after the counsel of God;

Horribly and speedily shall he come upon you: for a sharp judgment shall be to them that be in high places.

For mercy will soon pardon the meanest: but mighty men shall be mightily tormented.

For he which is Lord over all shall fear no man's person, neither shall he stand in awe of any man's greatness: for he hath made the small and great, and careth for all alike.

But a sore trial shall come upon the mighty.

Unto you therefore, O kings, do I speak, that ye may learn wisdom, and not fall away:

For they that keep holiness holily, shall be judged holy: and they that have learned such things shall find what to answer.

Wherefore set your affection upon my words: desire them, and ye shall be instructed.

Wisdom is glorious, and never fadeth away: yea, she is easily seen of them that love her, and found of such as seek her.

She preventeth them that desire her, in making herself first known unto them.

Whoso seeketh her early shall have no great travail: for he shall find her sitting at his doors.

To think therefore upon her is perfection of wisdom: and whoso watcheth for her shall quickly be without care.

For she goeth about seeking such as are worthy of her,

sheweth herself favourably unto them in the ways, and meeteth them in every thought.

For the very true beginning of her is the desire of discipline, and the care of discipline is love:

And love is the keeping of her laws; and the giving heed unto her laws is the assurance of incorruption;

And incorruption maketh us near unto God:

Therefore the desire of wisdom bringeth to a kingdom.

If your delight be then in thrones and sceptres, O ye kings of the people, honour wisdom, that ye may reign for evermore.

As for wisdom, what she is, and how she came up, I will tell you, and will not hide mysteries from you: but will seek her out from the beginning of her nativity, and bring the knowledge of her into light, and will not pass over the truth.

Neither will I go with consuming envy; for such a man shall have no fellowship with wisdom.

But the multitude of the wise is the welfare of the world: and a wise king is the upholding of the people.

Receive therefore instruction through my words, and it shall do you good.

Wisdom, vi

I myself also am a mortal man, like to all, and the offspring of him that was first made of the earth;

And in my mother's womb was fashioned to be flesh in the time of ten months, being compacted in blood, of the seed of man, and the pleasure that came with sleep.

And when I was born, I drew in the common air, and fell upon the earth, which is of like nature, and the first voice which I uttered was crying, as all others do.

I was nursed in swaddling-clothes, and that with cares.

For there is no king that had any other beginning of birth.

For all men have one entrance into life, and the like going out.

Wherefore, I prayed, and understanding was given me: I

called upon God, and the spirit of wisdom came to me.

I preferred her before sceptres and thrones, and esteemed riches nothing in comparison of her.

Neither compared I unto her any precious stone, because all gold in respect of her is as a little sand, and silver shall be counted as clay before her.

I loved her above health and beauty, and chose to have her instead of light: for the light that cometh from her never goeth out.

All good things together came to me with her, and innumerable riches in her hands.

And I rejoiced in them all, because wisdom goeth before them, and I knew not that she was the mother of them.

I learned diligently, and to communicate her liberally: I do not hide her riches.

For she is a treasure unto men, that never faileth: which they that use become the friends of God, being commended for the gifts that come from learning.

God hath granted me to speak as I would, and to conceive as is meet for the things that are given me: because it is he that leadeth unto wisdom, and directeth the wise.

For in his hand are both we and our words; all wisdom also, and knowledge of workmanship.

For he hath given me certain knowledge of the things that are, namely, to know how the world was made, and the operation of the elements:

The beginning, ending, and midst of the times: the alterations of the turnings of the sun, and the change of seasons:

The circuits of years, and the positions of stars:

The natures of living creatures, and the furies of wild beasts, the violence of winds, and the reasonings of men: the diversities of plants, and the virtues of roots:

And all such things as are either secret or manifest, them I know.

For wisdom, which is the worker of all things, taught me:

for in her is an understanding spirit, holy, one only, manifold, subtil, lively, clear, undefiled, plain, not subject to hurt, loving the thing that is good, quick, which cannot be letted, ready to do good.

Kind to man, steadfast, sure, free from care, having all power, overseeing all things, and going through all understanding, pure and most subtil spirits.

For wisdom is more moving than any motion: she passeth and goeth through all things by reason of her pureness.

For she is the breath of the power of God, and a pure influence flowing from the glory of the Almighty; therefore can no defiled thing fall into her.

For she is the brightness of the everlasting light, the unspotted mirror of the power of God, and the image of his goodness.

And being but one, she can do all things: and remaining in herself, she maketh all things new: and in all ages entering into holy souls, she maketh them friends of God and prophets.

For God loveth none but him that dwelleth with wisdom.

For she is more beautiful than the sun, and above all the order of stars: being compared with the light, she is found before it.

For after this cometh night: but vice shall not prevail against wisdom.

Wisdom, vii

Wisdom reacheth from one end to another mightily: and sweetly doth she order all things.

I loved her, and sought her out from my youth: I desired to make her my spouse, and I was a lover of her beauty.

In that she is conversant with God, she magnifieth her nobility: yea, the Lord of all things himself loved her.

For she is privy to the mysteries of the knowledge of God, and a lover of his works.

If riches be a possession to be desired in this life; what is richer than wisdom, that worketh all things?

And if prudence work; who of all that are, is a more cunning workman than she?

And if a man love righteousness, her labours are virtues: for she teacheth temperance and prudence, justice and fortitude: which are such things, as men can have nothing more profitable in their life.

If a man desire much experience, she knoweth things of old, and conjectureth aright what is to come: she knoweth the subtilties of speeches, and can expound dark sentences; she foreseeth signs and wonders, and the events of seasons and times.

Therefore I purposed to take her to me to live with me, knowing that she would be a counsellor of good things, and a comfort in cares and grief.

For her sake I shall have estimation among the multitude, and honour with the elders, though I be young.

I shall be found of a quick conceit in judgment and shall be admired in the sight of great men.

When I hold my tongue, they shall abide my leisure, and when I speak, they shall give good ear unto me: If I talk much, they shall lay their hands upon their mouth.

Moreover by the means of her I shall obtain immortality, and leave behind me an everlasting memorial to them that come after me.

I shall set the people in order, and the nations shall be subject unto me.

Horrible tyrants shall be afraid when they do but hear of me; I shall be found good among the multitude, and valiant in war.

After I have come into my house, I will repose myself with her: for her conversation hath no bitterness; and to live with her hath no sorrow, but mirth and joy.

Now, when I considered these things in myself, and pondered them in my heart, how that to be allied unto wisdom is immortality;

And great pleasure it is to have her friendship; and in the works of her hands are infinite riches; and in the exercise of conference with her, prudence; and in talking with her, a good report; I went about seeking how to take her to me.

For I was a witty child, and had a good spirit.

Yea rather, being good, I came into a body undefiled.

Nevertheless, when I perceived that I could not otherwise obtain her, except God gave her me; and that was a point of wisdom also to know whose gift she was; I prayed unto the Lord, and besought him, and with my whole heart I said,

Wisdom, viii

O God of my fathers, and Lord of mercy, who hast made all things with thy word,

And ordained men through thy wisdom, that he should have dominion over the creatures which thou hast made,

And order the world according to equity and righteousness, and execute judgment with an upright heart:

Give me wisdom, that sitteth by thy throne; and reject me not from among thy children:

For I thy servant, and son of thy handmaid, am a feeble person, and of a short time, and too young for the understanding of judgment and laws.

For though a man be never so perfect among the children of men, yet if thy wisdom be not with him, he shall be nothing regarded.

Thou hast chosen me to be a king of thy people, and a judge of thy sons and daughters:

Thou hast commanded me to build a temple upon thy holy mount, and an altar in the city wherein thou dwellest; a resemblance of the holy tabernacle, which thou hast prepared from the beginning.

And wisdom was with thee: which knoweth thy works, and was present when thou madest the world, and knew what was acceptable in thy sight, and right in thy commandments.

O send her out of thy holy heavens, and from the throne of thy glory, that being present she may labour with me, that I may know what is pleasing unto thee.

For she knoweth and understandeth all things, and she shall lead me soberly in my doings, and preserve me in her power.

So shall my works be acceptable, and then shall I judge thy people righteously, and be worthy to sit in my father's seat.

For what man is he that can know the counsel of God? or who can think what the will of the Lord is?

For the thoughts of mortal men are miserable, and our devices are but uncertain.

For the corruptible body presseth down the soul, and the earthly tabernacle weigheth down the mind that museth upon many things.

And hardly do we guess aright at things that are upon earth, and with labour do we find the things that are before us: but the things that are in heaven who hath searched out?

And thy counsel who hath known, except thou give wisdom and send thy Holy Spirit from above?

For so the ways of them which lived on the earth were reformed, and men were taught the things that are pleasing unto thee, and were saved through wisdom.

***Wisdom*, ix**

Aphorisms of Jeshu ben Sirah

ALL WISDOM cometh from the Lord, and is with him for ever.

Who can number the sand of the sea, and the drops of rain, and the days of eternity?

Who can find out the height of heaven, and the breadth of the earth, and the deep, and wisdom?

Wisdom hath been created before all things, and the understanding of prudence from everlasting.

The word of God most high is the fountain of wisdom; and her ways are everlasting commandments.

To whom hath the root of wisdom been revealed? or who hath known her wise counsels?

[Unto whom hath the knowledge of wisdom been made manifest? and who hath understood her great experience?]

There is one wise and greatly to be feared, the Lord sitting upon his throne.

He created her, and saw her, and numbered her, and poured her out upon all his works.

She is with all flesh according to his gift, and he hath given her to them that love him.

The fear of the Lord is honour, and glory, and gladness, and a crown of rejoicing.

The fear of the Lord maketh a merry heart, and giveth joy, and gladness, and a long life.

Whoso feareth the Lord, it shall go well with him at the last, and he shall find favour in the day of his death.

To fear the Lord is the beginning of wisdom: and it was created with the faithful in the womb.

She hath built an everlasting foundation with men, and

she shall continue with their seed.

To fear the Lord is fulness of wisdom, and filleth men with her fruits.

She filleth all their house with things desirable, and the garners with her increase.

The fear of the Lord is a crown of wisdom, making peace and perfect health to flourish; both which are the gifts of God: and it enlargeth their rejoicing that love him.

Wisdom raineth down skill and knowledge of understanding, and exalteth them to honour that hold her fast.

The root of wisdom is to fear the Lord, and the branches thereof are long life.

The fear of the Lord driveth away sins: and where it is present it turneth away wrath.

A furious man cannot be justified; for the sway of his fury shall be his destruction.

A patient man will bear for a time, and afterward joy shall spring up unto him.

He will hide his words for a time, and the lips of many shall declare his wisdom.

The parables of knowledge are in the treasures of wisdom: but godliness is an abomination to a sinner.

If thou desire wisdom, keep the commandments, and the Lord shall give her unto thee.

For the fear of the Lord is wisdom and instruction: and faith and meekness are his delight.

Distrust not the fear of the Lord when thou art poor: and come not unto him with a double heart.

Be not a hypocrite in the sight of men, and take good heed what thou speakest.

Exalt not thyself, lest thou fall, and bring dishonour upon thy soul, and so God discover thy secrets, and cast thee down in the midst of the congregation, because thou camest not in truth to the fear of the Lord, but thy heart is full of deceit.

My son, if thou come to serve the Lord, prepare thy soul for temptation.

Set thy heart aright, and constantly endure, and make not haste in time of trouble.

Cleave unto him, and depart not away, that thou mayest be increased at thy last end.

Whatsoever is brought upon thee, take cheerfully, and be patient when thou art changed to a low estate.

For gold is tried in the fire, and acceptable men in the furnace of adversity.

Believe in him, and he will help thee; order thy way aright and trust in him.

Ye that fear the Lord, wait for his mercy; and go not aside, lest ye fall.

Ye that fear the Lord, believe him; and your reward shall not fail.

Ye that fear the Lord, hope for good, and for everlasting joy and mercy.

Look at the generations of old, and see; did ever any trust in the Lord, and was confounded? or did any abide in his fear, and was forsaken? or whom did he ever despise, that called upon him?

For the Lord is full of compassion and mercy, long-suffering, and very pitiful, and forgiveth sins, and saveth in time of affliction.

Wo be to fearful hearts, and faint hands, and the sinner that goeth two ways!

Wo unto him that is faint-hearted! for he believeth not; therefore shall he not be defended.

Wo unto you that have lost patience! and what will ye do when the Lord shall visit you?

They that fear the Lord will not disobey his word; and they that love him will keep his ways.

They that fear the Lord will seek that which is well-pleasing unto him; and they that love him shall be filled with the law.

They that fear the Lord will prepare their hearts, and humble their souls in his sight,

Saying, We will fall into the hands of the Lord, and not into the hands of men: for as his majesty is, so is his mercy.

❧

Hear me your father, O children, and do thereafter, that ye may be safe.

For the Lord hath given the father honour over the children, and hath confirmed the authority of the mother over the sons.

Whoso honoureth his father maketh an atonement for his sins:

And he that honoureth his mother is as one that layeth up treasure.

Whoso honoureth his father shall have joy of his own children; and when he maketh his prayer, he shall be heard.

He that honoureth his father shall have a long life and he that is obedient unto the Lord shall be a comfort to his mother.

He that feareth the Lord will honour his father, and will do service unto his parents, as to his masters.

Honour thy father and mother both in word and deed, that a blessing may come upon thee from them.

For the blessing of the father establisheth the houses of children; but the curse of the mother rooteth out foundations.

Glory not in the dishonour of thy father; for thy father's dishonour is no glory unto thee.

For the glory of a man is from the honour of his father; and a mother in dishonour is a reproach to the children.

My son, help thy father in his age, and grieve him not as long as he liveth.

And if his understanding fail, have patience with him; and despise him not when thou art in thy full strength.

For the relieving of thy father shall not be forgotten: and instead of sins it shall be added to build thee up.

In the day of thine affliction it shall be remembered; thy sins also shall melt away, as the ice in the fair warm weather.

He that forsaketh his father is as a blasphemer; and he that angereth his mother is cursed of God.

My son, go on with thy business in meekness; so shalt thou be beloved of him that is approved.

The greater thou art, the more humble thyself, and thou shalt find favour before the Lord.

Many are in high place, and of renown: but mysteries are revealed unto the meek.

For the power of the Lord is great, and he is honoured of the lowly.

Seek not out the things that are too hard for thee, neither search the things that are above thy strength.

But what is commanded thee, think thereupon with reverence; for it is not needful for thee to see with thine eyes the things that are in secret.

Be not curious in unnecessary matters: for more things are shewed unto thee than men understand.

For many are deceived by their own vain opinion; and an evil suspicion hath overthrown their judgment.

Without eyes thou shalt want light: profess not the knowledge therefore that thou hast not.

A stubborn heart shall fare evil at the last; and he that loveth danger shall perish therein.

An obstinate heart shall be laden with sorrows: and the wicked man shall heap sin upon sin.

In the punishment of the proud there is no remedy; for the plant of wickedness hath taken root in him.

The heart of the prudent will understand a parable; and an attentive ear is the desire of a wise man.

Water will quench a flaming fire; and alms maketh an atonement for sins.

And he that requiteth good turns is mindful of that which may come hereafter; and when he falleth, he shall find a stay.

My son, defraud not the poor of his living, and make not the needy eyes to wait long.

Make not a hungry soul sorrowful; neither provoke a man in his distress.

Add not more trouble to a heart that is vexed; and defer not to give to him that is in need.

Reject not the supplication of the afflicted; neither turn away thy face from a poor man.

Turn not away thine eye from the needy, and give him none occasion to curse thee:

For if he curse thee in the bitterness of his soul, his prayer shall be heard of him that made him.

Get thyself the love of the congregation, and bow thy head to a great man.

Let it not grieve thee to bow down thine ear to the poor, and give him a friendly answer with meekness.

Deliver him that suffereth wrong from the hand of the oppressor; and be not faint-hearted when thou sittest in judgment.

Be as a father unto the fatherless, and instead of a husband unto their mother: so shalt thou be as a son of the Most High, and he shall love thee more than thy mother doth.

Wisdom exalteth her children, and layeth hold of them that seek her.

He that loveth her loveth life; and they that seek to her early shall be filled with joy.

He that holdeth her fast shall inherit glory; and wheresoever she entereth, the Lord will bless.

They that serve her shall minister to the Holy One: and them that love her the Lord doth love.

Whoso giveth ear unto her, shall judge the nations: and he that attendeth unto her shall dwell securely.

If a man commit himself unto her he shall inherit her; and his generation shall hold her in possession.

For at the first she will walk with him by crooked ways, and bring fear and dread upon him, and torment him with her discipline, until she may trust his soul, and try him by her laws.

Then will she return the straight way unto him, and comfort him, and shew him her secrets.

But if he go wrong, she will forsake him, and give him over to his own ruin.

Observe the opportunity, and beware of evil; and be not ashamed when it concerneth thy soul.

For there is a shame that bringeth sin; and there is a shame which is glory and grace.

Accept no person against thy soul, and let not the reverence of any man cause thee to fall.

And refrain not to speak, when there is occasion to do good, and hide not thy wisdom in her beauty.

For by speech wisdom shall be known: and learning by the word of the tongue.

In no wise speak against the truth; but be abashed of the error of thine ignorance.

Be not ashamed to confess thy sins; and force not the course of the river.

Make not thyself an underling to a foolish man; neither accept the person of the mighty.

Strive for the truth unto death, and the Lord shall fight for thee.

Be not hasty in thy tongue, and in thy deeds slack and remiss.

Be not as a lion in thy house, nor frantic among thy servants.

Let not thy hand be stretched out to receive, and shut when thou shouldest repay.

❧

Set not thy heart upon thy goods; and say not, I have enough for my life.

Follow not thine own mind and thy strength, to walk in the ways of thy heart:

And say not, Who shall control me for my works? for the Lord will surely revenge thy pride.

Say not, I have sinned, and what harm hath happened unto me? for the Lord is long-suffering, he will in no wise let thee go.

Concerning propitiation, be not without fear to add sin unto sin;

And say not, His mercy is great; he will be pacified for the multitude of my sins: for mercy and wrath come from him, and his indignation resteth upon sinners.

Make no tarrying to turn to the Lord, and put not off from day to day: for suddenly shall the wrath of the Lord come forth, and in thy security thou shalt be destroyed, and perish in the day of vengeance.

Set not thy heart upon goods unjustly gotten: for they shall not profit thee in the days of calamity.

Winnow not with every wind, and go not into every way: for so doth the sinner that hath a double tongue.

Be steadfast in thine understanding; and let thy word be the same.

Be swift to hear; and let thy life be sincere; and with patience give answer.

If thou hast understanding, answer thy neighbour; if not, lay thy hand upon thy mouth.

Honour and shame is in talk: and the tongue of man is his fall.

Be not called a whisperer, and lie not in wait with thy tongue: for a foul shame is upon the thief, and an evil condemnation upon the double tongue.

Be not ignorant of any thing in a great matter or a small.

❧

Instead of a friend become not an enemy; [for thereby] thou shalt inherit an ill name, shame, and reproach: even so shall a sinner that hath a double tongue.

Extol not thyself in the counsel of thine own heart; that thy soul be not torn in pieces as a bull [straying alone.]

Thou shalt eat up thy leaves, and lose thy fruit, and leave thyself as a dry tree.

A wicked soul shall destroy him that hath it, and shall make him to be laughed to scorn of his enemies.

Sweet language will multiply friends: and a fair speaking tongue will increase kind greetings.

Be in peace with many: nevertheless have but one counsellor of a thousand.

If thou wouldest get a friend, prove him first, and be not hasty to credit him.

For some man is a friend for his own occasion, and will not abide in the day of thy trouble.

And there is a friend, who being turned to enmity and strife, will discover thy reproach.

Again, some friend is a companion at the table, and will not continue in the day of thine affliction.

But in thy prosperity he will be as thyself, and will be bold over thy servants.

If thou be brought low, he will be against thee, and will hide himself from thy face.

Separate thyself from thine enemies, and take heed of thy friends.

A faithful friend is a strong defence: and he that hath found such a one hath found a treasure.

Nothing doth countervail a faithful friend, and his excellency is invaluable.

A faithful friend is the medicine of life; and they that fear the Lord shall find him.

Whoso feareth the Lord shall direct his friendship aright: for as he is, so shall his neighbour be also.

My son, gather instruction from thy youth up: so shalt thou find wisdom till thine old age.

Come unto her as one that plougheth and soweth, and wait for her good fruits: for thou shalt not toil much in labouring about her, but thou shalt eat of her fruits right soon.

She is very unpleasant to the unlearned: he that is without understanding will not remain with her.

She will lie upon him as a mighty stone of trial; and he will cast her from him ere it be long.

For wisdom is according to her name, and she is not manifest unto many.

Give ear, my son, receive mine advice, and refuse not my counsel,

And put thy feet into her fetters, and thy neck into her chain.

Bow down thy shoulder, and bear her, and be not grieved with her bonds.

Come unto her with thy whole heart, and keep her ways with all thy power.

Search, and seek, and she shall be made known unto thee: and when thou has got hold of her, let her not go.

For at the last thou shalt find her rest, and that shall be turned to thy joy.

Then shall her fetters be a strong defence for thee, and her chains a robe of glory.

For there is a golden ornament upon her, and her bands are purple lace.

Thou shalt put her on as a robe of honour, and shalt put her about thee as a crown of joy.

My son, if thou wilt, thou shalt be taught: and if thou wilt apply thy mind, thou shalt be prudent.

If thou love to hear, thou shalt receive understanding: and if thou bow thine ear, thou shalt be wise.

Stand in the multitude of the elders; and cleave unto him that is wise.

Be willing to hear every godly discourse; and let not the parables of understanding escape thee.

And if thou seest a man of understanding, get thee betimes unto him, and let thy foot wear the steps of his door.

Let thy mind be upon the ordinances of the Lord, and meditate continually in his commandments: he shall establish thy heart, and give thee wisdom at thine own desire.

Do no evil, so shall no harm come unto thee.

Depart from the unjust, and iniquity shall turn away from thee.

My son, sow not upon the furrows of unrighteousness, and thou shalt not reap them seven-fold.

Seek not of the Lord pre-eminence, neither of the king the seat of honour.

Justify not thyself before the Lord; and boast not of thy wisdom before the king.

Seek not to be judge, being not able to take away iniquity; lest at any time thou fear the prison of the mighty, and lay a stumbling-block in the way of thine uprightness.

Offend not against the multitude of a city, and then thou shalt not cast thyself down among the people.

Bind not one sin upon another; for in one thou shalt not be unpunished.

Say not, God will look upon the multitude of mine oblations, and when I offer to the most high God, he will accept it.

Be not faint-hearted when thou makest thy prayer, and neglect not to give alms.

Laugh no man to scorn in the bitterness of his soul: for there is one which humbleth and exalteth.

Devise not a lie against thy brother: neither do the like to thy friend.

Use not to make any manner of lie: for the custom thereof is not good.

Use not many words in a multitude of elders, and make not much babbling when thou prayest.

Hate not laborious work, neither husbandry, which the Most High hath ordained.

Number not thyself among the multitude of sinners, but remember that wrath will not tarry long.

Humble thy soul greatly: for the vengeance of the ungodly is fire and worms.

Change not a friend for any good, by no means; neither a

faithful brother for the gold of Ophir.

Forego not a wise and good woman: for her grace is above gold.

Whereas thy servant worketh truly, entreat him not evil, nor the hireling that bestoweth himself wholly for thee.

Let thy soul love a good servant, and defraud him not of liberty.

Hast thou cattle? have an eye to them: and if they be for thy profit, keep them with thee.

Hast thou children? instruct them, and bow down their neck from their youth.

Hast thou daughters? have a care of their body, and shew not thyself cheerful toward them.

Marry thy daughter, and so shalt thou have performed a weighty matter: but give her to a man of understanding.

Hast thou a wife after thy mind? forsake her not: but give not thyself over to a light woman.

Honour thy father with thy whole heart, and forget not the sorrows of thy mother.

Remember that thou wast begotten of them, and how canst thou recompense them the things that they have done for thee?

Fear the Lord with all thy soul, and reverence his priests.

Love him that made thee with all thy strength, and forsake not his ministers.

Fear the Lord, and honour the priest; and give him his portion, as it is commanded thee; the first-fruits, and the trespass-offering, and the gift of the shoulders, and the sacrifice of sanctification, and the first-fruits of the holy things.

And stretch thy hand unto the poor, that thy blessing may be perfected.

A gift hath grace in the sight of every man living, and for the dead detain it not.

Fail not to be with them that weep, and mourn with them that mourn.

Be not slow to visit the sick: for that shall make thee to be loved.

Whatsoever thou takest in hand, remember the end, and thou shalt never do amiss.

❧

Strive not with a mighty man, lest thou fall into his hands.

Be not at variance with a rich man, lest he overweigh thee: for gold hath destroyed many, and perverted the hearts of kings.

Strive not with a man that is full of tongue, and heap not wood upon his fire.

Jest not with a rude man, lest thine ancestors be disgraced.

Reproach not a man that turneth from sin, but remember that we are all worthy of punishment.

Dishonour not a man in his old age: for even some of us wax old.

Rejoice not over thy greatest enemy being dead, but remember that we die all.

Despise not the discourse of the wise, but acquaint thyself with their proverbs: for of them thou shalt learn instruction, and how to serve great men with ease.

Miss not the discourse of the elders: for they also learned of their fathers, and of them thou shalt learn understanding, and to give answer as need requireth.

Kindle not the coals of a sinner, lest thou be burnt with the flame of his fire.

Rise not up [in anger] at the presence of an injurious person, lest he lie in wait to entrap thee in thy words.

Lend not unto him that is mightier than thyself: for if thou lendest him, count it but lost.

Be not surety above thy power: for if thou be surety, take care to pay it.

Go not to law with a judge, for they will judge for him according to his honour.

Travel not by the way with a bold fellow, lest he become grievous unto thee: for he will do according to his own will, and thou shalt perish with him through his folly.

Strive not with an angry man, and go not with him into a solitary place: for blood is as nothing in his sight, and where there is no help, he will overthrow thee.

Consult not with a fool, for he cannot keep counsel.

Do no secret thing before a stranger; for thou knowest not what he will bring forth.

Open not thy heart to every man, lest he requite thee with a shrewd turn.

⁂

Be not jealous over the wife of thy bosom, and teach her not an evil lesson against thyself.

Give not thy soul unto a woman to set her foot upon thy substance.

Meet not with a harlot, lest thou fall into her snares.

Use not much the company of a woman that is a singer, lest thou be taken with her attempts.

Gaze not on a maid, that thou fall not by those things that are precious in her.

Give not thy soul unto harlots, that thou lose not thine inheritance.

Look not round about thee in the streets of the city, neither wander thou in the solitary places thereof.

Turn away thine eye from a beautiful woman, and look not upon another's beauty; for many have been deceived by the beauty of a woman; for herewith love is kindled as a fire.

Sit not at all with another man's wife, nor sit down with her in thine arms, and spend not thy money with her at the wine; lest thy heart incline unto her, and so through thy desire thou fall into destruction.

Forsake not an old friend; for the new is not comparable to him: a new friend is as new wine; when it is old, thou shalt drink it with pleasure.

Envy not the glory of a sinner: for thou knowest not what shall be his end.

Delight not in the thing that the ungodly have pleasure in: but remember they shall not go unpunished unto their grave.

Keep thee far from the man that hath power to kill; so shalt thou not doubt the fear of death: and if thou come unto him, make no fault, lest he take way thy life presently: remember that thou goest in the midst of snares, and that thou walkest upon the battlements of the city.

As near as thou canst, guess at thy neighbour, and consult with the wise.

Let thy talk be with the wise, and all thy communication in the law of the Most High.

And let just men eat and drink with thee: and let thy glorying be in the fear of the Lord.

For the hand of the artificer the work shall be commended: and the wise ruler of the people for his speech.

A man of an ill tongue is dangerous in his city; and he that is rash in his talk shall be hated.

A wise judge will instruct his people; and the government of a prudent man is well ordered.

As the judge of the people is himself, so are his officers; and what manner of man the ruler of the city is, such are all they that dwell therein.

An unwise king destroyeth his people; but through the prudence of them which are in authority, the city shall be inhabited.

The power of the earth is in the hand of the Lord, and in due time he will set over it one that is profitable.

In the hand of God is the prosperity of man: and upon the person of the scribe shall he lay his honour.

Bear not hatred to thy neighbour for every wrong; and do nothing at all by injurious practices.

Pride is hateful before God and man: and by both doth one commit iniquity.

Because of unrighteous dealings, injuries, and riches got by deceit, the kingdom is translated from one people to another.

Why is earth and ashes proud? There is not a more wicked thing than a covetous man: for such a one setteth his own soul to sale; because while he liveth, he casteth away his bowels.

The physician cutteth off a long disease; and he that is today a king, tomorrow shall die.

For when a man is dead, he shall inherit creeping things, beasts, and worms.

The beginning of pride is when one departeth from God, and his heart is turned away from his Maker.

For pride is the beginning of sin, and he that hath it shall pour out abomination: and therefore the Lord brought upon them strange calamities, and overthrew them utterly.

The Lord hath cast down the thrones of proud princes, and set up the meek in their stead.

The Lord hath plucked up the roots of the proud nations, and planted the lowly in their place.

The Lord overthrew countries of the heathen, and destroyed them to the foundations of the earth.

He took some of them away, and destroyed them, and hath made their memorial to cease from the earth.

Pride was not made for men, nor furious anger for them that are born of a woman.

They that fear the Lord are a sure seed, and they that love him an honorable plant: they that regard not the law are a dishonourable seed; they that transgress the commandments are a deceivable seed.

Among brethren he that is chief is honourable; so are they that fear the Lord, in his eyes.

The fear of the Lord goeth before the obtaining of authority: but roughness and pride is the losing thereof.

Whether he be rich, noble, or poor, their glory is the fear of the Lord.

It is not meet to despise the poor man that hath understanding; neither is it convenient to magnify a sinful man.

Great men, and judges, and potentates, shall be honoured; yet is there none of them greater than he that feareth the Lord.

Unto the servant that is wise shall they that are free do service: and he that hath knowledge will not grudge when he is reformed.

Be not overwise in doing thy business; and boast not thyself in the time of thy distress.

Better is he that laboureth, and aboundeth in all things, than he that boasteth himself and wanteth bread.

My son, glorify thy soul in meekness, and give it honour according to the dignity thereof.

Who will justify him that sinneth against his own soul? and who will honour him that dishonoureth his own life?

The poor man is honoured for his skill, and the rich man is honoured for his riches.

He that is honoured in poverty, how much more in riches? and he that is dishonourable in riches, how much more in poverty?

Wisdom lifteth up the head of him that is of low degree, and maketh him to sit among great men.

❧

Commend not a man for his beauty, neither abhor a man for his outward appearance.

The bee is little among such as fly; but her fruit is the chief of sweet things.

Boast not of thy clothing and raiment, and exalt not thyself in the day of honour: for the works of the Lord are wonderful, and his works among men are hidden.

Many kings have sat down upon the ground; and one that was never thought of hath worn the crown.

Many mighty men have been greatly disgraced; and the

honourable delivered into other men's hands.

Blame not before thou hast examined the truth: understand first, and then rebuke.

Answer not before thou hast heard the cause; neither interrupt men in the midst of their talk.

Strive not in a matter that concerneth thee not; and sit not in judgment with sinners.

My son, meddle not with many matters: for if thou meddle much, thou shalt not be innocent: and if thou follow after, thou shalt not obtain, neither shalt thou escape by fleeing.

There is one that laboureth, and taketh pains, and maketh haste, and is so much the more behind.

Again, there is another that is slow, and hath need of help, wanting ability, and full of poverty; yet the eye of the Lord looked upon him for good, and set him up from his low estate,

And lifted up his head from misery; so that many that saw it marvelled at him.

Prosperity and adversity, life and death, poverty and riches, come of the Lord.

Wisdom, knowledge, and understanding of the law, are of the Lord: love, and the way of good works, are from him.

Error and darkness had their beginning together with sinners: and evil shall wax old with them that glory therein.

The gift of the Lord remaineth with the godly, and his favour bringeth prosperity for ever.

There is that waxeth rich by his wariness and pinching, and this is the portion of his reward:

Whereas he saith, I have found rest, and now will eat continually of my goods; and yet he knoweth not what time shall come upon him, and that he must leave those things to others, and die.

Be steadfast in thy covenant, and be conversant therein, and wax old in thy work.

Marvel not at the works of sinners; but trust in the Lord,

and abide in thy labour: for it is an easy thing in the sight of the Lord, on the sudden to make a poor man rich.

The blessing of the Lord is in the reward of the godly, and suddenly he maketh his blessing to flourish.

Say not, What profit is there of my service? and what good things shall I have hereafter?

Again, say not, I have enough, and possess many things, and what evil can come to me hereafter?

In the day of prosperity there is a forgetfulness of affliction: and in the day of affliction there is no more remembrance of prosperity.

For it is an easy thing unto the Lord in the day of death to reward a man according to his ways.

The affliction of an hour maketh a man forget pleasure: and in his end his deeds shall be discovered.

Judge none blessed before his death: for a man shall be known in his children.

Bring not every man into thy house: for the deceitful man hath many trains.

Like as a partridge taken [and kept] in a cage, so is the heart of the proud; and like a spy, watcheth he for thy fall:

For he lieth in wait, and turneth good into evil, and in things worthy praise will lay blame upon thee.

Of a spark of fire, a heap of coals is kindled: and a sinful man layeth wait for blood.

Take heed of a mischievous man, for he worketh wickedness; lest he bring upon thee a perpetual blot.

Receive a stranger into thy house, and he will disturb thee, and turn thee out of thine own.

❧

When thou wilt do good, know to whom thou doest it; so shalt thou be thanked for thy benefits.

Do good to the godly man, and thou shalt find a recompense; and if not from him, yet from the Most High.

There can no good come to him that is always occupied in evil nor to him that giveth no alms.

Give to the godly man, and help not a sinner.

Do well unto him that is lowly, but give not to the ungodly; hold back thy bread, and give it not unto him, lest he overmaster thee thereby: for [else] thou shalt receive twice as much evil for all the good thou shalt have done unto him.

For the Most High hateth sinners, and will repay vengeance unto the ungodly, and keepeth them against the mighty day of their punishment.

Give unto the good, and help not the sinner.

A friend cannot be known in prosperity; and an enemy cannot be hid in adversity.

In the prosperity of a man, enemies will be grieved: but in his adversity, even a friend will depart.

Never trust thine enemy: for like as iron rusteth, so is his wickedness.

Though he humble himself, and go crouching, yet take good heed and beware of him, and thou shalt be unto him as if thou hadst wiped a looking-glass, and thou shalt know that his rust hath not been altogether wiped away.

Set him not by thee, lest, when he hath overthrown thee, he stand up in thy place; neither let him sit at thy right hand, lest he seek to take thy seat, and thou at the last remember my words, and be pricked therewith.

Who will pity the charmer that is bitten with a serpent, or any such as come nigh wild beasts?

So one that goeth to a sinner, and is defiled with him in his sins, who will pity?

For a while he will abide with thee, but if thou begin to fall, he will not tarry.

An enemy speaketh sweetly with his lips, but in his heart he imagineth how to throw thee into a pit: he will weep with his eyes, but if he find opportunity, he will not be satisfied with blood.

If adversity come upon thee, thou shalt find him there first; and though he pretend to help thee, yet shall he undermine thee.

He will shake his head, and clap his hands, and whisper much, and change his countenance.

❧

He that toucheth pitch shall be defiled therewith; and he that hath fellowship with a proud man shall be like unto him.

Burden not thyself above thy power while thou livest; and have no fellowship with one that is mightier and richer than thyself: for how agree the kettle and the earthen pot together? for if the one be smitten against the other, it shall be broken.

The rich man hath done wrong, and yet he threateneth withal: the poor is wronged, and he must entreat also.

If thou be for his profit, he will use thee: but if thou have nothing, he will forsake thee.

If thou have any thing, he will live with thee: yea, he will make thee bare, and will not be sorry for it.

If he have need of thee, he will deceive thee, and smile upon thee and put thee in hope; he will speak thee fair, and say, What wantest thou?

And he will shame thee by his meats, until he have drawn thee dry twice or thrice, and at the last he will laugh thee to scorn: afterward, when he seeth thee, he will forsake thee, and shake his head at thee.

Beware that thou be not deceived, and brought down in thy jollity.

If thou be invited of a mighty man, withdraw thyself, and so much the more will he invite thee.

Press thou not upon him, lest thou be put back; stand not far off, lest thou be forgotten.

Affect not to be made equal unto him in talk, and believe not his many words: for with much communication will he tempt thee, and smiling upon thee will get out thy secrets:

But cruelly he will lay up thy words, and will not spare to do thee hurt, and to put thee in prison.

Observe, and take good heed, for thou walkest in peril of thy overthrowing: when thou hearest these things, awake in thy sleep.

Love the Lord all thy life, and call upon him for thy salvation.

Every beast loveth his like, and every man loveth his neighbour.

All flesh consorteth according to kind, and a man will cleave to his like.

What fellowship hath the wolf with the lamb? so the sinner with the godly.

What agreement is there between a hyena and a dog? and what peace between the rich and the poor?

As the wild ass is the lion's prey in the wilderness: so the rich eat up the poor.

As the proud hate humility: so doth the rich abhor the poor.

A rich man beginning to fall is held up of his friends: but a poor man being down is thrust also away by his friends.

When a rich man is fallen, he hath many helpers: he speaketh things not to be spoken, and yet men justify him: the poor man slipped, and yet they rebuked him too; he spake wisely, and could have no place.

When a rich man speaketh, every man holdeth his tongue, and look, what he saith, they extol it to the clouds: but if the poor man speak, they say, What fellow is this? and if he stumble, they will help to overthrow him.

Riches are good unto him that hath no sin, and poverty is evil in the mouth of the ungodly.

The heart of a man changeth his countenance, whether it be for good or evil: and a merry heart maketh a cheerful countenance.

A cheerful countenance is a token of a heart that is in prosperity; and the finding out of parables is a wearisome labour of the mind.

❧

Blessed is the man that hath not slipped with his mouth, and is not pricked with the multitude of sins.

Blessed is he whose conscience hath not condemned him, and who is not fallen from his hope in the Lord.

Riches are not comely for a niggard: and what should an envious man do with money?

He that gathereth by defrauding his own soul, gathereth for others, that shall spend his goods riotously.

He that is evil to himself, to whom will he be good? he shall not take pleasure in his goods.

There is none worse than he that envieth himself; and this is a recompense of his wickedness.

And if he doeth good, he doeth it unwillingly; and at the last he will declare his wickedness.

The envious man hath a wicked eye; he turneth away his face, and despiseth men.

A covetous man's eye is not satisfied with his portion; and the iniquity of the wicked drieth up his soul.

A wicked eye envieth [his] bread, and he is a niggard at his table.

My son, according to thy ability do good to thyself, and give the Lord his due offering.

Remember that death will not be long in coming, and that the covenant of the grave is not shewed unto thee.

Do good unto thy friend before thou die, and according to thy ability stretch out thy hand, and give to him.

Defraud not thyself of the good day, and let not the part of a good desire overpass thee.

Shalt thou not leave thy travails unto another? and thy labours to be divided by lot?

Give, and take, and sanctify thy soul; for there is no seeking of dainties in the grave.

All flesh waxeth old as a garment: for the covenant from the beginning is, Thou shalt die the death.

As of the green leaves on a thick tree, some fall, and some grow; so is the generation of flesh and blood, one cometh to an end, and another is born.

Every work rotteth and consumeth away, and the worker thereof shall go withal.

Blessed is the man that doth meditate good things in wisdom, and that reasoneth of holy things by his understanding.

He that considereth her ways in his heart shall also have understanding in her secrets.

Go after her as one that traceth, and lie in wait in her ways.

He that pryeth in at her windows shall also hearken at her doors.

He that doth lodge near her house shall also fasten a pin in her walls.

He shall pitch his tent nigh unto her, and shall lodge in a lodging where good things are.

He shall set his children under her shelter, and shall lodge under her branches.

By her he shall be covered from heat, and in her glory shall he dwell.

❧

He that feareth the Lord will do good; and he that hath the knowledge of the law shall obtain her.

And as a mother shall she meet him, and receive him as a wife married of a virgin.

With the bread of understanding shall she feed him, and give him the water of wisdom to drink.

He shall be stayed upon her, and shall not be moved; and shall rely upon her, and shall not be confounded.

She shall exalt him above his neighbours, and in the midst of the congregation shall she open his mouth.

He shall find joy and a crown of gladness, and she shall cause him to inherit an everlasting name.

But foolish men shall not attain unto her, and sinners shall not see her.

For she is far from pride, and men that are liars cannot remember her.

Praise is not seemly in the mouth of a sinner, for it was not sent him of the Lord.

For praise shall be uttered in wisdom, and the Lord will prosper it.

Say not thou, It is through the Lord that I fell away; for thou oughtest not to do the things that he hateth.

Say not thou, He hath caused me to err: for he hath no need of the sinful man.

The Lord hateth all abomination; and they that fear God love it not.

He himself made man from the beginning, and left him in the hand of his counsel;

If thou wilt, to keep the commandments, and to perform acceptable faithfulness.

He hath set fire and water before thee: stretch forth thy hand unto whether thou wilt.

Before man is life and death; and whether him liketh shall be given him.

For the wisdom of the Lord is great, and he knoweth every work of man.

He hath commanded no man to do wickedly, neither hath he given any man license to sin.

❧

Desire not a multitude of unprofitable children, neither delight in ungodly sons.

Though they multiply, rejoice not in them, except the fear of the Lord be with them.

Trust not thou in their life, neither respect their multitude: for one that is just is better than a thousand; and better it is to die without children, then to have them that are ungodly.

For by one that hath understanding shall the city be replenished: but the kindred of the wicked shall speedily become desolate.

Many such things have I seen with mine eyes, and mine ear hath heard greater things than these.

In the congregation of the ungodly shall a fire be kindled; and in a rebellious nation wrath is set on fire.

He was not pacified toward the old giants who fell away in the strength of their foolishness.

Neither spared he the place where Lot sojourned, but abhorred them for their pride.

He pitied not the people of perdition, who were taken away in their sins:

Nor the six hundred thousand footmen, who were gathered together in the hardness of their hearts.

And if there be one stiff-necked among the people, it is marvel if he escape unpunished: for mercy and wrath are with him; he is mighty to forgive and to pour out displeasure.

As his mercy is great so is his correction also: he judgeth a man according to his works.

The sinner shall not escape with his spoils: and the patience of the godly shall not be frustrated.

Make way for every work of mercy: for every man shall find according to his works.

The Lord hardened Pharaoh, that he should not know him, that his powerful works might be known to the world.

His mercy is manifest to every creature; and he hath separated his light from the darkness with an adamant.

Say not thou, I will hide myself from the Lord: shall any remember me from above? I shall not be remembered among so many people: for what is my soul among such an infinite number of creatures?

Behold, the heaven, and the heaven of heavens, the deep, and the earth, and all that therein is, shall be moved when he shall visit.

The mountains also and foundations of the earth shall be

shaken with trembling when the Lord looketh upon them.

No heart can think upon these things worthily: and who is able to conceive his ways?

It is a tempest which no man can see: for the most part of his works are hid.

Who can declare the works of his justice? or who can endure them? for his covenant is afar off, and the trial of all things is in the end.

He that wanteth understanding, will think upon vain things: and a foolish man erring, imagineth follies.

My son, hearken unto me, and learn knowledge, and mark my words with thy heart.

I will shew forth doctrine in weight, and declare his knowledge exactly.

The works of the Lord are done in judgment from the beginning: and from the time he made them he disposed the parts thereof.

He garnished his works for ever, and in his hand are the chief of them unto all generations: they neither labour, nor are weary, nor cease from their works.

None of them hindereth another, and they shall never disobey his word.

After this the Lord looked upon the earth, and filled it with his blessings.

With all manner of living things hath he covered the face thereof; and they shall return into it again.

❧

The Lord created man of the earth and turned him into it again. He gave them few days and a short time, and power also over the things therein.

He endued them with strength by themselves, and made them according to his image.

And put the fear of man upon all flesh, and gave him dominion over beasts and fowls.

[They received the use of the five operations of the Lord, and in the sixth place he imparted them understanding, and in the seventh speech, an interpreter of the cogitations thereof.]

Counsel, and a tongue, and eyes, ears, and a heart gave he them to understand.

Withal he filled them with the knowledge of understanding, and shewed them good and evil.

He set his eye upon their hearts, that he might shew them the greatness of his works.

He gave them to glory in his marvellous acts for ever, that they might declare his works with understanding.

And the elect shall praise his holy name.

Besides this, he gave them knowledge, and the law of life for a heritage.

He made an everlasting covenant with them, and shewed them his judgments.

Their eyes saw the majesty of his glory, and their ears heard his glorious voice.

And he said unto them, Beware of all unrighteousness; and he gave every man commandment concerning his neighbour.

Their ways are ever before him, and shall not be hid from his eyes.

Every man from his youth is given to evil; neither could they make to themselves fleshly hearts for stony.

For in the division of the nations of the whole earth, he set a ruler over every people; but Israel is the Lord's portion.

Whom, being his first-born, he nourisheth with discipline, and giving him the light of his love, doth not forsake him.

Therefore all their works are as the sun before him, and his eyes are continually upon their ways.

None of their unrighteous deeds are hid from him, but all their sins are before the Lord.

But the Lord being gracious,and knowing his workmanship, neither left nor forsook them, but spared them.

The alms of a man is as a signet with him, and he will keep

the good deeds of man as the apple of the eye, and give repentance to his sons and daughters.

Afterward he will rise up and reward them, and render their recompense upon their heads.

But unto them that repent, he granted them return, and comforted those that failed in patience.

Return unto the Lord, and forsake thy sins, make thy prayer before his face, and offend less.

Turn again to the Most High, and turn away from iniquity: for he will lead thee out of darkness into the light of health; and hate thou abomination vehemently.

Who shall praise the Most High in the grave, instead of them which live and give thanks?

Thanksgiving perisheth from the dead, as from one that is not: the living and sound in heart shall praise the Lord.

How great is the loving-kindness of the Lord our God, and his compassion unto such as turn unto him in holiness!

For all things cannot be in men, because the son of man is not immortal.

What is brighter than the sun? yet the light thereof faileth: and flesh and blood will imagine evil.

He vieweth the power of the height of heaven, and all men are but earth and ashes.

❧

He that liveth for ever created all things in general.

The Lord only is righteous, and there is none other but he.

Who governeth the world with the palm of his hand, and all things obey his will: for he is the King of all, by his power dividing holy things among them from profane.

To whom hath he given power to declare his works? and who shall find out his noble acts?

Who shall number the strength of his majesty? and who shall also tell out his mercies?

As for the wondrous works of the Lord, there may nothing

be taken from them, neither may any thing be put unto them, neither can the ground of them be found out.

When a man hath done, then he beginneth; and when he leaveth off, then he shall be doubtful.

What is man, and whereto serveth he? what is his good, and what is his evil?

The number of a man's days at the most are a hundred years.

As a drop of water unto the sea, and a gravel-stone in comparison of the sand; so are a thousand years to the days of eternity.

Therefore is God patient with them, and poureth forth his mercy upon them.

He saw and perceived their end to be evil; therefore he multiplied his compassion.

The mercy of man is toward his neighbour; but the mercy of the Lord is upon all flesh: he reproveth, and nurtureth, and teacheth, and bringeth again, as a shepherd his flock.

He hath mercy on them that receive discipline, and that diligently seek after his judgments.

My son, blemish not thy good deeds, neither use uncomfortable words when thou givest any thing.

Shall not the dew assuage the heat? so is a word better than a gift.

Lo, is not a word better than a gift? but both are with a gracious man.

A fool will upbraid churlishly, and a gift of the envious consumeth the eyes.

Learn before thou speak, and use physick or ever thou be sick.

Before judgment examine thyself, and in the day of visitation thou shalt find mercy.

Humble thyself before thou be sick, and in the time of sins shew repentance.

Let nothing hinder thee to pay thy vow in due time, and

defer not until death to be justified.

Before thou prayest, prepare thyself; and be not as one that tempteth the Lord.

Think upon the wrath that shall be at the end, and the time of vengeance, when he shall turn away his face.

When thou hast enough, remember the time of hunger, and when thou art rich, think upon poverty and need.

From the morning until the evening the time is changed, and all things are soon done before the Lord.

A wise man will fear in every thing, and in the day of sinning he will beware of offense: but a fool will not observe time.

Every man of understanding knoweth wisdom, and will give praise unto him that found her.

They that were of understanding in sayings, became also wise themselves, and poured forth exquisite parables.

Go not after thy lusts, but refrain thyself from thine appetites.

If thou givest thy soul the desires that please her, she will make thee a laughing-stock to thine enemies that malign thee.

Take not pleasure in much good cheer, neither be tied to the expense thereof.

Be not made a beggar by banqueting upon borrowing, when thou hast nothing in thy purse: for thou shalt lie in wait for thine own life and be talked on.

❧

A labouring man that is given to drunkenness shall not be rich: and he that contemneth small things shall fall by little and little.

Wine and women will make men of understanding to fall away: and he that cleaveth to harlots will become impudent.

Moths and worms shall have him to heritage, and a bold man shall be taken away.

He that is hasty to give credit is light-minded; and he that sinneth shall offend against his own soul.

Whoso taketh pleasure in wickedness shall be condemned: but he that resisteth pleasures crowneth his life.

He that can rule his tongue shall live without strife; and he that hateth babbling shall have less evil.

Rehearse not unto another that which is told unto thee, and thou shalt fare never the worse.

Whether it be to a friend or foe, talk not of other men's lives; and if thou canst without offense reveal them not.

For he heard and observed thee, and when time cometh he will hate thee.

If thou hast heard a word, let it die with thee; and be bold, it will not burst thee.

A fool travaileth with a word, as a woman in labour of a child.

As an arrow that sticketh in a man's thigh, so is a word within a fool's belly.

Admonish a friend, it may be he hath not done it: and if he have done it, that he do it no more.

Admonish thy friend, it may be he hath not said it: and if he have, that he speak it not again.

Admonish a friend: for many times it is a slander, and believe not every tale.

There is one that slippeth in his speech, but not from his heart; and who is he that hath not offended with his tongue?

Admonish thy neighbour before thou threaten him; and not being angry give place to the law of the Most High.

The fear of the Lord is the first step to be accepted [of him,] and wisdom obtaineth his love.

The knowledge of the commandments of the Lord is the doctrine of life: and they that do things that please him shall receive the fruit of the tree of immortality.

The fear of the Lord is all wisdom; and in all wisdom is the performance of the law, and the knowledge of his omnipotency.

If a servant say to his master, I will not do as it pleaseth thee; though afterward he do it, he angereth him that nourisheth him.

The knowledge of wickedness is not wisdom, neither at any time the counsel of sinners prudence.

There is a wickedness, and the same an abomination: and there is a fool wanting in wisdom.

He that hath small understanding, and feareth God, is better than one that hath much wisdom, and transgresseth the law of the Most High.

There is an exquisite subtilty, and the same is unjust; and there is one that turneth aside to make judgment appear; and there is a wise man that justifieth in judgment.

There is a wicked man that hangeth down his head sadly; but inwardly he is full of deceit,

Casting down his countenance, and making as if he heard not: where he is not known, he will do thee a mischief before thou be aware.

And if for want of power he be hindered from sinning, yet when he findeth opportunity he will do evil.

A man may be known by his look, and one that hath understanding by his countenance, when thou meetest him.

A man's attire, and excessive laughter, and gait, shew what he is.

❧

There is a reproof that is not comely: again, some man holdeth his tongue, and he is wise.

It is much better to reprove, than to be angry secretly: and he that confesseth his fault shall be preserved from hurt.

How good is it, when thou art reproved, to shew repentance! for so shalt thou escape wilful sin.

As is the lust of a eunuch to deflower a virgin; so is he that executeth judgment with violence.

There is one that keepeth silence, and is found wise: and another by much babbling becometh hateful.

Some man holdeth his tongue, because he hath not to

answer: and some keepeth silence, knowing his time.

A wise man will hold his tongue till he see opportunity: but a babbler and a fool will regard no time.

He that useth many words shall be abhorred; and he that taketh to himself authority therein shall be hated.

There is a sinner that hath good success in evil things; and there is a gain that turneth to loss.

There is a gift that shall not profit thee; and there is a gift whose recompense is double.

There is an abasement because of glory; and there is that lifteth up his head from a low estate.

There is that buyeth much for a little, and repayeth it seven-fold.

A wise man by his words maketh himself beloved: but the graces of fools shall be poured out.

The gift of a fool shall do thee no good when thou hast it; neither yet of the envious for his necessity: for he looketh to receive many things for one.

He giveth little, and upbraideth much; he openeth his mouth like a crier; to-day he lendeth, and to-morrow will he ask it again: such a one is to be hated of God and man.

The fool saith, I have no friends, I have no thanks for all my good deeds, and they that eat my bread speak evil of me.

How oft, and of how many shall he be laughed to scorn! for he knoweth not aright what it is to have; and it is all one unto him as if he had it not.

To slip upon a pavement is better than to slip with the tongue: so the fall of the wicked shall come speedily.

An unseasonable tale will always be in the mouth of the unwise.

A wise sentence shall be rejected when it cometh out of a fool's mouth; for he will not speak it in due season.

There is that is hindered from sinning through want: and when he taketh rest, he shall not be troubled.

There is that destroyeth his own soul through bashfulness,

and by accepting of persons overthroweth himself.

There is that for bashfulness promiseth to his friend, and maketh him his enemy for nothing.

A lie is a foul blot in a man, yet it is continually in the mouth of the untaught.

A thief is better than a man that is accustomed to lie: but they both shall have destruction to heritage.

The disposition of a liar is dishonourable, and his shame is ever with him.

A wise man shall promote himself to honour with his words: and he that hath understanding will please great men.

He that tilleth his land shall increase his heap: and he that pleaseth great men shall get pardon for iniquity.

Presents and gifts blind the eyes of the wise, and stop up his mouth that he cannot reprove.

Wisdom that is hid, and treasure that is hoarded up, what profit is in them both?

Better is he that hideth his folly than a man that hideth his wisdom.

Necessary patience in seeking the Lord is better than he that leadeth his life without a guide.

❧

My son, hast thou sinned? do so no more, but ask pardon for thy former sins.

Flee from sin as from the face of a serpent: for if thou comest too near it, it will bite thee: the teeth thereof are as the teeth of a lion, slaying the souls of men.

All iniquity is as a two-edged sword, the wounds whereof cannot be healed.

To terrify and do wrong will waste riches: thus the house of proud men shall be made desolate.

A prayer out of a poor man's mouth reacheth to the ears of God, and his judgment cometh speedily.

He that hateth to be reproved is in the way of sinners: but

he that feareth the Lord will repent from his heart.

An eloquent man is known far and near; but a man of understanding knoweth when he slippeth.

He that buildeth his house with other men's money is like one that gathereth himself stones for the tomb of his burial.

The congregation of the wicked is like tow wrapped together: and the end of them is a flame of fire to destroy them.

The way of sinners is made plain with stones, but at the end thereof is the pit of hell.

He that keepeth the law of the Lord getteth the understanding thereof: and the perfection of the fear of the Lord is wisdom.

He that is not wise will not be taught: but there is a wisdom which multiplieth bitterness.

The knowledge of a wise man shall abound like a flood: and his counsel is like a pure fountain of life.

The inner parts of a fool are like a broken vessel, and he will hold no knowledge as long as he liveth.

If a skilful man hear a wise word, he will commend it, and add unto it: but as soon as one of no understanding heareth it, it displeaseth him, and he casteth it behind his back.

The talking of a fool is like a burden in the way: but grace shall be found in the lips of the wise.

They inquire at the mouth of the wise man in the congregation, and they shall ponder his words in their heart.

As is a house that is destroyed, so is wisdom to a fool: and the knowledge of the unwise is as talk without sense.

Doctrine unto fools is as fetters on the feet, and like manacles on the right hand.

A fool lifteth up his voice with laughter; but a wise man doth scarce smile a little.

Learning is unto a wise man as an ornament of gold, and like a bracelet upon his right arm.

A foolish man's foot is soon in his [neighbour's] house: but a man of experience is ashamed of him.

A fool will peep in at the door into the house: but he that is well nurtured will stand without.

It is the rudeness of a man to hearken at the door: but a wise man will be grieved with the disgrace.

The lips of talkers will be telling such things as pertain not unto them: but the words of such as have understanding are weighed in the balance.

The heart of fools is in their mouth: but the mouth of the wise is in their heart.

When the ungodly curseth Satan, he curseth his own soul.

A whisperer defileth his own soul, and is hated wheresoever he dwelleth.

❧

A slothful man is compared to a filthy stone, and every one will hiss him out to his disgrace.

A slothful man is compared to the filth of a dunghill: every man that takes it up will shake his hand.

An evil-nurtured son is the dishonour of his father that begat him: and a [foolish] daughter is born to his loss.

A wise daughter shall bring an inheritance to her husband: but she that liveth dishonestly is her father's heaviness.

She that is bold dishonoureth both her father and her husband, but they both shall despise her.

A tale out of season [is as] music in mourning: but stripes and correction of wisdom are never out of time.

Whoso teacheth a fool is as one that glueth a potsherd together, and as he that waketh one from a sound sleep.

He that telleth a tale to a fool speaketh to one in a slumber; when he hath told his tale, he will say, What is the matter?

If children live honestly, and have wherewithal, they shall cover the baseness of their parents.

But children, being haughty, through disdain and want of nurture do stain the nobility of their kindred.

Weep for the dead, for he hath lost the light: and weep for the fool, for he wanteth understanding: make little weeping for the dead, for he is at rest: but the life of the fool is worse than death.

Seven days do men mourn for him that is dead; but for a fool and an ungodly man all the days of his life.

Talk not much with a fool, and go not to him that hath no understanding: beware of him, lest thou have trouble, and thou shalt never be defiled with his fooleries: depart from him, and thou shalt find rest, and never be disquieted with madness.

What is heavier than lead? and what is the name thereof, but a fool?

Sand, and salt, and a mass of iron, is easier to bear than a man without understanding.

As timber girt and bound together in a building cannot be loosed with shaking; so the heart that is established by advised counsel shall fear at no time.

A heart settled upon a thought of understanding is as a fair plastering on the wall of a gallery.

Pales set on a high place will never stand against the wind: so a fearful heart in the imagination of a fool cannot stand against any fear.

He that pricketh the eye will make tears to fall: and he that pricketh the heart maketh it to shew her knowledge.

Whoso casteth a stone at the birds frayeth them away: and he that upbraideth his friend breaketh friendship.

Though thou drewest a sword at thy friend, yet despair not: for there may be a returning [to favour.]

If thou hast opened thy mouth against thy friend, fear not; for there may be a reconciliation: except for upbraiding, or pride, or disclosing of secrets, or a treacherous wound: for, for these things every friend will depart.

Be faithful to thy neighbour in his poverty, that thou mayest rejoice in his prosperity: abide steadfast unto him in the time of his trouble, that thou mayest be heir with him in his heritage: for a mean estate is not always to be contemned: nor the rich that is foolish to be had in admiration.

As the vapour and smoke of a furnace goeth before the fire; so reviling before blood.

I will not be ashamed to defend a friend; neither will I hide myself from him.

And if any evil happen unto me by him, every one that heareth it will beware of him.

Who shall set a watch before my mouth, and a seal of wisdom upon my lips, that I fall not suddenly by them, and that my tongue destroy me not?

O Lord, Father and Governor of all my whole life, leave me not to their counsels, and let me not fall by them.

Who will set scourges over my thoughts, and the discipline of wisdom over my heart? that they spare me not for mine ignorances, and it pass not by my sins:

Lest mine ignorances increase, and my sins abound to my destruction, and I fall before mine adversaries, and mine enemy rejoice over me, whose hope is far from thy mercy.

O Lord, Father and God of my life, give me not a proud look, but turn away from thy servants always a haughty mind.

Turn away from me vain hopes and concupiscence, and thou shalt hold him up that is desirous always to serve thee.

Let not the greediness of the belly nor the lust of the flesh take hold of me; and give not over me thy servant into an impudent mind.

Hear, O ye children, the discipline of the mouth: he that keepeth it shall never be taken in his lips.

The sinner shall be left in his foolishness: both the evil speaker and the proud shall fall thereby.

Accustom not thy mouth to swearing; neither thyself to the naming of the Holy One.

For as a servant that is continually beaten shall not be without a blue mark: so he that sweareth and nameth God continually shall not be faultless.

A man that useth much swearing shall be filled with iniquity, and the plague shall never depart from his house: if he shall offend, his sin shall be upon him: and if he acknowledge not his sin, he maketh a double offense: and if he swear in vain, he shall not be innocent, but his house shall be full of calamities.

There is a word that is clothed about with death: God grant that it be not found in the heritage of Jacob; for all such things shall be far from the godly, and they shall not wallow in their sins.

Use not thy mouth to intemperate swearing, for therein is the word of sin.

Remember thy father and thy mother, when thou sittest among great men. Be not forgetful before them, and so thou by thy custom become a fool, and wish that thou hadst not been born, and curse the day of thy nativity.

The man that is accustomed to opprobrious words will never be reformed all the days of his life.

Two sorts of men multiply sin, and the third will bring wrath: a hot mind is as a burning fire, it will never be quenched till it be consumed: a fornicator in the body of his flesh will never cease till he hath kindled a fire.

All bread is sweet to a whoremonger, he will not leave off till he die.

A man that breaketh wedlock, saying thus in his heart, Who seeth me? I am compassed about with darkness, the walls cover me, and nobody seeth me; what need I to fear? the Most High will not remember my sins:

Such a man only feareth the eyes of men, and knoweth not that the eyes of the Lord are ten thousand times brighter than the sun, beholding all the ways of men, and considering the most secret parts.

He knew all things ere ever they were created; so also after they were perfected he looked upon them all.

This man shall be punished in the streets of the city, and where he suspecteth not he shall be taken.

Thus shall it go also with the wife that leaveth her husband, and bringeth in an heir by another.

For first she hath disobeyed the law of the Most High; and secondly, she hath trespassed against her own husband; and thirdly, she hath played the whore in adultery, and brought children by another man.

She shall be brought out into the congregation, and inquisition shall be made of her children.

Her children shall not take root, and her branches shall bring forth no fruit.

She shall leave her memory to be cursed, and her reproach shall not be blotted out.

And they that remain shall know that there is nothing better than the fear of the Lord, and that there is nothing sweeter than to take heed unto the commandments of the Lord.

It is great glory to follow the Lord, and to be received of him is long life.

Wisdom shall praise herself, and shall glory in the midst of her people.

In the congregation of the Most High shall she open her mouth, and triumph before his power.

I came out of the mouth of the Most High, and covered the earth as a cloud.

I dwelt in high places, and my throne is in a cloudy pillar.

I alone compassed the circuit of heaven, and walked in the bottom of the deep.

In the waves of the sea, and in all the earth, and in every people and nation, I got a possession.

With all these I sought rest: and in whose inheritance shall I abide?

So the Creator of all things gave me a commandment, and he that made me caused my tabernacle to rest, and said, Let thy dwelling be in Jacob, and thine inheritance in Israel.

He created me from the beginning before the world, and I shall never fail.

In the holy tabernacle I served before him; and so was I established in Zion.

Likewise in the beloved city he gave me rest, and in Jerusalem was my power.

And I took root in an honourable people, even in the portion of the Lord's inheritance.

I was exalted like a cedar in Libanus, and as a cypress-tree upon the mountains of Hermon.

I was exalted like a palm-tree in Engaddi, and as a rose-plant in Jericho, as a fair olive-tree in a pleasant field, and grew up as a plane-tree by the water.

I gave a sweet smell like cinnamon and aspalathus, and I yielded a pleasant odour like the best myrrh, as galbanum, and onyx, and sweet storax, and as the fume of frankincense in the tabernacle.

As the turpentine-tree I stretched out my branches, and my branches are the branches of honour and grace.

As the vine brought I forth a pleasant savour, and my flowers are the fruit of honour and riches.

I am the mother of fair love, and fear, and knowledge, and holy hope: I therefore, being eternal, am given to all my children which are named of him.

Come unto me, all ye that be desirous of me, and fill yourselves with my fruits.

For my memorial is sweeter than honey, and mine inheritance than the honeycomb.

They that eat me shall yet be hungry, and they that drink me shall yet be thirsty.

He that obeyeth me shall never be confounded, and they that work by me shall not do amiss.

All these things are the book of the covenant of the most high God, even the law which Moses commanded for a heritage unto the congregations of Jacob.

Faint not to be strong in the Lord: that he may confirm you, cleave unto him: for the Lord Almighty is God alone, and besides him there is no other Saviour.

He filleth all things with his wisdom, as Phison and as Tigris in the time of the new fruits.

He maketh the understanding to abound like Euphrates, and as Jordan in the time of the harvest.

He maketh the doctrine of knowledge appear as the light, and as Geon in the time of vintage.

The first man knew her not perfectly: no more shall the last find her out.

For her thoughts are more than the sea, and her counsels profounder than the great deep.

I also came out as a brook from a river, and as a conduit into a garden.

I said, I will water my best garden, and will water abundantly my garden-bed: and lo, my brook became a river, and my river became a sea.

I will yet make doctrine to shine as the morning, and will send forth her light afar off.

I will yet pour out doctrine as prophecy, and leave it to all ages for ever.

Behold that I have not laboured for myself only, but for all them that seek wisdom.

❧

In three things I was beautified, and stood up beautiful both before God and men: the unity of brethren, the love of neighbours, a man and a wife that agree together.

Three sorts of men my soul hateth, and I am greatly offended at their life: a poor man that is proud, a rich man that is a liar, and an old adulterer that doteth.

If thou hast gathered nothing in thy youth, how canst thou find any thing in thine age?

O how comely a thing is judgment for gray hairs, and for ancient men to know counsel!

O how comely is the wisdom of old men, and understanding and counsel to men of honour!

Much experience is the crown of old men, and the fear of God is their glory.

There be nine things which I have judged in my heart to be happy, and the tenth I will utter with my tongue: A man that hath joy of his children; and he that liveth to see the fall of his enemy:

Well is him that dwelleth with a wife of understanding, and that hath not slipped with his tongue, and that hath not served a man more unworthy than himself:

Well is him that hath found prudence, and he that speaketh in the ears of them that will hear:

O how great is he that findeth wisdom! yet is there none above him that feareth the Lord.

But the love of the Lord passeth all things for illumination: he that holdeth it, whereto shall he be likened?

The fear of the Lord is the beginning of his love: and faith is the beginning of cleaving unto him.

[Give me] any plague, but the plague of the heart: and any wickedness, but the wickedness of a woman:

And any affliction, but the affliction from them that hate me: and any revenge, but the revenge of enemies.

There is no head above the head of a serpent; and there is no wrath above the wrath of an enemy.

I had rather dwell with a lion and a dragon, than to keep house with a wicked woman.

The wickedness of a woman changeth her face and darkeneth her countenance like sackcloth.

Her husband shall sit among his neighbours; and when he heareth it shall sigh bitterly.

All wickedness is but little to the wickedness of a woman: let the portion of a sinner fall upon her.

As the climbing of a sandy way is to the feet of the aged, so is a wife full of words to a quiet man.

Stumble not at the beauty of a woman, and desire her not for pleasure.

A woman, if she maintain her husband, is full of anger, impudence, and much reproach.

A wicked woman abateth the courage, maketh a heavy countenance and a wounded heart: a woman that will not comfort her husband in distress maketh weak hands and feeble knees.

Of the woman came the beginning of sin, and through her we all die.

Give the water no passage; neither a wicked woman liberty to gad abroad.

If she go not as thou wouldest have her, cut her off from thy flesh, and give her a bill of divorce, and let her go.

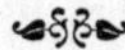

Blessed is the man that hath a virtuous wife, for the number of his days shall be double.

A virtuous woman rejoiceth her husband, and he shall fulfil the years of his life in peace.

A good wife is a good portion, which shall be given in the portion of them that fear the Lord.

Whether a man be rich or poor, if he have a good heart toward the Lord, he shall at all times rejoice with a cheerful countenance.

There be three things that my heart feareth; and for the fourth I was sore afraid: the slander of a city, and gathering together of an unruly multitude, and a false accusation: all these are worse than death.

But a grief of heart and sorrow is a woman that is jealous over another woman, and a scourge of the tongue which communicateth with all.

An evil wife is a yoke shaken to and fro; he that hath hold of her is as though he held a scorpion.

A drunken woman and a gadder abroad causeth great anger, and she will not cover her own shame.

The whoredom of a woman may be known in her haughty looks and eyelids.

If thy daughter be shameless, keep her in straitly, lest she abuse herself through overmuch liberty.

Watch over an impudent eye: and marvel not if she trespass against thee.

She will open her mouth as a thirsty traveller when he hath found a fountain, and drink of every water near her; by every hedge she will sit down, and open her quiver against every arrow.

The grace of a wife delighteth her husband, and her discretion will fatten his bones.

A silent and loving woman is a gift of the Lord; and there is nothing so much worth as a mind well instructed.

A shamefaced and a faithful woman is a double grace, and her continent mind cannot be valued.

As the sun when it ariseth in the high heaven; so is the beauty of a good wife in the ordering of her house.

As the clear light is upon the holy candlestick; so is the beauty of the face in ripe age.

As the golden pillars are upon the sockets of silver; so are the fair feet with a constant heart.

My son, keep the flower of thine age sound; and give not thy strength to strangers.

When thou hast gotten a fruitful possession through all the field, sow it with thine own seed, trusting in the goodness of thy stock.

So thy race which thou leavest shall be magnified, having the confidence of their good descent.

A harlot shall be accounted as spittle, but a married

woman is a tower against death to her husband.

A wicked woman is given as a portion to a wicked man: but a godly woman is given to him that feareth the Lord.

A dishonest woman contemneth shame: but an honest woman will reverence her husband.

A shameless woman shall be accounted as a dog; but she that is shamefaced will fear the Lord.

A woman that honoureth her husband shall be judged wise of all; but she that dishonoureth him in her pride shall be counted ungodly of all.

A loud crying woman and a scold shall be sought out to drive away the enemies.

There be two things that grieve my heart; and the third maketh me angry: a man of war that suffereth poverty; and men of understanding that are not set by; and one that returneth from righteousness to sin; the Lord prepareth such a one for the sword.

A merchant shall hardly keep himself from doing wrong: and a huckster shall not be freed from sin.

❧

Many have sinned for a small matter; and he that seeketh for abundance will turn his eyes away.

As a nail sticketh fast between the joinings of the stones; so doth sin stick close between buying and selling.

Unless a man hold himself diligently in the fear of the Lord, his house shall soon be overthrown.

As when one sifteth with a sieve, the refuse remaineth; so the filth of man in his talk.

The furnace proveth the potter's vessels; so the trial of man is in his reasoning.

The fruit declareth if the tree have been dressed; so is the utterance of a conceit in the heart of man.

Praise no man before thou hearest him speak; for this is the trial of men.

If thou followest righteousness, thou shalt obtain her, and put her on, as a glorious long robe.

The birds will resort unto their like; so will truth return unto them that practise in her.

As the lion lieth in wait for the prey; so sin for them that work iniquity.

The discourse of a godly man is always with wisdom; but a fool changeth as the moon.

If thou be among the indiscreet observe the time; but be continually among men of understanding.

The discourse of fools is irksome, and their sport is in the wantonness of sin.

The talk of him that sweareth much maketh the hair stand upright; and their brawls make one stop his ears.

The strife of the proud is blood-shedding, and their revilings are grievous to the ear.

Whoso discovereth secrets loseth his credit; and shall never find a friend to his mind.

Love thy friend, and be faithful unto him: but if thou betrayest his secrets, follow no more after him.

For as a man hath destroyed his enemy; so hast thou lost the love of thy neighbour.

As one that letteth a bird go out of his hand, so hast thou let thy neighbour go, and shalt not get him again.

Follow after him no more, for he is too far off; he is as a roe escaped out of the snare.

As for a wound, it may be bound up; and after reviling there may be reconcilement: but he that betrayeth secrets is without hope.

He that winketh with the eyes worketh evil: and he that knoweth him will depart from him.

When thou art present he will speak sweetly, and will admire thy words: but at the last he will writhe his mouth, and slander thy sayings.

I have hated many things, but nothing like him; for the

Lord will hate him.

Whoso casteth a stone on high casteth it on his own head; and a deceitful stroke shall make wounds.

Whoso diggeth a pit shall fall therein: and he that setteth a trap shall be taken therein.

He that worketh mischief, it shall fall upon him, and he shall not know whence it cometh.

Mockery and reproach are from the proud; but vengeance as a lion, shall lie in wait for them.

They that rejoice at the fall of the righteous shall be taken in the snare; and anguish shall consume them before they die.

Malice and wrath, even these are abominations; and the sinful man shall have them both.

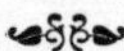

He that revengeth shall find vengeance from the Lord, and he will surely keep his sins [in remembrance.]

Forgive thy neighbour the hurt that he hath done unto thee, so shall thy sins also be forgiven when thou prayest.

One man beareth hatred against another, and doth he seek pardon from the Lord?

He sheweth no mercy to a man, which is like himself: and doth he ask forgiveness of his own sins?

If he that is but flesh nourish hatred, who will entreat for pardon of his sins?

Remember thy end and let enmity cease; [remember] corruption and death, and abide in the commandments.

Remember the commandments, and bear no malice to thy neighbour: [remember] the covenant of the Highest, and wink at ignorance.

Abstain from strife, and thou shalt diminish thy sins: for a furious man will kindle strife.

A sinful man disquieteth friends, and maketh debate among them that be at peace.

As the matter of the fire is, so it burneth: and as a man's

strength is, so is his wrath; and according to his riches his anger riseth; and the stronger they are which contend, the more they will be inflamed.

A hasty contention kindleth a fire: and a hasty fighting sheddeth blood.

If thou blow the spark, it shall burn: if thou spit on it, it shall be quenched: and both these come out of thy mouth.

Curse the whisperer and doubletongued: for such have destroyed many that were at peace.

A backbiting tongue hath disquieted many, and driven them from nation to nation: strong cities hath it pulled down, and overthrown the houses of great men.

A backbiting tongue hath cast out virtuous women, and deprived them of their labours.

Whoso hearkeneth unto it shall never find rest, and never dwell quietly.

The stroke of the whip maketh marks in the flesh: but the stroke of the tongue breaketh the bones.

Many have fallen by the edge of the sword: but not so many as have fallen by the tongue.

Well is he that is defended from it, and hath not passed through the venom thereof; who hath not drawn the yoke thereof, nor hath been bound in her hands.

For the yoke thereof is a yoke of iron, and the bands thereof are bands of brass.

The death thereof is an evil death, the grave were better than it.

It shall not have rule over them that fear God, neither shall they be burned with the flame thereof.

Such as forsake the Lord shall fall into it; and it shall burn in them, and not be quenched; it shall be sent upon them as a lion, and devour them as a leopard.

Look that thou hedge thy possession about with thorns, and bind up thy silver and gold:

And weigh thy words in a balance, and make a door and

bar for thy mouth.

Beware thou slide not by it, lest thou fall before him that lieth in wait.

❧

He that is merciful will lend unto his neighbour; and he that strengtheneth his hand keepeth the commandments.

Lend to thy neighbour in time of his need, and pay thou thy neighbour again in due season.

Keep thy word, and deal faithfully with him, and thou shalt always find the thing that is necessary for thee.

Many, when a thing was lent them, reckoned it to be found, and put them to trouble that helped them.

Till he hath received, he will kiss a man's hand; and for his neighbor's money he will speak submissly: but when he should repay, he will prolong the time, and return words of grief, and complain of the time.

If he prevail, he shall hardly receive the half, and he will count as if he had found it: if not, he hath deprived him of his money, and he hath gotten him an enemy without cause: he payeth him with cursings and railings; and for honour he will pay him disgrace.

Many therefore have refused to lend for other men's ill dealing, fearing to be defrauded.

Yet have thou patience with a man in poor estate, and delay not to shew him mercy.

Help the poor for the commandment's sake, and turn him not away because of his poverty.

Lose thy money for thy brother and thy friend, and let it not rust under a stone to be lost.

Lay up thy treasure according to the commandments of the Most High, and it shall bring thee more profit than gold.

Shut up alms in thy storehouses; and it shall deliver thee from all affliction.

It shall fight for thee against thine enemies better than a mighty shield and strong spear.

An honest man is surety for his neighbour: but he that is impudent will forsake him.

Forget not the friendship of thy surety, for he hath given his life for thee.

A sinner will overthrow the good estate of his surety:

And he that is of an unthankful mind will leave him [in danger] that delivered him.

Suretiship hath undone many of good estate, and shaken them as a wave of the sea: mighty men hath it driven from their houses, so that they wandered among strange nations.

A wicked man transgressing the commandments of the Lord shall fall into suretiship: and he that undertaketh and followeth other men's business for gain shall fall into suits.

Help thy neighbour according to thy power, and beware that thou thyself fall not into the same.

The chief thing for life is water, and bread, and clothing, and a house to cover shame.

Better is the life of a poor man in a mean cottage, than delicate fare in another man's house.

Be it little or much, hold thee contented, that thou hear not the reproach of thy house.

For it is a miserable life to go from house to house: for where thou art a stranger, thou darest not open thy mouth.

Thou shalt entertain, and feast, and have no thanks: moreover, thou shalt hear bitter words:

Come, thou stranger, and furnish a table, and feed me of that thou hast ready.

Give place, thou stranger, to an honourable man; my brother cometh to be lodged, and I have need of my house.

These things are grievous to a man of understanding; the upbraiding of houseroom, and reproaching of the lender.

❧

He that loveth his son causeth him oft to feel the rod, that he may have joy of him in the end.

He that chastiseth his son shall have joy in him, and shall rejoice in him among his acquaintance.

He that teacheth his son grieveth the enemy: and before his friends he shall rejoice of him.

Though his father die, yet he is as though he were not dead: for he hath left one behind him that is like himself.

While he lived, he saw and rejoiced in him: and when he died he was not sorrowful.

He left behind him an avenger against his enemies, and one that shall requite kindness to his friends.

He that maketh too much of his son shall bind up his wounds; and his bowels will be troubled at every cry.

A horse not broken becometh headstrong: and a child left to himself will be wilful.

Cocker thy child, and he shall make thee afraid: play with him, and he will bring thee to heaviness.

Laugh not with him, lest thou have sorrow with him, and lest thou gnash thy teeth in the end.

Give him no liberty in his youth, and wink not at his follies.

Bow down his neck while he is young, and beat him on the sides while he is a child, lest he wax stubborn, and be disobedient unto thee, and so bring sorrow to thy heart.

Chastise thy son, and hold him to labour, lest his lewd behaviour be an offence unto thee.

Better is the poor, being sound and strong of constitution, than a rich man that is afflicted in his body.

Health and good estate of body are above all gold, and a strong body above infinite wealth.

There is no riches above a sound body, and no joy above the joy of the heart.

Death is better than a bitter life or continual sickness.

Delicates poured upon a mouth shut up, are as messes of meat set upon a grave.

What good doeth the offering unto an idol? for neither can it eat nor smell: so is he that is persecuted of the Lord.

He seeth with his eyes and groaneth, as a eunuch that embraceth a virgin and sigheth.

Give not over thy mind to heaviness, and afflict not thyself in thine own counsel.

The gladness of the heart is the life of man, and the joyfulness of a man prolongeth his days.

Love thine own soul, and comfort thy heart, remove sorrow far from thee: for sorrow hath killed many, and there is no profit therein.

Envy and wrath shorten the life, and carefulness bringeth age before the time.

A cheerful and good heart will have a care of his meat and diet.

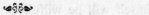

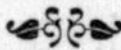

Watching for riches consumeth the flesh, and the care thereof driveth away sleep.

Watching care will not let a man slumber, as a sore disease breaketh sleep.

The rich hath great labour in gathering riches together; and when he resteth, he is filled with his delicates.

The poor laboureth in his poor estate; and when he leaveth off, he is still needy.

He that loveth gold shall not be justified, and he that followeth corruption shall have enough thereof.

Gold hath been the ruin of many, and their destruction was present.

It is a stumbling-block unto them that sacrifice unto it, and every fool shall be taken therewith.

Blessed is the rich that is found without blemish, and hath not gone after gold.

Who is he? and we will call him blessed: for wonderful things hath he done among his people.

Who hath been tried thereby, and found perfect? then let him glory. Who might offend, and hath not offended? or done evil, and hath not done it?

His goods shall be established, and the congregation shall declare his alms.

If thou sit at a bountiful table, be not greedy upon it, and say not, There is much meat on it.

Remember that a wicked eye is an evil thing: and what is created more wicked than an eye? therefore it weepeth upon every occasion.

Stretch not thy hand whithersoever it looketh, and thrust it not with him into the dish.

Judge of thy neighbour by thyself: and be discreet in every point.

Eat, as it becometh a man, those things which are set before thee; and devour not, lest thou be hated.

Leave off first for manner's sake; and be not unsatiable, lest thou offend.

When thou sittest among many, reach not thy hand out first of all.

A very little is sufficient for a man well nurtured, and he fetcheth not his wind short upon his bed.

Sound sleep cometh of moderate eating: he riseth early, and his wits are with him: but the pain of watching, and choler, and pangs of the belly, are with an unsatiable man.

And if thou hast been forced to eat, arise, go forth, vomit, and thou shalt have rest.

My son, hear me, and despise me not, and at the last thou shalt find as I told thee: in all thy works be quick, so shall there no sickness come unto thee.

Whoso is liberal of his meat, men shall speak well of him; and the report of his good house-keeping will be believed.

But against him that is a niggard of his meat the whole city shall murmur; and the testimonies of his niggardness shall not be doubted of.

Shew not thy valiantness in wine; for wine hath destroyed many.

The furnace proveth the edge by dipping: so doth wine the hearts of the proud by drunkenness.

Wine is as good as life to a man, if it be drunk moderately: what is life then to a man that is without wine? for it was made to make men glad.

Wine measurably drunk and in season, bringeth gladness of the heart, and cheerfulness of the mind:

But wine drunken with excess maketh bitterness of the mind, with brawling and quarrelling.

Drunkenness increaseth the rage of a fool till he offend: it diminisheth strength, and maketh wounds.

Rebuke not thy neighbour at the wine, and despise him not in his mirth: give him no despiteful words, and press not upon him with urging him [to drink.]

❧

If thou be made the master [of a feast,] lift not thyself up, but be among them as one of the rest, take diligent care for them, and hold yourself down.

And when thou hast done all thy office, take thy place that thou mayest be merry with them, and receive a crown for thy well-ordering of the feast.

Speak, thou art the elder, for it becometh thee, but with sound judgment; and hinder not music.

Pour not out words where there is a musician, and shew not forth wisdom out of time.

A concert of music in a banquet of wine is as a signet of carbuncle set in gold.

As a signet of an emerald set in a work of gold, so is the melody of music with pleasant wine.

Speak, young man, if there be need of thee: and yet scarcely when thou are twice asked.

Let thy speech be short, comprehending much in few words; be as one that knoweth and yet holdeth his tongue.

If thou be among great men, make not thyself equal with

them; and when ancient men are in place use not many words.

Before the thunder goeth lightning; and before a shamefaced man shall go favour.

Rise up betimes, and be not the last; but get thee home without delay.

There take thy pastime, and do what thou wilt: but sin not by proud speech.

And for these things bless him that made thee, and hath replenished thee with his good things.

Whoso feareth the Lord will receive his discipline; and they that seek him early shall find favour.

He that seeketh the law shall be filled therewith: but the hypocrite will be offended thereat.

They that fear the Lord shall find judgment, and shall kindle justice as a light.

A sinful man will not be reproved, but findeth an excuse according to his will.

A man of counsel will be considerate; but a strange and proud man is not daunted with fear, even when of himself he hath done without counsel.

Do nothing without advice; and when thou hast once done, repent not.

Go not in a way wherein thou mayest fall, and stumble not among the stones.

Be not confident in a plain way.

And beware of thy own children.

In every good work trust thy own soul; for this is the keeping of the commandments.

He that believeth in the Lord taketh heed to the commandment: and he that trusteth in him shall fare never the worse.

❧

There shall no evil happen unto him that feareth the Lord; but in temptation even again he will deliver him.

A wise man hateth not the law; but he that is a hypocrite therein is as a ship in a storm.

A man of understanding trusteth in the law; and the law is faithful unto him, as an oracle.

Prepare what to say, and so thou shalt be heard: and bind up instruction, and then make answer.

The heart of the foolish is like a cart-wheel; and his thoughts are like a rolling axle-tree.

A stallion horse is as a mocking friend, he neigheth under every one that sitteth upon him.

Why doth one day excel another, when as all the light of every day in the year is of the sun?

By the knowledge of the Lord they were distinguished: and he altered seasons and feasts.

Some of them hath he made high days, and hallowed them, and some of them hath he made ordinary days.

And all men are from the ground, and Adam was created of earth.

In much knowledge the Lord hath divided them, and made their ways diverse.

Some of them hath he blessed and exalted, and some of them hath he sanctified, and set near himself: but some of them hath he cursed and brought low, and turned out of their places.

As the clay is in the potter's hand, to fashion it at his pleasure; so man is in the hand of him that made him, to render to them as liketh him best.

Good is set against evil, and life against death: so is the godly against the sinner, and the sinner against the godly.

So look upon all the works of the Most High; and there are two and two, one against another.

I waked up last of all, as one that gathereth after the grape-gatherers: by the blessing of the Lord I profited, and filled my wine-press like a gatherer of grapes.

Consider that I laboured not for myself only, but for all

them that seek learning.

Hear me, O ye great men of the people, and hearken with your ears, ye rulers of the congregation.

Give not thy son and wife, thy brother and friend, power over thee while thou livest, and give not thy goods to another: lest it repent thee, and thou entreat for the same again.

As long as thou livest and hast breath in thee, give not thyself over to any.

For better it is that thy children should seek to thee, than that thou shouldest stand to thy courtesy.

In all thy works keep to thyself the pre-eminence; leave not a stain in thine honour.

At the time when thou shalt end thy days, and finish thy life, distribute thine inheritance.

Fodder, a wand, and burdens, are for the ass; and bread, correction, and work, for a servant.

If thou set thy servant to labour, thou shalt find rest: but if thou let him go idle, he shall seek liberty.

A yoke and a collar to bow the neck: so are tortures and torments for an evil servant.

Send him to labour, that he be not idle; for idleness teacheth much evil.

Set him to work, as is fit for him: if he be not obedient, put on more heavy fetters.

But be not excessive toward any; and without discretion do nothing.

If thou have a servant, let him be unto thee as thyself, because thou hast bought him with a price.

If thou have a servant, entreat him as a brother: for thou hast need of him, as of thine own soul: if thou entreat him evil, and he run from thee, which way wilt thou go to seek him?

The hopes of a man void of understanding are vain and false: and dreams lift up fools.

Whoso regardeth dreams is like him that catcheth at a shadow, and followeth after the wind.

The vision of dreams is the resemblance of one thing to another, even as the likeness of a face to a face.

Of an unclean thing what can be cleansed? and from that thing which is false what truth can come?

Divinations, and soothsayings, and dreams, are vain: and the heart fancieth, as a woman's heart in travail.

If they be not sent from the Most High in thy visitation, set not thy heart upon them.

For dreams have deceived many, and they have failed that put their trust in them.

The law shall be found perfect without lies: and wisdom is perfection to a faithful mouth.

A man that hath travelled knoweth many things; and he that hath much experience will declare wisdom.

He that hath no experience knoweth little: but he that hath travelled is full of prudence.

When I travelled, I saw many things; and I understood more than I can express.

I was oft-times in danger of death: yet I was delivered because of these things.

The spirit of those that fear the Lord shall live; for their hope is in him that saveth them.

Whoso feareth the Lord shall not fear nor be afraid; for he is his hope.

Blessed is the soul of him that feareth the Lord: to whom doth he look? and who is his strength?

For the eyes of the Lord are upon them that love him, he is their mighty protection and strong stay, a defense from heat, and a cover from the sun at noon, a preservative from stumbling, and a help from falling.

He raiseth up the soul, and lighteneth the eyes: he giveth

health, life, and blessing.

He that sacrificeth of a thing wrongfully gotten, his offering is ridiculous; and the gifts of unjust men are not accepted.

The Most High is not pleased with the offerings of the wicked; neither is he pacified for sin by the multitude of sacrifices.

Whoso bringeth an offering of the goods of the poor, doeth as one that killeth the son before his father's eyes.

The bread of the needy is their life: he that defraudeth him therefore is a man of blood.

He that taketh away his neighbour's living slayeth him; and he that defraudeth the labourer of his hire is a bloodshedder.

When one buildeth, and another pulleth down, what profit have they then but labour?

When one prayeth, and another curseth, whose voice will the Lord hear?

He that washeth himself after the touching of a dead body, if he touch it again, what availeth his washing?

So it is with a man that fasteth for his sins, and goeth again, and doeth the same: who will hear his prayer? or what doth his humbling profit him?

⁂

He that keepeth the law bringeth offerings enough: he that taketh heed to the commandment offereth a peace-offering.

He that requiteth a good turn offereth fine flour; and he that giveth alms sacrificeth praise.

To depart from wickedness is a thing pleasing to the Lord; and to forsake unrighteousness is a propitiation.

Thou shalt not appear empty before the Lord.

For all these things [are to be done] because of the commandment.

The offering of the righteous maketh the altar fat, and the

sweet savour thereof is before the Most High.

The sacrifice of a just man is acceptable, and the memorial thereof shall never be forgotten.

Give the Lord his honour with a good eye, and diminish not the first-fruits of thy hands.

In all thy gifts shew a cheerful countenance, and dedicate thy tithes with gladness.

Give unto the Most High according as he hath enriched thee; and as thou hast gotten, give with a cheerful eye.

For the Lord recompenseth, and will give thee seven times as much.

Do not think to corrupt with gifts; for such he will not receive: and trust not to unrighteous sacrifices; for the Lord is judge, and with him is no respect of persons.

He will not accept any person against a poor man, but will hear the prayer of the oppressed.

He will not despise the supplication of the fatherless; nor the widow, when she poureth out her complaint.

Do not the tears run down the widow's cheeks? and is not her cry against him that causeth them to fall?

He that serveth the Lord shall be accepted with favour, and his prayer shall reach unto the clouds.

The prayer of the humble pierceth the clouds: and till it come nigh, he will not be comforted; and will not depart, till the Most High shall behold to judge righteously, and execute judgment.

For the Lord will not be slack, neither will the Mighty be patient toward them till he have smitten in sunder the loins of the unmerciful, and repaid vengeance to the heathen; till he have taken away the multitude of the proud, and broken the sceptre of the unrighteous;

Till he have rendered to every man according to his deeds, and to the works of men according to their devices; till he have judged the cause of his people, and made them to rejoice in his mercy.

Mercy is seasonable in the time of affliction, as clouds of rain in time of drought.

❧

Have mercy upon us, O Lord God of all, and behold us:

And send thy fear upon all the nations that seek not after thee.

Lift up thy hand against the strange nations, and let them see thy power.

As thou wast sanctified in us before them: so be thou magnified among them before us.

And let them know thee, as we have known thee, that there is no God but only thou, O God.

Shew new signs, and make other strange wonders: glorify thy hand and thy right arm, that they may set forth thy wondrous works.

Raise up indignation, and pour out wrath: take away the adversary, and destroy the enemy.

Make the time short, remember the covenant, and let them declare thy wonderful works.

Let him that escapeth be consumed by the rage of the fire; and let them perish that oppress the people.

Smite in sunder the heads of the rulers of the heathen, that say, There is none other but we.

Gather all the tribes of Jacob together, and inherit thou them, as from the beginning.

O Lord, have mercy upon the people that is called by thy name, and upon Israel, whom thou hast named thy first-born.

O be merciful unto Jerusalem, thy holy city, the place of thy rest.

Fill Zion with thine unspeakable oracles, and thy people with thy glory.

Give testimony unto those that thou hast possessed from the beginning, and raise up prophets that have been in thy name.

Reward them that wait for thee, and let thy prophets be found faithful.

O Lord, hear the prayer of thy servants, according to the blessings of Aaron over thy people, that all they which dwell upon the earth may know that thou art the Lord, the eternal God.

The belly devoureth all meats, yet is one meat better than another.

As the palate tasteth divers kinds of venison: so doth a heart of understanding false speeches.

A froward heart causeth heaviness: but a man of experience will recompense him.

A woman will receive every man, yet is one daughter better than another.

The beauty of a woman cheereth the countenance, and a man loveth nothing better.

If there be kindness, meekness, and comfort in her tongue, then is not her husband like other men.

He that getteth a wife, beginneth a possession, a help like unto himself, and a pillar of rest.

Where no hedge is, there the possession is spoiled: and he that hath no wife will wander up and down mourning.

Who will trust a thief well appointed, that skippeth from city to city? so [who will believe] a man that hath no house, and lodgeth wheresoever the night taketh him?

❧

Every friend saith, I am his friend also, but there is a friend which is only a friend in name.

Is it not a grief unto death, when a companion and friend is turned to an enemy?

O wicked imagination, whence camest thou in to cover the earth with deceit?

There is a companion, which rejoiceth in the prosperity

of a friend, but in the time of trouble will be against him.

There is a companion, which helpeth his friend for the belly, and taketh up the buckler against the enemy.

Forget not thy friend in thy mind, and be not unmindful of him in thy riches.

Every counsellor extolleth counsel; but there is some that counselleth for himself.

Beware of a counsellor, and know before what need he hath; for he will counsel for himself; lest he cast the lot upon thee.

And say unto thee, Thy way is good: and afterward he stand on the other side, to see what shall befall thee.

Consult not with one that suspecteth thee: and hide thy counsel from such as envy thee.

Neither consult with a woman touching her of whom she is jealous; neither with a coward in matters of war; nor with a merchant concerning exchange; nor with a buyer of selling; nor with an envious man of thankfulness; nor with an unmerciful man touching kindness; nor with the slothful for any work; nor with a hireling for a year of finishing work; nor with an idle servant of much business: hearken not unto these in any matter of counsel.

But be continually with a godly man, whom thou knowest to keep the commandments of the Lord, whose mind is according to thy mind, and will sorrow with thee, if thou shalt miscarry.

And let the counsel of thine own heart stand: for there is no man more faithful unto thee than it.

For a man's mind is sometime wont to tell him more than seven watchmen, that sit above in a high tower.

And above all this pray to the Most High, that he will direct thy way in truth.

Let reason go before every enterprise, and counsel before every action.

The countenance is a sign of changing of the heart.

Four manner of things appear: good and evil, life and death: but the tongue ruleth over them continually.

There is one that is wise and teacheth many, and yet is unprofitable to himself.

There is one that sheweth wisdom in words, and is hated: he shall be destitute of all food.

For grace is not given him from the Lord; because he is deprived of all wisdom.

Another is wise to himself; and the fruits of understanding are commendable in his mouth.

A wise man instructeth his people; and the fruits of his understanding fail not.

A wise man shall be filled with blessing; and all they that see him shall count him happy.

The days of the life of man may be numbered: but the days of Israel are innumerable.

A wise man shall inherit glory among his people, and his name shall be perpetual.

My son, prove thy soul in thy life, and see what is evil for it, and give not that unto it.

For all things are not profitable for all men, neither hath every soul pleasure in every thing.

Be not unsatiable in any dainty thing, nor too greedy upon meats.

For excess of meats bringeth sickness, and surfeiting will turn into choler.

By surfeiting have many perished; but he that taketh heed prolongeth his life.

❧

Honour a physician with the honour due unto him for the uses which ye may have of him: for the Lord hath created him.

For of the Most High cometh healing, and he shall receive honour of the king.

The skill of the physician shall lift up his head: and in the sight of great men he shall be in admiration.

The Lord hath created medicines out of the earth; and he that is wise will not abhor them.

Was not the water made sweet with wood, that the virtue thereof might be known?

And he hath given men skill, that he might be honoured in his marvellous works.

With such doth he heal [men,] and taketh away their pains.

Of such doth the apothecary make a confection; and of his works there is no end; and from him is peace over all the earth.

My son, in thy sickness be not negligent: but pray unto the Lord, and he will make thee whole.

Leave off from sin, and order thy hands aright, and cleanse thy heart from all wickedness.

Give a sweet savour, and a memorial of fine flour; and make a fat offering, as not being.

Then give place to the physician, for the Lord hath created him: let him not go from thee, for thou hast need of him.

There is a time when in their hands there is good success.

For they shall also pray unto the Lord, that he would prosper that which they give for ease and remedy to prolong life.

He that sinneth before his Maker, let him fall into the hand of the physician.

My son, let tears fall down over the dead, and begin to lament, as if thou hadst suffered great harm thyself; and then cover his body according to the custom, and neglect not his burial.

Weep bitterly, and make great moan, and use lamentation, as he is worthy, and that a day or two, lest thou be evil spoken of: and then comfort thyself for thy heaviness.

For of heaviness cometh death, and the heaviness of the heart breaketh strength.

In affliction also sorrow remaineth: and the life of the poor is the curse of the heart.

Take no heaviness to heart: drive it away, and remember the last end.

Forget it not, for there is no turning again: thou shalt not do him good, but hurt thyself.

Remember my judgment: for thine also shall be so; yesterday for me, and to-day for thee.

When the dead is at rest, let his remembrance rest; and be comforted for him, when his spirit is departed from him.

The wisdom of a learned man cometh by opportunity of leisure: and he that hath little business shall become wise.

How can he get wisdom that holdeth the plough, and that glorieth in the goad, that driveth oxen, and is occupied in their labours, and whose talk is of bullocks?

He giveth his mind to make furrows; and is diligent to give the kine fodder.

So every carpenter and workmaster, that laboureth night and day: and they that cut and grave seals, and are diligent to make great variety, and give themselves to counterfeit imagery, and watch to finish a work:

The smith also sitting by the anvil, and considering the iron work, the vapour of the fire wasteth his flesh, and he fighteth with the heat of the furnace: the noise of the hammer and the anvil is ever in his ears, and his eyes look still upon the pattern of the thing that he maketh; he setteth his mind to finish his work, and watcheth to polish it perfectly:

So doth the potter sitting at his work, and turning the wheel about with his feet, who is always carefully set at his work, and maketh all his work by number;

He fashioneth the clay with his arm, and boweth down his strength before his feet; he applieth himself to lead it over; and he is diligent to make clean the furnace.

All these trust to their hands: and every one is wise in his work.

Without these cannot a city be inhabited: and they shall not dwell where they will, nor go up and down:

They shall not be sought for in public council, nor sit high in the congregation: they shall not sit on the judges' seat, nor understand the sentence of judgment: they cannot declare justice and judgment; and they shall not be found where parables are spoken.

But they will maintain the state of the world, and [all] their desire is in the work of their craft.

❧

But he that giveth his mind to the law of the Most High, and is occupied in the meditation thereof, will seek out the wisdom of all the ancient, and be occupied in prophecies.

He will keep the sayings of the renowned men: and where subtil parables are, he will be there also.

He will seek out the secrets of grave sentences, and be conversant in dark parables.

He shall serve among great men, and appear before princes; he will travel through strange countries; for he hath tried the good and the evil among men.

He will give his heart to resort early to the Lord that made him, and will pray before the Most High, and will open his mouth in prayer, and make supplication for his sins.

When the great Lord will, he shall be filled with the spirit of understanding: he shall pour out wise sentences, and give thanks unto the Lord in his prayer.

He shall direct his counsel and knowledge, and in his secrets shall he meditate.

He shall shew forth that which he hath learned, and shall glory in the law of the covenant of the Lord.

Many shall commend his understanding; and so long as the world endureth it shall not be blotted out; his memorial shall not depart away, and his name shall live from generation to generation.

Nations shall show forth his wisdom, and the congregation shall declare his praise.

If he die, he shall leave a greater name than a thousand: and if he live, he shall increase it.

Yet have I more to say, which I have thought upon; for I am filled as the moon at the full.

Hearken unto me ye holy children, and bud forth as a rose growing by the brook of the field.

And give ye a sweet savour as frankincense, and flourish as a lily, send forth a smell, and sing a song of praise, bless the Lord in all his works.

Magnify his name, and shew forth his praise with the songs of your lips, and with harps, and in praising him ye shall say after this manner:

All the works of the Lord are exceeding good, and whatsoever he commandeth shall be accomplished in due season.

And none may say, What is this? wherefore is that? for a time convenient they shall all be sought out: at his commandment the waters stood as a heap, and at the words of his mouth the receptacles of waters.

At his commandment is done whatsoever pleaseth him; and none can hinder when he will save.

The works of all flesh are before him, and nothing can be hid from his eyes.

He seeth from everlasting to everlasting; and there is nothing wonderful before him.

A man need not to say, What is this? wherefore is that? for he hath made all things for their uses.

His blessing covered the dry land as a river, and watered it as a flood.

As he hath turned the waters into saltness: so shall the heathen inherit his wrath.

As his ways are plain unto the holy; so are they stumblingblocks unto the wicked.

For the good are good things created from the beginning:

so evil things for sinners.

The principal things for the whole use of man's life are water, fire, iron, and salt, flour of wheat, honey, milk, and the blood of the grape and oil and clothing.

All these things are for good to the godly: so to the sinners they are turned into evil.

There be spirits that are created for vengeance which in their fury lay on sore strokes; in the time of destruction they pour out their force, and appease the wrath of him that made them.

Fire, and hail, and famine, and death, all these were created for vengeance;

Teeth of wild beasts, and scorpions, serpents, and the sword, punishing the wicked to destruction.

They shall rejoice in this commandment, and they shall be ready upon earth, when need is; and when their time is come, they shall not transgress his word.

Therefore from the beginning I was resolved, and thought upon these things, and have left them in writing.

All the works of the Lord are good: and he will give every needful thing in due season.

So that a man cannot say, This is worse than that: for in time they shall all be well approved.

And therefore praise ye the Lord with the whole heart and mouth, and bless the name of the Lord.

❧

Great travail is created for every man, and a heavy yoke is upon the sons of Adam, from the day that they go out of their mother's womb, till the day that they return to the mother of all things.

Their imagination of things to come, and the day of death, [trouble] their thoughts, and [cause] fear of heart;

From him that sitteth on a throne of glory, unto him that is humbled in earth and ashes;

From him that weareth purple and a crown, unto him that is clothed with a linen frock.

Wrath, and envy, trouble, and unquietness, fear of death, and anger, and strife, and in the time of rest upon his bed, his night-sleep, to change his knowledge.

A little or nothing is his rest, and afterward he is in his sleep, as in a day of keeping watch, troubled in the vision of his heart, as if he were escaped out of a battle.

When all is safe, he awaketh, and marvelleth that the fear was nothing.

[Such things happen] unto all flesh, both man and beast, and that is seven-fold more upon sinners.

Death, and bloodshed, strife, and sword, calamities, famine, tribulation, and the scourge;

These things are created for the wicked and for their sakes came the flood.

All things that are of the earth shall turn to the earth again: and that which is of the waters doth return into the sea.

All bribery and injustice shall be blotted out: but true dealing shall endure for ever.

The goods of the unjust shall be dried up like a river, and shall vanish with noise, like a great thunder in rain.

While he openeth his hand he shall rejoice: so shall transgressors come to nought.

The children of the ungodly shall not bring forth many branches: but are as unclean roots upon a hard rock.

The weed growing upon every water and bank of a river, shall be pulled up before all grass.

Bountifulness is as a most fruitful garden, and mercifulness endureth for ever.

To labour, and to be content with that a man hath, is a sweet life: but he that findeth a treasure is above them both.

Children and the building of a city continue a man's name: but a blameless wife is counted above them both.

Wine and music rejoice the heart: but the love of wisdom

is above them both.

The pipe and the psaltery make sweet melody: but a pleasant tongue is above them both.

Thine eye desireth favour and beauty: but more than both, corn while it is green.

A friend and companion never meet amiss: but above both is a wife with her husband.

Brethren and help are against time of trouble: but alms shall deliver more than them both.

Gold and silver make the foot stand sure: but counsel is esteemed above them both.

Riches and strength lift up the heart: but the fear of the Lord is above them both: there is no want in the fear of the Lord, and it needeth not to seek help.

The fear of the Lord is a fruitful garden, and covereth him above all glory.

My son, lead not a beggar's life; for better it is to die than to beg.

The life of him that dependeth on another man's table is not to be counted for a life; for he polluteth himself with other men's meat: but a wise man well nurtured will beware thereof.

Begging is sweet in the mouth of the shameless: but in his belly there shall burn a fire.

❧

O death, how bitter is the remembrance of thee to a man that liveth at rest in his possessions, unto the man that hath nothing to vex him, and that hath prosperity in all things: yea, unto him that is yet able to receive meat!

O death, acceptable is thy sentence unto the needy, and unto him whose strength faileth, that is now in the last age, and is vexed with all things, and to him that despaireth, and hath lost patience!

Fear not the sentence of death, remember them that have

been before thee, and that come after; for this is the sentence of the Lord over all flesh.

And why art thou against the pleasure of the Most High? there is no inquisition in the grave, whether thou have lived ten, or a hundred, or a thousand years.

The children of sinners are abominable children, and they that are conversant in the dwelling of the ungodly.

The inheritance of sinners' children shall perish, and their posterity shall have a perpetual reproach.

The children will complain of an ungodly father, because they shall be reproached for his sake.

Wo be unto you, ungodly men, which have forsaken the law of the most high God! for if ye increase it shall be to your destruction:

And if ye be born, ye shall be born to a curse: and if ye die, a curse shall be your portion.

All that are of the earth shall turn to earth again: so the ungodly shall go from a curse to destruction.

The mourning of men is about their bodies: but an ill name of sinners shall be blotted out.

Have regard to thy name; for that shall continue with thee above a thousand great treasures of gold.

A good life hath but few days: but a good name endureth for ever.

My children keep discipline in peace: for wisdom that is hid, and a treasure that is not seen, what profit is in them both?

A man that hideth his foolishness is better than a man that hideth his wisdom.

Therefore be shamefaced according to my word: for it is not good to retain all shamefacedness; neither is it altogether approved in every thing.

Be ashamed of whoredom before father and mother: and of a lie before a prince and a mighty man;

Of an offense before a judge and ruler; of iniquity before

a congregation and people; of unjust dealing before thy partner and friend;

And of theft in regard of the place where thou sojournest, and in regard of the truth of God and his covenant; and to lean with thine elbow upon the meat; and of scorning to give and take.

And of silence before them that salute thee; and to look upon a harlot;

And to turn away thy face from thy kinsman; or to take away a portion or a gift; or to gaze upon another man's wife;

Or to be over-busy with his maid, and come not near her bed; or of upbraiding speeches before friends; and after thou hast given, upbraid not;

Or of iterating and speaking again that which thou hast heard, and of revealing of secrets.

So shalt thou be truly shamefaced, and find favour before all men.

⁂

Of these things be not ashamed, and accept no person to sin thereby:

Of the law of the Most High, and his covenant and of judgment to justify the ungodly;

Of reckoning with thy partners and travellers; or of the gift of the heritage of friends;

Of exactness of balance and weights; or of getting much or little;

And of merchants' indifferent selling; of much correction of children; and to make the side of an evil servant to bleed. Sure keeping is good, where an evil wife is; and shut up, where many hands are.

Deliver all things in number and weight; and put all in writing that thou givest out, or receivest in.

Be not ashamed to inform the unwise and foolish, and the extreme aged that contendeth with those that are young:

thus shalt thou be truly learned, and approved of all men living.

The father waketh for the daughter, when no man knoweth; and the care for her taketh away sleep: when she is young, lest she pass away the flower of her age; and being married, lest she should be hated.

In her virginity, lest she should be defiled and gotten with child in her father's house; and having a husband, lest she should misbehave herself; and when she is married, lest she should be barren.

Keep a sure watch over a shameless daughter, lest she make thee a laughing-stock to thine enemies, and a byword in the city, and a reproach among the people, and make thee ashamed before the multitude.

Behold not every body's beauty, and sit not in the midst of women.

For from garments cometh a moth, and from women wickedness.

Better is the churlishness of a man than a courteous woman, a woman, I say, which bringeth shame and reproach.

I will now remember the works of the Lord, and declare the things that I have seen: In the words of the Lord are his works.

The sun that giveth light looketh upon all things, and the work thereof is full of the glory of the Lord.

The Lord hath not given power to the saints to declare all his marvellous works, which the Almighty Lord firmly settled, that whatsoever is, might be established for his glory.

He seeketh out the deep, and the heart, and considereth their crafty devices: for the Lord knoweth all that may be known, and he beholdeth the signs of the world.

He declareth the things that are past, and for to come, and revealeth the steps of hidden things.

No thought escapeth him, neither any word is hidden from him.

He hath garnished the excellent works of his wisdom, and he is from everlasting to everlasting: unto him may nothing be added, neither can he be diminished, and he hath no need of any counsellor.

O how desirable are all his works! and that a man may see even to a spark.

All these things live and remain for ever for all uses, and they are all obedient.

All things are double one against another: and he hath made nothing imperfect.

One thing establisheth the good of another: and who shall be filled with beholding his glory?

❧

The pride of the height, the clear firmament, the beauty of heaven, with his glorious shew;

The sun when it appeareth, declaring at his rising a marvellous instrument, the work of the Most High:

At noon it parcheth the country, and who can abide the burning heat thereof?

A man blowing a furnace is in works of heat, but the sun burneth the mountains three times more; breathing out fiery vapours, and sending forth bright beams, it dimmeth the eyes.

Great is the Lord that made it; and at his commandment it runneth hastily.

He made the moon also to serve in her season for a declaration of times, and a sign of the world.

From the moon is the sign of feasts, a light that decreaseth in her perfection.

The month is called after her name, increasing wonderfully in her changing, being an instrument of the armies above, shining in the firmament of heaven.

The beauty of heaven, the glory of the stars, an ornament giving light in the highest places of the Lord.

At the commandment of the Holy One they will stand in

their order, and never faint in their watches.

Look upon the rainbow, and praise him that made it; very beautiful it is in the brightness thereof.

It compasseth the heaven about with a glorious circle, and the hands of the Most High have bended it.

By his commandment he maketh the snow to fall apace, and sendeth swiftly the lightnings of his judgment.

Through this the treasures are opened: and clouds fly forth as fowls.

By his great power he maketh the clouds firm, and the hailstones are broken small.

At his sight the mountains are shaken, and at his will the south wind bloweth.

The noise of the thunder maketh the earth to tremble: so doth the northern storm and the whirlwind: as birds flying he scattereth the snow, and the falling down thereof is as the lighting of grasshoppers:

The eye marvelleth at the beauty of the whiteness thereof, and the heart is astonished at the raining of it.

The hoar-frost also as salt he poureth on the earth, and being congealed, it lieth on the top of sharp stakes.

When the cold north wind bloweth, and the water is congealed into ice, it abideth upon every gathering together of water, and clotheth the water as with a breastplate.

It devoureth the mountains, and burneth the wilderness, and consumeth the grass as fire.

A present remedy of all is a mist coming speedily: a dew coming after heat, refresheth.

By his counsel he appeaseth the deep, and planteth islands therein.

They that sail on the sea, tell of the danger thereof; and when we hear it with our ears, we marvel thereat.

For therein be strange and wondrous works, variety of all kinds of beasts and whales created.

By him the end of them hath prosperous success, and by

his word all things consist.

We may speak much, and yet come short: wherefore in sum, he is all.

How shall we be able to magnify him? for he is great above all his works.

The Lord is terrible and very great, and marvellous in his power.

When ye glorify the Lord, exalt him as much as ye can; for even yet will he far exceed: and when ye exalt him, put forth all your strength, and be not weary; for ye can never go far enough.

Who hath seen him that he might tell us? and who can magnify him as he is?

There are yet hid greater things than these be, for we have seen but a few of his works.

For the Lord hath made all things; and to the godly hath he given wisdom.

❧

I will thank thee, O Lord and King, and praise thee, O God my Saviour: I do give praise unto thy name:

For thou art my defender and helper, and hast preserved my body from destruction, and from the snare of the slanderous tongue, and from the lips that forge lies, and hast been my helper against mine adversaries:

And hast delivered me, according to the multitude of thy mercies and greatness of thy name, from the teeth of them that were ready to devour me, and out of the hands of such as sought after my life, and from the manifold afflictions which I had;

From the choking of fire on every side, and from the midst of the fire which I kindled not;

From the depth of the belly of hell, from an unclean tongue, and from lying words.

By an accusation to the king from an unrighteous tongue,

my soul drew near even unto death, my life was near to the hell beneath.

They compassed me on every side, and there was no man to help me: I looked for the succour of men, but there was none.

Then thought I upon thy mercy, O Lord, and upon thine acts of old, how thou deliverest such as wait for thee, and savest them out of the hands of the enemies.

Then lifted I up my supplication from the earth, and prayed for deliverance from death.

I called upon the Lord, the Father of my Lord, that he would not leave me in the days of my trouble, and in the time of the proud, when there was no help.

I will praise thy name continually, and will sing praise with thanksgiving; and so my prayer was heard:

For thou savedst me from destruction, and deliveredst me from the evil time: therefore will I give thanks, and praise thee, and bless thy name, O Lord.

When I was yet young, or ever I went abroad, I desired wisdom openly in my prayer.

I prayed for her before the temple, and will seek her out even to the end.

Even from the flower till the grape was ripe, hath my heart delighted in her: my foot went the right way, from my youth up sought I after her.

I bowed down mine ear a little, and received her, and gat much learning.

I profited therein, therefore will I ascribe the glory unto him that giveth me wisdom.

For I purposed to do after her, and earnestly I followed that which is good; so shall I not be confounded.

My soul hath wrestled with her, and in my doings I was exact: I stretched forth my hands to the heaven above, and bewailed my ignorances of her.

I directed my soul unto her, and I found her in pureness:

I have had my heart joined with her from the beginning, therefore shall I not be forsaken.

My heart was troubled in seeking her: therefore have I gotten a good possession.

The Lord hath given me a tongue for my reward, and I will praise him therewith.

Draw near unto me, ye unlearned, and dwell in the house of learning.

Wherefore are ye slow, and what say ye of these things, seeing your souls are very thirsty?

I opened my mouth, and said Buy her for yourselves without money.

Put your neck under the yoke, and let your soul receive instruction: she is hard at hand to find.

Behold with your eyes, how that I have had but little labour, and have gotten unto me much rest.

Get learning with a great sum of money, and get much gold by her.

Let your soul rejoice in his mercy, and be not ashamed of his praise.

Work your work betimes, and in his time he will give you your reward.

The Love Songs of King Solomon

THE SONG OF SONGS, which is Solomon's.

Let him kiss me with the kisses of his mouth: for thy love is better than wine.

Because of the savour of thy good ointments thy name is as ointment poured forth, therefore do the virgins love thee.

Draw me, we will run after thee: the king hath brought me into his chambers: we will be glad and rejoice in thee, we will remember thy love more than wine: the upright love thee.

I am black, but comely, O ye daughters of Jerusalem, as the tents of Kedar, as the curtains of Solomon.

Look not upon me, because I am black, because the sun hath looked upon me: my mother's children were angry with me; they made me the keeper of the vineyards; but mine own vineyard have I not kept.

Tell me, O thou whom my soul loveth, where thou feedest, where thou makest thy flock to rest at noon: for why should I be as one that turneth aside by the flocks of thy companions?

If thou know not, O thou fairest among women, go thy way forth by the footsteps of the flock, and feed thy kids beside the shepherds' tents.

I have compared thee, O my love, to a company of horses in Pharaoh's chariots.

Thy cheeks are comely with rows of jewels, thy neck with chains of gold.

We will make thee borders of gold with studs of silver.

While the king sitteth at his table, my spikenard sendeth forth the smell thereof.

A bundle of myrrh is my wellbeloved unto me; he shall lie all night betwixt my breasts.

My beloved is unto me as a cluster of camphire in the vineyards of Engedi.

Behold, thou art fair, my love; behold, thou art fair; thou hast doves' eyes.

Behold, thou art fair, my beloved, yea pleasant: also our bed is green.

The beams of our house are cedar, and our rafters of fir.

❧

I am the rose of Sharon, and the lily of the valleys.

As the lily among thorns, so is my love among the daughters.

As the apple tree among the trees of the wood, so is my beloved among the sons. I sat down under his shadow with great delight, and his fruit was sweet to my taste.

He brought me to the banqueting house, and his banner over me was love.

Stay me with flagons, comfort me with apples: for I am sick of love.

His left hand is under my head and his right hand doth embrace me.

I charge you, O ye daughters of Jerusalem, by the roes, and by the hinds of the field, that ye stir not up, nor awake my love, till he please.

The voice of my beloved! Behold, he cometh leaping upon the mountains, skipping upon the hills.

My beloved is like a roe or a young hart: behold, he standeth behind our wall, he looketh forth at the windows, shewing himself through the lattice.

My beloved spake, and said unto me: Rise up, my love, my fair one, and come away.

For, lo, the winter is past, the rain is over and gone;

The flowers appear on the earth; the time of the singing of

birds is come, and the voice of the turtle is heard in our land;

The fig tree putteth forth her green figs, and the vines with the tender grape give a good smell. Arise, my love, my fair one, and come away.

O my dove, that art in the clefts of the rock, in the secret places of the stairs, let me see thy countenance, let me hear thy voice; for sweet is thy voice, and thy countenance is comely.

Take us the foxes, the little foxes, that spoil the vines: for our vines have tender grapes.

My beloved is mine, and I am his: he feedeth among the lilies.

Until the day break, and the shadows flee away, turn, my beloved, and be thou like a roe or a young hart upon the mountains of Bether.

❧

By night on my bed I sought him whom my soul loveth: I sought him, but I found him not.

I will rise now, and go about the city in the streets, and in the broad ways I will seek him whom my soul loveth: I sought him, but I found him not.

The watchmen that go about the city found me: to whom I said, saw ye him whom my soul loveth?

It was but a little that I passed from them, but I found him whom my soul loveth: I held him, and would not let him go, until I had brought him into my mother's house, and into the chamber of her that conceived me.

I charge you, O ye daughters of Jerusalem, by the roes, and by the hinds of the field, that ye stir not up, nor awake my love, till he please.

Who is this that cometh out of the wilderness like pillars of smoke, perfumed with myrrh and frankincense, with all powders of the merchant?

Behold his bed, which is Solomon's; threescore valiant men

are about it, of the valiant of Israel.

They all hold swords, being expert in war: every man hath his sword upon his thigh because of fear in the night.

King Solomon made himself a chariot of the wood of Lebanon.

He made the pillars thereof of silver, the bottom thereof of gold, the covering of it of purple, the midst thereof being paved with love, for the daughters of Jerusalem.

Go forth, O ye daughters of Zion, and behold king Solomon with the crown wherewith his mother crowned him in the day of his espousals, and in the day of the gladness of his heart

⁂

Behold, thou art fair, my love; behold, thou art fair; thou hast doves' eyes within thy locks: thy hair is as a flock of goats, that appear from mount Gilead.

Thy teeth are like a flock of sheep that are even shorn, which came up from the washing; whereof every one bear twins, and none is barren among them.

Thy lips are like a thread of scarlet, and thy speech is comely: thy temples are like a piece of a pomegranate within thy locks.

Thy neck is like the tower of David builded for an armoury, whereon there hang a thousand bucklers, all shields of mighty men.

Thy two breasts are like two young roes that are twins, which feed among the lilies.

Until the day break, and the shadows flee away, I will get me to the mountain of myrrh, and to the hill of frankincense.

Thou art all fair, my love; there is no spot in thee.

Come with me from Lebanon, my spouse, with me from Lebanon: look from the top of Amana, from the top of Shenir and Hermon, from the lions' dens, from the mountains of the leopards.

Thou hast ravished my heart, my sister, my spouse; thou hast ravished my heart with one of thine eyes, with one chain of thy neck.

How fair is thy love, my sister, my spouse! how much better is thy love than wine! and the smell of thine ointments than all spices!

Thy lips, O my spouse, drop as the honeycomb: honey and milk are under thy tongue; and the smell of thy garments is much like the smell of Lebanon.

A garden inclosed is my sister, my spouse; a spring shut up, a fountain sealed.

Thy plants are an orchard of pomegranates, with pleasant fruits; camphire, with spikenard,

Spikenard and saffron; calamus and cinnamon, with all trees of frankincense; myrrh and aloes, with all the chief spices:

A fountain of gardens, a well of living waters, and streams from Lebanon.

Awake, O north wind; and come, thou south; blow upon my garden, that the spices thereof may flow out. Let my beloved come into his garden, and eat his pleasant fruits.

❧

I am come into my garden, my sister, my spouse: I have gathered my myrrh with my spice; I have eaten my honeycomb with my honey; I have drunk my wine with my milk: eat, O friends; drink, yea, drink abundantly, O beloved.

I sleep, but my heart waketh: it is the voice of my beloved that knocketh, saying: Open to me, my sister, my love, my dove, my undefiled: for my head is filled with dew, and my locks with the drops of the night.

I have put off my coat; how shall I put it on? I have washed my feet; how shall I defile them?

My beloved put in his hand by the hole of the door, and my bowels were moved for him.

I rose up to open to my beloved; and my hands dropped with myrrh, and my fingers with sweet smelling myrrh, upon the handles of the lock.

I opened to my beloved; but my beloved had withdrawn himself, and was gone: my soul failed when he spake: I sought him, but I could not find him; I called him, but he gave me no answer.

The watchmen that went about the city found me, they smote me, they wounded me; the keepers of the walls took away my veil from me.

I charge you, O daughters of Jerusalem, if ye find my beloved, that ye tell him, that I am sick of love.

What is thy beloved more than another beloved, O thou fairest among women? What is thy beloved more than another beloved, that dost so charge us?

My beloved is white and ruddy, the chiefest among ten thousand.

His head is as the most fine gold, his locks are bushy, and black as a raven.

His eyes are as the eyes of doves by the rivers of waters, washed with milk, and fitly set.

His cheeks are as a bed of spices, as sweet flowers: his lips like lilies, dropping sweet smelling myrrh.

His hands are as gold rings set with the beryl: his belly is as bright ivory overlaid with sapphires.

His legs are as pillars of marble, set upon sockets of fine gold: his countenance is as Lebanon, excellent as the cedars.

His mouth is most sweet: yea he is altogether lovely. This is my beloved, and this is my friend, O daughters of Jerusalem.

❧

Whither is thy beloved gone, O thou fairest among women? Whither is thy beloved turned aside? that we may seek him with thee.

My beloved is gone down into his garden, to the beds of

spices, to feed in the gardens, and to gather lilies.

I am my beloved's, and my beloved is mine: he feedeth among the lilies.

Thou art beautiful, O my love, as Tirzah, comely as Jerusalem, terrible as an army with banners.

Turn away thine eyes from me, for they have overcome me: thy hair is as a flock of goats that appear from Gilead.

Thy teeth are as a flock of sheep which go up from the washing, whereof every one beareth twins, and there is not one barren among them.

As a piece of a pomegranate are thy temples within thy locks.

There are threescore queens, and fourscore concubines, and virgins without number.

My dove, my undefiled is but one; she is the only one of her mother, she is the choice one of her that bare her. The daughters saw her, and blessed her; yea, the queens and the concubines, and they praised her.

Who is she that looketh forth as the morning, fair as the moon, clear as the sun, and terrible as an army with banners?

I went down into the garden of nuts to see the fruits of the valley, and to see whether the vine flourished, and the pomegranates budded.

Or ever I was aware, my soul made me like the chariots of Amminadib.

Return, return, O Shulamite; return, return, that we may look upon thee. What will ye see in the Shulamite? As it were the company of two armies.

❧

How beautiful are thy feet with shoes, O prince's daughter! The joints of thy thigh are like jewels, the work of the hands of a cunning workman.

Thy navel is like a round goblet, which wanteth not liquor: thy belly is like a heap of wheat set about with lilies.

Thy two breasts are like two young roes that are twins.

Thy neck is as a tower of ivory; thine eyes like the fish-pools in Heshbon, by the gate of Bathrabbim: thy nose is as the tower of Lebanon which looketh toward Damascus.

Thine head upon thee is like Carmel, and the hair of thine head like purple; the king is held in the galleries.

How fair and how pleasant art thou, O love, for delights!

This thy stature is like to a palm tree, and thy breasts to clusters of grapes.

I said, I will go up to the palm tree, I will take hold of the boughs thereof: now also thy breasts shall be as clusters of the vine, and the smell of thy nose like apples;

And the roof of thy mouth like the best wine for my beloved, that goeth down sweetly, causing the lips of those that are asleep to speak.

I am my beloved's, and his desire is toward me.

Come, my beloved, let us go forth into the field; let us lodge in the villages.

Let us get up early to the vineyards; let us see if the vine flourish, whether the tender grape appear, and the pomegranates bud forth: there will I give thee my loves.

The mandrakes give a smell, and at our gates are all manner of pleasant fruits, new and old, which I have laid up for thee, O my beloved.

⁂

O that thou wert as my brother, that sucked the breasts of my mother! When I should find thee without, I would kiss thee; yea, I should not be despised.

I would lead thee, and bring thee into my mother's house, who would instruct me: I would cause thee to drink of spiced wine of the juice of my pomegranate.

His left hand should be under my head, and his right hand should embrace me.

I charge you, O daughters of Jerusalem, that ye stir not up, nor awake my love, until he please.

Who is this that cometh up from the wilderness, leaning upon her beloved? I raised thee up under the apple tree: there thy mother brought thee forth: there she brought forth that bare thee.

Set me as a seal upon thine heart, as a seal upon thine arm: for love is strong as death; jealousy is cruel as the grave: the coals thereof are coals of fire, which hath a most vehement flame.

Many waters cannot quench love, neither can the floods drown it: if a man would give all the substance of his house for love, it would utterly be contemned.

We have a little sister, and she hath no breasts: what shall we do for our sister in the day when she shall be spoken for?

If she be a wall, we will build upon her a palace of silver: and if she be a door, we will inclose her with boards of cedar.

I am a wall, and my breasts like towers: then was I in his eyes as one that found favour.

Solomon had a vineyard at Baalhamon; he let out the vineyard unto keepers; every one for the fruit thereof was to bring a thousand pieces of silver.

My vineyard, which is mine, is before me: thou, O Solomon, must have a thousand, and those that keep the fruit thereof two hundred.

Thou that dwellest in the gardens, the companions hearken to thy voice: cause me to hear it.

Make haste, my beloved, and be thou like to a roe or to a young hart upon the mountains of spices.